Fantasy and Symbol

STUDIES IN ANTHROPOLOGY

Under the Consulting Editorship of E. A. Hammel,
UNIVERSITY OF CALIFORNIA, BERKELEY

Andrei Simić, THE PEASANT URBANITES: A Study of Rural-Urban Mobility in Serbia

John U. Ogbu, THE NEXT GENERATION: An Ethnography of Education in an Urban Neighborhood

Bennett Dyke and Jean Walters MacCluer (Eds.), COMPUTER SIMULATION IN HUMAN POPULATION STUDIES

Robbins Burling, THE PASSAGE OF POWER: Studies in Political Succession

Piotr Sztompka, SYSTEM AND FUNCTION: Toward a Theory of Society

William G. Lockwood, EUROPEAN MOSLEMS: Economy and Ethnicity in Western Bosnia

Günter Golde, CATHOLICS AND PROTESTANTS: Agricultural Modernization in Two German Villages

Peggy Reeves Sanday (Ed.), ANTHROPOLOGY AND THE PUBLIC INTEREST: Fieldwork and Theory

Carol A. Smith (Ed.), REGIONAL ANALYSIS, Volume I: Economic Systems, and Volume II: Social Systems

Raymond D. Fogelson and Richard N. Adams (Eds.), THE ANTHROPOLOGY OF POWER: Ethnographic Studies from Asia, Oceania, and the New World

Frank Henderson Stewart, FUNDAMENTALS OF AGE-GROUP SYSTEMS

Larissa Adler Lomnitz, NETWORKS AND MARGINALITY: Life in a Mexican Shantytown

Benjamin S. Orlove, ALPACAS, SHEEP, AND MEN: The Wool Export Economy and Regional Society in Southern Peru

Harriet Ngubane, BODY AND MIND IN ZULU MEDICINE: An Ethnography of Health and Disease in Nyuswa-Zulu Thought and Practice

George M. Foster, Thayer Scudder, Elizabeth Colson, and Robert Van Kemper (Eds.), LONG-TERM FIELD RESEARCH IN SOCIAL ANTHROPOLOGY

R. H. Hook (Ed.), FANTASY AND SYMBOL: Studies in Anthropological Interpretation

Essays in honour of
George Devereux

George Devereux

Fantasy and Symbol

Studies in Anthropological Interpretation

edited by
R. H. HOOK
Department of Anthropology
Research School of Pacific Studies
Australian National University
Canberra
Australia

1979

ACADEMIC PRESS
LONDON NEW YORK SAN FRANCISCO
A Subsidiary of Harcourt Brace Jovanovich, Publishers

Academic Press Inc. (London) Ltd
24–28 Oval Road
London NW1

US edition published by
Academic Press Inc.
111 Fifth Avenue,
New York, New York 10003

British Library Cataloguing in Publication Data

Fantasy and Symbol. – (Studies in anthropology).
1. Symbolism – Addresses, essays, lectures
2. Symbolism (Psychology) – Addresses, essays, lectures
I. Devereux, George II. Hook, R H
III. Psychoanalysis and the Interpretation of Symbolic Behavior *(Conference), Canberra, 1975*
IV. Series

301.2′1 GN452.5 78–67899

ISBN 0-12-355480-2

Typeset in Great Britain by Kelmscott Press Ltd., London EC4
Printed in Great Britain by Whitstable Litho Ltd., Whitstable, Kent

Contributors

L. BRYCE BOYER is a practising psychoanalyst and Member of the American Psychoanalytic Association. He is Associate Director, Psychiatric Residency Training, Herrick Memorial Hospital, Berkeley, California, USA.

ARIANE DELUZ is Chargé de Recherches, Centre Nationale de la Recherche Scientifique, Laboratoire d'Anthropologie Sociale, Paris, France.

A. L. EPSTEIN is Professor of Social Anthropology, University of Sussex, and was formerly Professor of Anthropology in the Research School of Pacific Studies, Australian National University, Canberra, Australia.

MEYER FORTES is Emeritus Professor of Social Anthropology, Kings College, University of Cambridge, England.

DEREK FREEMAN is Professor of Anthropology in the Research School of Pacific Studies, Australian National University, Canberra, Australia.

ALFRED GELL is Senior Lecturer, Department of Prehistory and Anthropology, Faculty of Arts, Australian National University, Canberra, Australia.

L. R. HIATT is Reader in the Department of Anthropology, University of Sydney, Sydney, Australia.

R. H. HOOK is a practising psychoanalyst and Associate Member of the Australian Psychoanalytical Society. He is a Visiting Fellow in the Research School of Pacific Studies, Australian National University, Canberra, Australia.

MICHAEL JACKSON is Senior Lecturer in the Department of Social Anthropology and Maori Studies, Massey University, Palmerston North, New Zealand.

WESTON LA BARRE is James B. Duke Professor of Anthropology Emiritus at Duke University, Durham, North Carolina, USA.

CLAUDE LÉVI-STRAUSS is Professor of Anthropology at the Collège de France, Paris, France.

MARGARET MEAD was, until her death in November 1978, Curator Emeritus of Ethnology, American Museum of Natural History, New York, USA.

Preface

This collection of papers in honour of George Devereux had its origin in a symposium on "Psychoanalysis and the Interpretation of Symbolic Behaviour" of the Anthropology Section at the 46th Congress of the Australian and New Zealand Association for the Advancement of Science (ANZAAS) held in Canberra in 1975. George Devereux, then Visiting Fellow in the Department of Anthropology in the Research School of Pacific Studies at the Australian National University, was the principal speaker at this symposium, his paper (which appears in this volume) being entitled "Fantasy and Symbol as Dimensions of Reality".

It was subsequently proposed that the papers contributed to this very stimulating symposium be published in a volume that would commemorate the varied and distinguished career, as anthropologist and psychoanalyst, of Professor George Devereux. Several of his colleagues and students were also invited to contribute.

In the hands of these contributors the book has grown into its present form. In one way or another, all contributors deal with symbolic behaviour and its interpretation and, as the reader will quickly appreciate, many of the papers have a psychoanalytic orientation, the psychoanalytic interpretation of symbolic behaviour and the complementarity of psychological and sociological accounts of cultural phenomena being topics of prime interest to George Devereux.

The preparation of this volume was carried out in the Department of Anthropology in the Research School of Pacific Studies of the Australian National University, in which the editor is a Visiting Fellow. It could never have been accomplished without the very ready assistance, advice and encouragement of Derek Freeman, Professor of Anthropology in this Department, who also arranged for the inclusion of the symposium on "Psychoanalysis and the Interpretation of Symbolic Behaviour" in the ANZAAS programme of 1975. The President of the Anthropology Section at the 46th ANZAAS Congress was Professor Meyer Fortes and his support of the decision to publish the papers presented and his continuing interest and assistance in the work of preparation of the volume is gratefully acknowledged. I am particularly indebted to Dr Ariane Deluz for her sketch of George Devereux's career and also for the very considerable assistance given in dealing with matters requiring attention in Paris. Miss Judith Wilson, Research Assistant in the Department of Anthropology, has rendered invaluable assistance in proof-reading the papers and in preparing them for publication; her extensive experience enabled her to give advice in such matters as classical and other references and on detailed points of translation or interpretation.

A special acknowledgement is necessary of Professor Weston La Barre's kindness and generosity in making available the photograph of George Devereux which appears as a frontispiece, presenting him in a passionately intellectual, inquiring mood. Many other people have offered very valuable assistance and advice and, although it is not possible to name them individually, they have my sincere appreciation and thanks.

December 1978. R. H. HOOK

Contents

Introduction

R. H. Hook

For if symbolic behavior is even half as important as Freud, for example, suggested, symbolic anthropology is the custodian of the richest of all the mines which are worked by the science of man.

MELFORD E. SPIRO

Ainsi, de ses multiples expériences, en ethnopsychiatrie, en psychanalyse, dans le domaine de l'histoire grecque, et en ethnologie, Devereux tire une série de règles méthodologiques comme une philosophie générale des sciences de l'homme . . . un homme lucide au milieu des pièges – combatif, voire agressif, contre ceux qui se laissent prendre à ces pièges, mais sachant tirer, des obstacles recontrés, la possibilité d'une science de l'homme authentiquement objective.

ROGER BASTIDE

THE LINKING OF symbolic behaviour with the name of Freud is, of course, hardly an accident: no one has done more for the understanding of symbolism than has the father of psychoanalysis. The capacity for symbol formation and symbolic thinking, and related phantasy,[1] perhaps the oldest specifically human phenomena, resisted all attempts to penetrate its real significance and meaning prior to Freud's systematic and scientific study of symbolism in what is, perhaps, his major single theoretical achievement, *The Interpretation of Dreams*, which appeared in 1899, but not in English until 1913, when

[1] The use of two different spellings of phantasy/fantasy, which at first sight may appear capricious, is discussed on page 271 of this volume in my paper, "Phantasy and Symbol".

it was translated by A. A. Brill (Strachey, 1953, pp. xi–xii).

Charles Rycroft (1977) points out that Freud did not at first attach much importance to symbolism in *The Interpretation of Dreams* and that it was only in the fourth edition (1914) that it was given separate treatment and a section to itself when material from the 1909 and 1911 editions, included under a different heading ("Typical Dreams"), was taken, along with further new material, to form the added section ("Representation by Symbols in Dreams – Some Further Typical Dreams", Section (E) of Chapter VI) (Strachey, 1953, p. 350, footnote). But this observation does not detract from the pioneering importance of Freud's work on symbolism.

It has been taken as an excess that psychoanalysts sometimes use words like "true" and "real" in discussion, for example, of such things as symbols and meanings, but the offence may be diminished or seen to arise from insufficient care in the choice of words, or the limitation of language when it is recognized that what is intended is not that other symbols are "false" or other meanings "unreal", but that psychoanalysts wish to indicate a specially important role for the *unconscious* meaning or *primary process* symbol – but obviously the same difficulty arises with all such words, including "primary", "primal" and "fundamental"; even "primitive" and the notions associated with it have gone through some surprising vagaries, as is indicated in Rycroft's discussion of Ernest Jones's use of the word in such expressions as "primitive civilizations" and "the primitive mind" (Rycroft, 1977, p. 134). Discussion of Jones's concept of "true" symbols – as distinct from "symbolism in the widest sense"– makes up a large part of Rycroft's case against the traditional psychoanalytic theory of symbolism, which he claims "has created well-nigh insuperable barriers between itself and other humane disciplines" (Rycroft, 1977, p. 139). Whilst agreeing with the thrust of Rycroft's argument against too restrictive a definition of symbolism, one might still wonder whether such barriers as do exist might not rest on other foundations, too numerous and complex to review here, but of which at least one is resistance to the psychoanalytic extension of the concept "neurotic"– and indeed, also its counterpart "psychotic"– to more universal incidence, at least in regard to defence mechanisms universally used, and of clinical significance only in certain circumstances, when the use of such mechanisms leads to overt illness or dysfunction.

But is not such a claim to special relevance for the psychological approach to the understanding of symbols and phantasy extravagant, when even a cursory glance at Sir Raymond Firth's extensive study of symbols (Firth, 1973) would show that the psychological is but one of many approaches? Moreover, the social anthropologist could complain that such an emphasis on psychoanalysis seems to ignore the sociological side of the equation.

It is not necessary here to review the relationships between anthropology and psychology,[1] but it might approriately be observed that the debate has frequently been bedevilled by the assumption, often no more than implicit, that psychological and sociological explanations each exhaust the material to be explained and are, moreover, mutually exclusive, so that a psychological explanation makes a sociological explanation irrelevant, and vice versa. The logic of the relationship between sociological explanation and psychological explanation has been one of George Devereux's major theoretical interests and is discussed in *Ethnopsychanalyse Complémentariste* (1972). His conclusions, which derive largely from the application of the physical principle of complementarity to the problems of the human sciences, as Ariane Deluz indicates (this volume, p. 14),[2] were worked out over an extended period of time. In a review of *Ethnopsychanalyse Complémentariste*, at that time Devereux's latest book, Alain Besançon (1973) summarized Devereux's conclusions in the form of thirteen propositions or *theorems*. For convenient reference they are listed here (my translation):

1. It is both possible and necessary to explain in different ways behaviour already accounted for within another frame of reference.
2. It is the possibility of explaining fully a given human phenomenon in at least two (complementary) ways which demonstrates, on the one hand, that the phenomenon in question is at once both real and explicable and, on the other, that each of these two explanations is complete (and therefore valid) within its own frame of reference.
3. Two types of inquiry, leading to two complementary explanations, may not be carried out, nor even thought, simultaneously.

[1] It has been done by others more competent. Reference might be made to two recent discussions of this subject: "Custom and Conscience in Anthropological Perspective" (Meyer Fortes, 1977); and *Symbols and Sentiments* (Ioan Lewis, 1977, Introduction).

[2] See also Bohr (1963).

Corollary: Interdisciplinarity of a synthesizing or parallel kind is not possible. What is possible, and indeed obligatory, is a non-synthesizing and non-simultaneous pluridisciplinarity.

4. The total interdependence of sociological and of psychological data (both created out of the same raw facts) assures the absolute autonomy of both the psychological and the sociological discourse. No psychology, however perfect, can permit the formulation of sociological laws, nor can sociology extended to its extreme limits ever arrive at a formulation of psychological laws.

5. Every attempt at explanation within a single frame of reference is subject to the law of diminishing returns. Explanation pushed too far, like experiment pushed too far, destroys or explains away the phenomenon it seeks to study, which, precisely because of this explanation, ceases to be that which one claimed to explain. Beyond a certain limit theory becomes tautological and "explains" nothing but itself.

6. There is, then, a threshold beyond which the object of explanation, within one frame of reference, disappears and is replaced by another object belonging to the complementary discourse (to the sociological as regards psychology, for example, or vice versa).

7. An intensive analysis of the core, the context, and the implications of a single institution or of a single psyche will permit the formulation of universal propositions, which will be identical with those arrived at by an extensive study of the variations of the same cultural trait in a large number of societies or individuals. This may be thought of as the equivalent of the ergodic hypothesis: the score obtained by tossing a single coin a large number of times is the same as would be obtained by tossing simultaneously a number of coins equal to the number of tosses of the single coin.

Corollary: As in psychoanalysis, it is possible to treat as free associations to a central theme either data pertaining to other areas of a culture, one of whose specific traits is being studied, or comparable material pertaining to the same segment or trait in other cultures.

8. Were anthropologists to draw up an exhaustive list of all known types of cultural behaviour, it would correspond, item for item, with an equally complete list of drives, desires and fantasies obtained by psychoanalytic means in a clinical setting. Conversely, a complete list of desires, drives and fantasies obtained by psychoanalytic means in a clinical setting would correspond, item for item, with a

list of all known cultural beliefs and procedures.

9. What exists in one society openly, or even in an institutionalized form, exists in another society in a state of repression. For example, a fantasy such as that of the "inverted penis" may appear in one society as psychotic behaviour, in another as myth, as belief in a third, and also as the analysed fantasy of a psychoanalyst who may identify it on all the levels on which it may manifest, or, on the contrary, conceal itself.

10. What is operant motivation in sociological discourse is instrumental motivation in psychological discourse, and vice versa. For example, in the Hungarian uprising of 1956, a certain rebel might have killed a policeman from an unconscious hatred of the father (operant motive in psychology but instrumental motive in sociology) and have done this believing himself to be authorized to do so by society (instrumental motive in psychology but operant motive in sociology).

11. It follows that social movements are possible, not because all the individuals who participate in them are motivated in an identical manner, but because a variety of identically subjective motives are able to find ego-syntonic expression in the same kind of collective activity.

12. If by an endogenous stress is understood the situation in which a quantitatively minimal stimulus arising from outside the organism triggers a massive response within the organism, and by exogenous stress that in which a minimal impulse coming from within the organism triggers a massive reaction in the environment, then the minimal stimulus is, in both cases, the element of closure of a configuration. It structures a series of existing predispositions, giving them a meaning and mobilizing them *en bloc*. What separates the "inside" from the "outside" is a continuous (Jordan) curve of a special sort, a series of cuts (analogous with the Dedekind cut), "mobile" and created *de novo* at each instant by events which, by occurring "on" it, create it. Homeostasis ensures only the stability of an organism within certain limits, in terms of, and in consequence of, these events.

13. This model, applicable to the organism, can also be applied to social processes. A society – defined as the ordering of individuals within a space that is structured precisely by their existence – subjected to the pressure of external forces will tend to maintain its

structure. It can do so only by modifying certain of its features. If its structure is flexible, its modification can be minimal and the society will return to a state related to its former state. If, on the other hand, it is too rigid, the modifications required will be too great and the society will collapse under the impact of the stress.

These theorems define the method of complementarity, which is not intended to be taken as a theory but as a means of coordinating theories. This has the merit of putting an end to the (often prejudiced) assumption that one explanation necessarily excludes another, even though situated on a different level of discourse or within a different frame of reference; that it is a matter of *either* this explanation *or* that. Unless logically incompatible or contradictory, both may be correct – what is true on the level of the unconscious does not negate what holds on the level of the conscious, and what is true on the rational level is not necessarily incompatible with what holds on the non-rational level.

The essays presented in this volume cover diverse ground and extend over many themes, though all are concerned in one way or another with the psychological and the sociological linked through the medium of a study of fantasy and symbol. Some, though by no means all, adopt a psychoanalytical approach to the material.

The universality of symbols is a central theme in George Devereux's discussion of the public and general availability of what at first sight might appear to be purely private symbols. Professor Devereux takes up the relevance of symbolization for human behaviour and shows the inadequacy of behaviour which is segmental and non-symbolic.

Bridging large tracts of time and space, Claude Lévi-Strauss shows symbolism in its universal aspect, a unique psychic process demonstrating remarkable consistency, even in detail, between cultures as distant as those of ancient Greece, Japan and the American Indian. A common article of diet, the bean, may have comparable symbolic significance for each. Professor Lévi-Strauss considers the significance of beans in rites and myths and examines the features which give them this significance, comparing them with the features of other plants also symbolically important and, after discussing the content of the fantasies associated with them, shows how they also mediate between opposite categories, in this case, female–male, death–life.

Margaret Mead considered the consequences of changes in available techniques for the development of theory, and the communication of observed experience across disciplinary boundaries, then reexamined the question of personality development and its assessment in differing cultures.

Whilst magic arrogantly commands impersonal, external reality, religion beseeches person-like spirits or the ghosts of persons, parents and ancestors: Weston La Barre traces both to their origin in the prolonged dependence of the human infant – accordingly, they are species specific for *homo sapiens*. Magic and religion also bear witness to a basic human characteristic: "it is not in the nature of man to submit blindly to what purports to be mystically inevitable".

Meyer Fortes expands this theme in the examination of the successive stages of Tallensi rituals for dealing with an evil "Predestiny" – perhaps more person-like than impersonal – a young woman's inability to bear children who survive, interweaving narrative and analysis into a fascinating account of the way in which ritual enables the individual to come to terms with the irresistible and irrevocable and permits, on the social level, adaptation to an otherwise intolerable situation.

Destiny, in another aspect – succession to power and chiefly office – is dealt with by Michael Jackson, also in an African context. Rivalry, hence hostility, may be experienced laterally or vertically, that is, within the same generation or between succeeding generations (half-brother to half-brother, or father to son, etc.). In the father–son situation, the son may be as reluctant to succeed (grow up) as the father is to be superseded (die). In the Kuranko narrative in which these conflicts are worked out, content and structure are complementary. Some will also see in the physical disabilities alluded to in the narrative a variant of the Oedipus situation: lameness, retardation, weakness=impotence; recovery, that is, achievement of potency ⟶death of the father, or, in other words, "If I am potent, my father will die".

Alfred Gell examines the concept "ego" from a "phenomenological" position, differentiating his concept of ego from the "too-featureless 'ego' of symbolic anthropology ... a detached bystander 'classifying out' an already constituted world". It needs to be differentiated also from the "ego" of psychoanalytic structural theory. The tool used by Dr Gell for reworking the concept ego is the notion of *taboo* which, Dr Gell argues, "stands for the negative, denying aspect of ego-hood" whilst the notion of *lapse*, which in his analysis corresponds to taboo, "stands for the reabsorption of the ego into the world".

Taboo is also a central theme of A. L. Epstein's detailed analysis of *tambu*, which in a special sense is also taboo, sacred and emotionally highly charged. Professor Epstein sets himself the task of inquiring why the traditional monetary system of the Tolai, shell-money, is so highly charged and called by the same name as that which is tabooed. He finds the answer in the association of *tambu* with faeces and what follows is an analysis, in the Tolai context, of the "anal character" and the role of money. Though careful to avoid assimilating features drawn from a different social context, Professor Epstein's study of *tambu*, as an alternative currency in a dual currency system, throws light on the psychological role of money in other societies.

In Chiricahua and Mescalero Apache socialization practices – which lead to the development of intense frustration in children at each stage of psychosexual development, eliciting infantile rage directed initially against their mothers – L. Bryce Boyer traces the early stages of the ensuing aggressiveness of the adult Apache. In the dreams and myths of the Apache recorded and analysed by Dr Bryce Boyer, stone, in different forms, appears as a symbol of oral aggression and sadism.

Derek Freeman develops the analysis of symbolism in his study of head-hunting as symbolic behaviour. A symbol with a difference, a detached part of the human body, becomes for the head-hunting Iban the grisly object of an aggressive cult. Of phallic significance – as a symbol of virility and fertility – head-hunting is related to anxieties about germination of the rice seed and, on another level, to the expansion of the Iban during the nineteenth century when head-hunting was still rife and advancement was achieved by incursions into enemy territory on head-hunting raids.

L. R. Hiatt takes up the symbolism of secret male cults and their meaning in terms of male–female rivalry – rivalry for priority in the possession of rituals, rivalry about procreative capacity. Men's envy of women's ability to bear children, which is not unrelated to men's fear of women, more specifically of women's sexuality and the female genital, is to be seen in Australian Aboriginal data. Dr Hiatt's study of secret male cults and their significance for male domination begins with an account of the opera, *The Magic Flute*, and the various interpretations of the libretto which have been put forward. Whether or not matriarchy preceded patriarchy historically may be a matter for debate but there can be little doubt that it does so ontogenetically and Dr Hiatt concludes that myths ascribing power to women "are more like dreams . . . in the present instance they express the memory, not of a prehistoric revolution, but of a crucial change in the early life of every individual male".

The final essay attempts a brief account of certain aspects of the development of the psychoanalytic theory of symbolism and the relation of symbol to fantasy, suggesting that both are typical elements of primary process thinking, itself the medium of dream and myth and, indeed, of all truly symbolic behaviour – linking with Devereux's conclusion that without symbolism human behaviour would be segmental and impoverished and man unable to make full contact with reality and therefore with himself.

References

BASTIDE, ROGER (1970). Preface. In *Essais d'Ethnopsychiatrie Générale* (G. Devereux), pp. vii–xix. Gallimard, Paris.

BESANÇON, ALAIN (1973). Review of *Ethnopsychanalyse Complémentariste. Annales: Economies, Sociétés, Civilisations*, **28,** no. 5, 1311–1313.

BOHR, NIELS (1963). *Essays 1958–1962 on Atomic Physics and Human Knowledge.* Interscience Publishers, New York.

DEVEREUX, GEORGE (1972). *Ethnopsychanalyse Complémentariste.* Flammarion, Paris.

DEVEREUX, GEORGE (1978). *Ethnopsychoanalysis: Psychoanalysis and Anthropology as Complementary Frames of Reference.* University of California Press, Berkeley, California. (English translation of *Ethnopsychanalyse Complémentariste.)*

FIRTH, RAYMOND (1973). *Symbols, Public and Private.* George Allen and Unwin, London.

FORTES, MEYER (1977). Custom and conscience in anthropological perspective. *The International Review of Psycho-Analysis*, **4,** 127–154.

FREUD, SIGMUND (1900). *The Interpretation of Dreams.* Standard Edition, vols 4 and 5 (1953). Hogarth Press, London.

LEWIS, IOAN (1977). *Symbols and Sentiments: Cross-cultural Studies in Symbolism.* Academic Press, London and New York.

RYCROFT, CHARLES (1977). Is Freudian symbolism a myth? In *Symbols and Sentiments: Cross-cultural Studies in Symbolism* (Ed. I. Lewis), pp. 129–140. Academic Press, London and New York.

SPIRO, MELFORD E. (1969). Discussion. In *Forms of Symbolic Action. Proceedings of the 1969 Annual Spring Meeting of the American Ethnological Society* (Ed. R. F. Spencer), pp. 208–214. University of Washington Press, Seattle and London.

STRACHEY, JAMES (1953). Editor's Introduction. In *The Interpretation of Dreams* (S. Freud), pp. xi–xxii. Standard Edition, vols 4 and 5. Hogarth Press, London.

George Devereux: A Portrait

Ariane Deluz

TIME AND AGAIN during recent years I have been told by both students and research workers familiar with the work of George Devereux how surprised they were to find a man belonging, at least in terms of his years, to the generation of their teachers. They had expected him to be of their own age. This indeed points to a very real time lag.

Devereux began writing in the 1930s but for a long time the value of his work was recognized by only a few scholars and, as he himself is well aware, it is only since the beginning of the present decade that he has been rejoined by the mainstream of science.

In the field of ethnopsychoanalysis, not only were George Devereux's predecessors few in number but they mostly lacked training in one or other discipline, psychoanalysis or anthropology. This was true of both Malinowski and Ernest Jones. Róheim alone had a dual training and was the first to collect for himself, in the field, the data which he then interpreted psychoanalytically, thereby founding the new science of ethnopsychoanalysis, though the basic principles had been laid down by Freud when he wrote *Totem and Taboo*. Róheim directed his attention primarily to the psychoanalysis of culture and to the shaping of personality. In non-Western societies, he was interested only in the "normal"; his clinical studies are related only to Western society. Complementary to but more systematic than that of Róheim, Devereux's approach led him to formulate a methodological basis for the young science of ethnopsychoanalysis – a term which he himself appears to have introduced – and, in addition, to establish the science of ethnopsychiatry by studying the psychopathological in non-Western societies.

In my endeavour to describe the personality of George Devereux and to trace his intellectual and scientific progress, I rely in the main on his autobiographical sketch in *The Making of Psychological Anthropology* (Spindler, George D. (ed.), 1978), on personal conversations with him, and on an interview which Margaret Mead kindly gave me. I used also a review of *Essais d'Ethnopsychiatrie Générale* by Alain Besançon, published in *La Quinzaine Littéraire* (1971) under the title, "Un méconnu: Devereux". The appearance of that review marked the beginning, at least in France, of a wider public recognition of George Devereux and an increase in the number of his students.

George Devereux, the son of a lawyer, was born in 1908 into a family which, according to tradition, originated in Lorraine. His home town, Lugos, was at that time part of Hungary. While still a young boy, George was confronted with multi-cultural situations and their inherent contradictions. In 1919, his home town, and official patriotism, changed sides and the lycée he attended also became Romanian. Consequently, he was obliged, while still young, to claim and to maintain a solid Hungarian identity, and it was on the basis of that identity that he was to build relationships with the many cultures in the midst of which he has had occasion to live since 1926.

He says that his boyhood and adolescence were unhappy, and it is probable that these early stresses lie behind the intuitions basic to certain of his papers, such as "The Voices of Children" (1965) and "The Cannibalistic Impulses of Parents" (1966). From childhood he reacted strongly against the "social and affective hypocrisy" to which he felt himself condemned. Sincerity, which he searched for and found in classical music, is one of the values to which he has always remained faithful – all his work bears witness to his intellectual honesty, as refreshing as it is abrupt.

After graduating from the lycée, George Devereux came to Paris in 1926 to seek "objective truth" in mathematical physics. But such was the state of physical theory taught at that time – before the epoch-making breakthrough achieved in 1927 by Werner Heisenberg and quickly taken up and elaborated by Neils Bohr – that it seemed to him to be in a theoretical cul-de-sac. Devereux gave up the study of physics and worked for the diploma in Malay of the Ecole Nationale des Langues Orientales Vivantes. The associated study of Malay life and custom, reinforced by an old love of the unfamiliar born of his early reading of such books as Friedrich Ratzel's *Völkerkunde* (1894), soon led him to anthropology, which he studied chiefly under Marcel Mauss but also with Lucien Lévy-Bruhl and Paul Rivet.

In 1932 Devereux obtained a Fellowship from the Rockefeller Foundation for the purpose of undertaking extensive fieldwork amongst the Sedang Moi of Vietnam. He prepared himself for this by doing preliminary fieldwork with the Hopi and Mohave Indians. Thus it was from R. H. Lowie and A. L. Kroeber that Devereux learned the craft of anthropological fieldwork, which he put into practice between 1932 and 1935 with the Sedang and, on many subsequent occasions, with the Mohave.

Ideas jotted down during the long evenings in a Sedang village became a frame of reference for his subsequent epistemological and theoretical studies. From this period date also the essential features of what he calls his "first" book, *From Anxiety to Method in the Behavioral Sciences*, though the book itself remained unpublished until 1967. In this book he brought out the crucial importance of countertransference in the behavioural sciences and showed that it is only by the joint study of both the observer and the observed that access is gained to the essence of the situation under observation. In this respect no other author has dissected the mechanism of countertransference nearly so rigorously as has George Devereux – and that was before becoming an analyst or even being analysed. Although he had been searching for a satisfactory psychological theory ever since the period in Paris (1926–32), he at first rejected psychoanalysis and reports that he did not understand Róheim's *Psycho-Analysis of Primitive Cultural Types* (1932), which he read whilst doing fieldwork with the Sedang in Vietnam. It was material furnished by Mohave informants during his 1938–39 field season that finally overcame his resistance to psychoanalysis, so closely did their ideas about psychiatry correspond with those of psychoanalysis. From then onwards Devereux found that he could easily integrate psychoanalysis with his own methodology, and subsequently went on to acquire a full psychoanalytic training.

From this same period of intellectual ferment of the thirties date many of Devereux's most important contributions to the principles underlying human sciences. Several articles, published in book form only as recently as 1972 (*Ethnopsychanalyse Complémentariste*), set out the theoretical bases of many of the ethnopsychiatric and ethnopsychoanalytic works which he wrote at the same time – *Reality and Dream, A Study of Abortion in Primitive Societies* and *Mohave Ethnopsychiatry*, to cite only works published prior to 1970.

Devereux shows that a relationship of complementarity exists between the socio-cultural and the psychological explanation of all human phenomena. It follows that explanations on these two levels of discourse, socio-cultural and psychological, cannot be offered at the same time, but also that, *within its own frame of reference*, each permits a complete explanation of a particular phenomenon. This position also establishes the logical impossibility of a synthesis of the two – an attempt which Devereux categorically rejects. In this way the impasse which confronted Devereux in his student days in Paris in 1926 was resolved and the solution – the consequence of the theories of Heisenberg and Bohr – incorporated into the sciences of man. In all his work Devereux never ceases to insist upon the relationship of complementarity: between psychological and sociological explanation; between, for example, aggressive drives of children and of parents; between culture and the human psyche; and between latent and manifest aspects of socio-cultural systems.

After returning from fieldwork amongst the Sedang in 1935, Devereux went through some very difficult years in the United States, both before and after the war, in which he volunteered for service. He found himself isolated, and for many reasons. Margaret Mead considered that had he been content to remain a specialist in the ethnography of South-East Asia he would probably have made a great impression on the Americans, for he was brilliant and anthropology was an established discipline. But what interested him most was the teaching of psychoanalysis to anthropologists – and such teaching had no recognized status in departments of anthropology. He was, moreover, a non-medical analyst, and his own analyst had been non-medical, at a time when psychoanalysis was no longer fashionable and was dominated by medical analysts. His psychoanalytic standing was inevitably suspect. What seems to me most important is the fact that at that time the culturalist trend was dominant in the United States in ethnopsychology and, even more so, in anthropology. Working with theories derived partly from psychoanalysis, but in fact more "neo-Freudian" in orientation, and often using their psychoanalytical training as a "screen", culturalists "adopted and then generalized that partial aspect of psychoanalysis which is the quest for experienced events and for the circumstances of child-rearing which have left an imprint on the first years of life" (Valabrega, 1957, p. 228: author's translation). This approach led to the replacement of psychoanalysis by a pseudo-sociology which explains nothing at all. For the culturalist, "explanation must be of the same nature as the facts to be explained – a postulate in contradiction with every principle of explanation in science" (Valabrega, 1957, p. 225: author's translation). Moreover, by accepting that every anthropological explanation must necessarily be limited to the interior of a given socio-cultural context, culturalists adopted a "localizing" attitude. In such an intellectual climate the works of Devereux, whose vigorous and scientific but non-academic style was just as disconcerting as his thought, was not so much attacked as passed over in silence. As George Devereux himself said to me on one occasion: "One of the reasons for my huge written output is the fact that for all those years I had no one to talk to. So I wrote."

The most thoroughly worked-out reply by George Devereux to the culturalists and to their psycho-sociological pseudo-syntheses appeared in 1961 in an article on the "modal personality" in which he analyses the diverse motivations of young Hungarians during the uprising of 1956 (Devereux, 1961b). At the end of that paper (translated into French and revised, 1972) he reminds the reader that "on the level of concrete research and explanation, one must undertake a double – but never simultaneous – analysis of the facts. This must be done in a manner which highlights well the *complementarity, strictu sensu*, of the two explanations, one of which is psychologistic and the other sociologistic" (Devereux, 1972, p. 129: author's translation). In 1956–57 Devereux was a member of a team studying the reactions of refugees after the failure of the Hungarian revolution. I heard Margaret Mead, in referring to his work on that occasion, praise Devereux's capacity to get inside the skin of his informant, whilst he himself expressed admiration for her capacity to compel him, by unexpected and penetrating questions, to express in words the essential features of the Hungarian personality – a good example of complementarity.

Not only was George Devereux busy writing from 1932 onwards, but from 1946 to 1959 he carried out important clinical work in various institutions before engaging in the private practice of psychoanalysis in New York from 1959 to 1963, when he was appointed professor at the Ecole des Hautes Etudes en Sciences Sociales (until 1975 called Ecole Pratique des Hautes Etudes, VIe Section) in Paris.

Though remaining aloof from any faction, Devereux felt more at home in the intellectual climate of Europe than in the United States. His affinity with the structuralism of Lévi-Strauss may be seen in an article published in 1965 (Devereux, 1965b) in which he proposed a psychological theory of kinship, complementary to the sociological theses of Claude Lévi-Strauss concerning the exchange of women. According to Devereux, "this exchange permits the indirect manifestation of homosexual impulses" (1965b, p. 243: author's translation) and "the institution of marriage has as its goal not the socially advantageous resolving of heterosexual problems, but the repelling of the threatening spectre of homosexuality which is a product of the oedipus complex" (1965b, p. 245: author's translation). One may think, as did Margaret Mead, that this represents a male point of view, but it is also the only psychological theory of kinship which offers a challenge. I would be inclined to say that if it is true that men exchange women it is also true that women exchange men and that it is by understanding under what conditions these ways of looking at the question can be articulated with each other that their effects can be best interpreted.

Since 1963 George Devereux has carved out for himself a niche in Hellenic studies, regarding Greek antiquity as the site of his last ethnographic fieldwork. In *Dreams in Greek Tragedy* (1976) he analyses the dreams contained in those Greek tragedies which have survived in a complete form, the rest of the tragedy in which the dream occurs being treated for purposes of interpretation as "free associations" to the dream. These dreams are then also correlated with comparable passages in other Greek texts, with Greek culture as a whole, and with comparable clinical material and ethnographic data. This latest *avatar* of George Devereux – as a Greek scholar – reminds us of his boldness and inventiveness.

George Devereux is one of those rare men of science of whom it may be said, "He is a scholar", but at the same time he is most sensitive to human warmth and friendship, as is well attested by the ties he has established with the students who attend his seminars in Paris. But, above all, "he has made the spirit of psychoanalysis so thoroughly his own that most of his propositions – even, indeed chiefly, the most scientific – in fact operate as interpretations. As such, they may be obliterated for a time by resistances, but once these are overcome they reorganize and clarify our understanding" (Besançon, 1971, p. 25: author's translation).

References

BESANÇON, ALAIN (1971). Un méconnu: Devereux. *La Quinzaine Littéraire*, 16–31 January, 25–26.

DEVEREUX, GEORGE (1951). *Reality and Dream: Psychotherapy of a Plains Indian.* International Universities Press, New York.

DEVEREUX, GEORGE (1955). *A Study of Abortion in Primitive Societies: A Typological, Distributional, and Dynamic Analysis of the Prevention of Birth in 400 Preindustrial Societies.* Julian Press, New York.

DEVEREUX, GEORGE (1961a). *Mohave Ethnopsychiatry and Suicide: The Psychiatric Knowledge and the Psychic Disturbances of an Indian Tribe* (Bureau of American Ethnology Bulletin No. 175). Government Printing Office, Washington, D.C.

DEVEREUX, GEORGE (1961b). Two types of modal personality models. In *Studying Personality Cross-Culturally* (Ed. Bert Kaplan), pp. 227–241. Row, Peterson and Company, Evanston, Illinois. (Also in *Ethnopsychanalyse Complémentariste* (1972), pp. 111–130. Flammarion, Paris.)

DEVEREUX, GEORGE (1965a). The voices of children: psychocultural obstacles to therapeutic communication. *American Journal of Psychotherapy*, **19**, 4–19. (Also in *Essais d'Ethnopsychiatrie Générale* (1970), pp. 124–142. Gallimard, Paris.)

DEVEREUX, GEORGE (1965b). Considérations ethnopsychanalytiques sur la notion de parenté. *L'Homme*, **5**, 224–247. (Also in *Ethnopsychanalyse Complémentariste* (1972), pp. 169–199. Flammarion, Paris.)

DEVEREUX, GEORGE (1966). The cannibalistic impulses of parents, and author's response. *Psychoanalytic Forum*, **1**, 114–124 and 129–130. (Also in *Essais d'Ethnopsychiatrie Générale* (1970), pp. 143–161. Gallimard, Paris.)

DEVEREUX, GEORGE (1967). *From Anxiety to Method in the Behavioral Sciences.* Mouton, The Hague and Paris.

DEVEREUX, GEORGE (1970). *Essais d'Ethnopsychiatrie Générale.* Gallimard, Paris. (English translation in preparation, University of Chicago Press, Chicago, Illinois.)

DEVEREUX, GEORGE (1972). *Ethnopsychanalyse Complémentariste.* Flammarion, Paris.

DEVEREUX, GEORGE (1976). *Dreams in Greek Tragedy: An Ethno-Psycho-Analytic Study*. University of California Press, Berkeley, California.

DEVEREUX, GEORGE (1978). *Ethnopsychoanalysis: Psychoanalysis and Anthropology as Complementary Frames of Reference*. University of California Press, Berkeley, California. (English translation of *Ethnopsychanalyse Complémentariste.*)

RATZEL, FRIEDRICH (1894). *Völkerkunde*. 3 volumes. Bibliographisches Institut, Leipzig.

RÓHEIM, GÉZA (1932). Psycho-analysis of primitive cultural types. *The International Journal of Psycho-Analysis*, **13**, 1–224.

SPINDLER, GEORGE D. (Ed.) (1978). *The Making of Psychological Anthropology*. University of California Press, Berkeley, California.

VALABREGA, J.-P. (1957). L'anthropologie psychanalytique. *La Psychanalyse*, 3, 221–245.

Fantasy and Symbol as Dimensions of Reality

George Devereux

FOR PRESENT PURPOSES I define the symbol as a special form of fantasy which, as a rule, stands for something having, or alleged to have, an existence, and susceptible of being designated by a conventional and specific signifier: for example by a word, which encompasses *all* of the signified, excepting only its symbolic connotations or potentialities. By contrast, the symbol of "something" designates, as a rule, not the essential objective totality of the thing symbolized, but only what it can mean, or can be made to mean, in a particular fantasmatic frame of references or context. Thus, the term "column" designates all the essential qualities of that object, which can *also* be a phallic symbol. I hold that it is at least heuristically useful to assume that "column" refers *(lato sensu)* to the *total* thing and column = phallus only to one of its fantasied segmental aspects, and that "column" and "symbol of the phallus" belong to different universes of discourse.

I do not propose to labour these heuristic distinctions, for that would only lead to metaphysical arguments – a type of discourse in which I do not feel at home. I therefore pass directly to concrete and operational considerations.

The first question to be asked when discussing symbolic behaviour is whether *non*-symbolic behaviour exists. Here, this question will be asked only as regards *human* behaviour. I am neither qualified, nor willing, to concern myself in any way with animals, for I cannot improvise solutions for problems outside my fields of competence. I write here as an ethnologist and psychoanalyst only and therefore feel entitled to use only the data and frames of reference of these two sciences.

In short, I do not propose to define in detail what is meant by "symbol". I only note that this very fashionable word is often manipulated in a somewhat Humpty-Dumpty-ish manner: it is made to mean whatever fits the intellectual game a particular person happens to be playing. In particular, this term increasingly tends to get mixed up with the conceptual ballet to which so much – but not all – of the presently popular science of signs, "semiology", is reducible. Specifically, I am not convinced that certain schools of semiology adequately distinguish "the signifier" from "the symbol", whenever both pertain – though in different ways – to the "same" signified "thing". The little I know of semiology, and that is very little indeed, leaves me with the possibly erroneous impression that this science is still bogged down, particularly as regards differentiating between signifier and symbolizer, in a kind of problem, or pseudo-problem, related to the one mooted already in Platon's *Kratylos*: is the name of a thing determined by and indeed part of the nature *(physis)* of that thing, or is it a purely conventional *(nomos)*, externally attributed, designation thereof? Fortunately, a further elucidation of these highly abstract and "philosophical", rather than properly scientific problems is outside the purview of the present discussion.

These remarks close the more or less speculative portion of my paper. In the rest I will discuss scientific, operationally meaningful problems only. My basic position is that there is no wholly non-symbolic human activity whatever. Our most basic activities, quite as much as our most recondite ones, always have an operative symbolic significance of one kind or another.

For example, it is by now fairly generally conceded that all dreams are largely symbolic and that every detail of a dream, including even such trivial activities as walking, eating, etc., in dream, may not be taken at face value in their interpretation but must be viewed as symbolic acts: almost as metaphors in the Aristotelian sense. It is fascinating in this context to consider, side by side, the Aristotelian conception of the metaphor as set forth in his *Poetics* (1459a5 ff.), and his notion of dream interpretation as explained in his *Divination in Dreams*

(464b5 ff.). The greatest gift of the poet, we are told, is his ability to devise metaphors: to construct symbolic representations of some sort of reality, be it a physical or an intrapsychic one. Conversely, it is evident that, for Aristoteles, dream interpretation, viewed as a series of operations, is practically the symmetrical opposite of metaphor construction. What the metaphor-creating poet (or dreamer) assembles, the dream interpreter disassembles. The poet or dreamer increases the gap between objective reality and its verbal representation by devising a metaphor, while the dream interpreter decreases it to the greatest possible extent.

It is, at any rate, quite clear that even the most commonplace dream element which, objectively, has an equally commonplace equivalent in real, waking life, also has a symbolic dimension. Thus, walking, which is a rhythmic activity, does not represent only locomotion in dream, no matter how much the dream's plot calls for dreamed walking. Because of its rhythmic character, walking in dream may symbolize, more or less crucially and focally, or else simply marginally, also coitus or sexual arousal. The same is true also of certain other highly rhythmic waking activities: first and foremost, of dancing. One may even compare post-orgastic dizziness to the type of dizziness one experiences after intensive waltzing, which involves a rotation about one's own axis, or else after trance-type dancing, where prolonged strenuous stamping and characteristic head bobbing bring about a particular type of vertigo resembling post-orgastic dizziness. I note in passing that the head bobbing one so often observes in trance dancing, and which I, like many others, observed in Haitian voodoo rituals, is represented also on a Greek bas-relief showing a dancing Mainad (British Museum).

I obviously cannot enumerate here, one by one, all the commonplace activities which can occur in ordinary dreams and then go on to indicate that each of them stands for something else, which is represented in dream in symbolic form only, in order to smuggle the symbolized (disguised) item past the selectively vigilant dream censor. I can, however, show that quite commonplace real activities, which symbolize something else in dream, can, even in their real, waking, purposeful, goal-oriented form, have affinities with what these activities symbolize in dream.

In English, to "go" with a person of the opposite sex, to *walk* with such a person, is a conventional and delicate way of alluding to an intended, or incipient, or actual sexual connection between the two. The German equivalent adds a further nuance to "walking": walking *out (ausgehen)*. In French, the first of these elements, the *walking*, recedes and becomes implicit: one "outs" or even "exits" with a person of the opposite sex: *Sortir avec une fille (un garçon)*. This infinitive is, content-wise, related to the English participle-noun, "outing". The added nuance ("out") corresponds to, or symbolizes, a very important aspect of courtship and sexual relations. Freud (1921) pointed out that society tends to resent the lovers' withdrawal of their libido from their group and its concentrated re-investment in the loved person.

Most societies had to come to terms with this psychological process, for without it society would cease to exist biologically. Of course, some "model" societies, beginning with Platon's *Republic*, have done all they could to reduce heterosexual love-making to an affectively sterile mounting of the female by the male. All have erected incest taboos, from which only the gods and, in some areas, the divine kings are exempt. Holding, with both Frazer and Freud, that the urge to commit incest must be very strong indeed to have given rise to so universal a taboo, I am inclined to see in this taboo partly – I repeat, partly – an attempt on the part of society to impede an excessive temporal prolongation of early intrafamilial affective bonding, as well as an extreme (and therefore desocializing) intensification of sexual bonding, which the permanent sexual receptiveness of the human female does render possible. Thus, in ancient Sparta there was, together with an un-Greek liberty of women, also a systematic attempt to minimize husband-wife intimacy and involvement. The waking life of the Spartan was spent amongst men; he visited his wife only at night and as secretively and sneakily as one visits a tabooed mistress. Some segments of our own society are also either unwilling or unable to cope with intense love relationships. In Nevile Shute's *Pastoral* (1944), a charming wartime novel about a Flight Lieutenant and a female Section Officer's very "proper" love affair, a senior WAAF officer tells the lovers that Royal Air Force rules were not made to cope with people in their state; that is, with deeply enamoured people.

These remarks amply demonstrate that even the simple act of "walking out" (with one's young woman) has, both psychoanalytically and sociologically, a fully interpretable symbolic meaning.

That both the words "walking" and "out", and even more the expression, "walking out *with*" hint at symbolic dimensions, particularly with respect to sexuality (and love, of course), explains – sufficiently to render the fact comprehensible within the universe of discourse adopted here – why, in dream, "walking" can be one way of symbolizing coitus. There are, of course, many other ways of symbolizing coitus or sexual arousal in dream (and elsewhere), but these other symbols could also be subjected to similar analyses.

I must now tackle the problem of the alleged difference between private and public symbols, discussed in a recent book by Sir Raymond Firth (1973). I am obliged to question the validity of that distinction on theoretical grounds.

I enunciated more than twenty years ago (Devereux, 1955; cf. 1972, Chapter 3) the principle that each person is a complete specimen of Man and each society a complete specimen of Society. The same range of items can be discovered by the study in depth of one person (or society) and by the cross-sectional study – using relatively superficial means, such as questionnaires – of many persons (or societies). Even fragmentary and usually superficial data concerning abortion in many societies permit one to draw up an inventory of everything a study in depth of abortion in one society or even in one person can reveal (Devereux, 1955). Similarly, types of sexual *conduct* which the Kinsey Reports show to be statistically frequent tend to correspond to the conscious *cravings* of most persons; forms of *conduct* which these reports reveal to be very rare tend to be present, as repressed *wishes*, in the unconscious of even normal heterosexuals. As regards societies, caninophobe traits are present at least in the marginal segments of our nominally caninophile culture ("man's best friend" *v.* "dirty dog", "bitch"), while in caninophobe Arab culture ("the dog is unclean") caninophily finds an expression in the recording of the purebred greyhound's pedigree in the family Koran (Devereux, 1970, p. 359). In short, under suitable conditions, everyone can fully empathize with everyone else: the anthropologist can, in principle, work with every tribe there is; the psychoanalyst can, in principle, understand any patient. The existence of cryptography, which includes both the encoding (symbolizing) of messages and the decoding of coded (symbolic) messages, demonstrates the same fact.

It was originally my intention to discuss here one of Stendhal's "private symbols": one of the neologistic cryptograms he used to record his ideas, opinions and private experiences. He meant these cryptic jottings to be incomprehensible "non-symbols" to the "spies" whom he so greatly dreaded, but also to serve him – and only him – as (symbolic) mnemotechnical devices. Unfortunately, the neologism (symbol) I had intended to discuss proved to be so complex that its detailed analysis would have taken too much space. Reserving my analysis of Stendhal's cryptogram "Earline" for another occasion, I note here only that it is almost certainly a neologism meaning "countess". What matters most is that a young admirer of Stendhal, who, like his idol, also used an idiosyncratic and improvised private code for the recording of certain personal matters, turned Stendhal's neologism, "Earline", into a "public symbol", by applying it to a countess with whom he had been intimate. I note, in fine, that Stendhal experts have decoded most of that author's cryptic jottings, or "private symbols" – many of them not by means of standard cryptographical analyses, but by learning to "free associate" the way Stendhal did.

Even more relevant in this context is Weston La Barre's admirable demonstration that all religions are simply the subsequently institutionalized, but originally subjective, delusions of ecstatic individuals, who had received a privately encoded symbolic "revelation", capable of being co-experienced by others as a revelation through the gradual transformation of the prophet's private symbols into public ones (La Barre, 1970).

The distinction between "public" and "private" symbols is made otiose also by the finding that public symbols of unknown meaning can be decoded exactly the way one decodes private symbols. Thus, there existed at Delphi the Stepterion festival, which Ploutarchos only recorded *(Greek Questions 12; On the Obsolescence of Oracles 15)* but did not explain. I will discuss one feature of this rite only: a table was set and then overturned. This rite appears to have had something to do with Apollon's slaying of the dragon Python who, before Apollon's takeover, had guarded the oracular shrine of Delphi on behalf of chthonian deities. We have two data to go on: both concern the cannibalization of children. One tradition reports that when a child was sacrified and its entrails offered to Zeus Lykaios (a name almost certainly connected with the word *lykos* (wolf), for the rite was connected with lykanthropy), Zeus – outraged, it is said, by this horrible sacrifice – upset the table which served as an altar. In Aischylos

(*Agamemnon*, 1601 f.), Thyestes kicks over the table on which a cannibalistic feast was served. In Seneca's *Thyestes* (989 ff.) too, the table shook as Thyestes vomited and then cursed the house of his brother Atreus. These data entitle one to assume that the upset table of the Delphic Stepterion also had something to do with a cannibalistic child sacrifice, whose aetiological myth had either been forgotten or which the amiable and humane Ploutarchos found too outrageous to record. Yet one can be certain that the teknophagic interpretation of the symbolism of the upset table is valid, for there exists one myth which explicitly links the ritual devouring of a child with Delphi.

According to Firmicus Maternus' treatise, *On the Errors of Pagan Religions* 6, the "first" Dionysos was rent and devoured in infancy by the Titans. Athena who, though present, could not prevent this deed, did not eat Dionysos' "heart", which was given to her as her share, but took it to Delphi where Zeus caused it to be placed inside a cult statue. Now, according to this account, what one should find at Delphi is the *heart* of Dionysos. Yet what, according to Ploutarchos, one does encounter in a major Delphic ritual is not the heart but the figwood phallos of Dionysos, placed in a winnowing basket, called *liknon* in Greek.

Lack of space prevents me from analysing this detail further and from showing that the salvaged "heart" is actually the salvaged phallos of Dionysos: of the *first* Dionysos (Zagreus). I must content myself with two brief indications. According to Klementos of Alexandria (*Protreptikos*, 2.19.4), the Kabeiroi, savage and archaic deities, carried around with them a box containing Dionysos' virile parts. This myth recalls the fact that the self-castrated Galloi, the priests of the Earth Goddess Kybele, put their own ablated organs into boxes, as did a certain Kumbabe (Loukianos, *de dea Syria*, 19 ff.). The second point is that in all classical literary sources the *second* Dionysos – whom, according to one tradition, Semele conceived "cannibalistically" by ingesting the ashes of his heart (or of his phallos?) (Hyginus, *Fabula* 167) – was systematically represented as effeminate (*gynnis*) and, as I have shown in a recent paper (Devereux, 1973), also as having a eunuchoid body build, that is, having abnormally long legs (Aischylos, *Fr.* 62 N^2).

I have cited this example not because I expect the reader to pay attention to the details of my analysis and conclusions, but in order to indicate that the decoding of what may, in the first approximation, be considered a *public* symbol, can be effected by the very same methods that can be used in the decoding of a supposedly *private* symbol, such as Stendhal's "Earline". I hold, in short, that the nature and genesis of so-called private symbols does not differ from that of so-called public symbols and that both can be decoded by recourse to identical methods and techniques. What one person or one culture can symbolize ("encode"), another can decode. One can usually discern the nature of what is represented symbolically and can, as a rule, specify also the decoding methods and techniques one used for this purpose.

I now propose to discuss briefly the third and last facet of symbolization and of symbolic behaviour in general. I start with a very simple fact. There are probably few words in the dictionary – if, indeed, there are any – which have no metaphorical uses at all. To keep to a word already discussed, "table" does not signify only a particular piece of furniture; one also speaks of "tableland", of *tabula rasa*, of "tabled" motions, of the "table" of multiplications, and so on. It is as though man forever rebelled against one of his species' most characteristic traits: against his capacity for specific, clearly circumscribed, segmental action and thinking. As a mathematician, one knows that "three" is simply the third integer and the third prime number; but, at the same time, one's cultural heritage causes one to assign certain cultural meanings to the number "three". For example, the Germans say, "All good things come in threes" *(Aller guten Dinge sind drei)*. One's religious background may also cause one to see in "three" a hint at the Holy Trinity. One's unconscious sees in "three" an allusion to the three parts of the male reproductive organ – already Ploutarchos *(Roman Questions* No. 2) says as much, almost in so many words; he visualized the number "two" as a feminine symbol and explained that the use of five nuptial torches symbolized the conjoining of the male "three" with the female "two".

Similarly, the male's tendency to take sexual initiatives, at times aggressively, explains why the Japanese speak of the penis as the "male dagger" and why spear, dagger, firearms, etc., all of which are primarily means of aggression, so often symbolize the male organ in daily parlance, in dream, in ritual, and so forth. The basic consideration appears to be that whereas semantically "table" or "dagger" denote highly specific objects, eliciting segmental, functionally specific, affectively circumscribed responses, manipulations, etc., the moment these terms are used symbolically they acquire a greatly broadened relevance and elicit infinitely more complexly motivated and affectively more variable and more resonant subjective responses and manipulations. Larger segments of the total personality become involved in a symbolic behaviour element than in an identical but (hypothetically) non-symbolic act.

As an aside, I note that great art often involves the blending of real things with their symbolic, fantasmatic significance. Winged Pegasos seems persuasive despite his biological, and even purely mechanical, impossibility, because both riding and flying represent coitus *for* and *in* the unconscious. Thus, since winged Pegasos represents both the reality of horses and the symbolic connotations of riding, it is able to "persuade" us. Having dealt with the Pegasos problem as paradigmatic of the depth-psychological realism of great art in a recent book (Devereux, 1976), I need not labour this point further and shall conclude my paper with certain theoretical inferences.

I propose to advance a hypothesis concerning, not the origins of symbols or of man's capacity to devise, use and decode symbols, but some psychological advantages of that capacity. Man is not only an extremely complexly organized creature, capable of highly specific and narrowly segmental acts but, perhaps precisely because such is his nature, also a being experiencing great difficulties in, so to speak, keeping himself together in one piece: in getting totally involved, in responding to specific stimuli not only segmentally, but wholly.

Like quicksilver, man is all too often dribbling away in every direction, by means of an overly narrow segmentalization of behaviour, etc. A good contemporary example is the increasingly prevalent tendency to indulge in mere fornication, devoid of affective overtones; or, on another level, to respond to a complex situation in a totally impersonal and circumscribed manner: "I wish I could help you in your plight, but paragraph 12 of article 270 of the code obliges me to . . ." – and that is all there is to it. A rose is a rose is a rose – period. All else is simply disconnected, or so it would seem, though I will return to this matter in a moment. But if a rose is also the rose of the Wars of the Roses and is apprehended as a suitable gift to one's beloved (and so forth), more of man-as-a-whole gets mobilized by the stimulus represented by a rose, and this broader, more comprehensive mobilization of man is recognized as an integral part of the stimulus (which now has also symbolic overtones and facets) and of the response to it as well. Thus, symbolization helps to hold man's segmental capacities together and fosters a broader direct involvement with the situation.

The key word here is *direct*. For even in a totally segmental response to a stimulus theoretically devoid ("plucked") of all symbolic dimensions, the rest of the person continues to be fully, albeit indirectly, stimulated and the exclusion – the casual or intentional disconnecting – of the rest of himself is, in fact, also a part of his global response to the supposedly non-symbolic, segmental stimulus. The crucial and destructive difference between a direct and an indirect (and reluctant) total mobilization of man by any stimulus is that the reluctant and indirect, and often unconscious, response of his supposedly excluded and uninvolved segments will radically vitiate his intentionally segmental response, decreasing its "objectivity" and functional appropriateness. Thus, coitus, spoliated of its other potentialities, will almost certainly be less absorbing and less gratifying for him (or her) than for an animal living in freedom. In such narrowly circumscribed situations the theoretically excluded segments of man still intervene, but in a manner which further impoverishes and distorts his segmental perception and response. In saying this, I simply carry one step further my previously published analysis of the distorting effects of absurd methodologies, which deliberately create a (fictitious) vacuum and call it objectivity (Devereux, 1967).

Side by side with this constricted perception of, and response to, a unidimensionally defined stimulus, from which one seeks to disconnect most of one's self, most of one's plenitude, one also brings about a self-destructive state of affairs. The uninvolved (or theoretically uninvolved) portion of one's self does not cease to operate. It simply splits off from reality and goes off on a "bender"... into a dreamlike and almost schizophrenoid state, operating apart from external stimuli which, as noted, become constricted to the point of unidimensionality.

I had such an experience on my arrival in Canberra from Paris, as a result of a combination of influenza and severe jet-lag. My total stimulability, my capacity to apprehend situations multidimensionally, was almost abolished. The moment I was able to entrust myself to my host's kindly care, I observed first an incapacity to operate in the framework of a time-span exceeding a few minutes. On talking over afterwards my behaviour while in a state of jet-lag exhaustion, my host told me that I had spoken rationally, but also that what I had said had no real continuity. I appear to have skipped from one thing to another, in response to the stimulus of the instant. My "temporal ego" (Devereux 1966) had been momentarily impaired.

On another level, I noted that whenever I was not the recipient of a stimulus directly addressed to me – that is, whenever I was not directly spoken to – part of my mind began to dream. Thus, I knew that I was sitting at a table and eating; I was also aware of my host's presence, but only in a remote sort of way. With my eyes open, part of my mind was periodically slipping "sideways", into a dreamlike, or at least hypnagogic, state – for the first, and I hope the last, time in my life, for it was not a pleasant experience. Also, though I was able to set in motion the machinery of my good upbringing, I could hear myself say "please" and "thank you" as if I were only a suitably programmed computer. At least twenty-four hours elapsed before I could once more apprehend those I met as multidimensional persons and not as mere "partial objects". So far as I know, I did nothing silly during the first twenty-four hours, but I also know that every person and thing I encountered during that period was experienced as unidimensional and non-symbolic and that successive events were apprehended as discrete: not as sequential, not as components of a temporal pattern. My time perception was not that of the historian but that of the chronicler (Devereux, 1975; 1978, Ch. 11).

Such, I believe, would be our perception of persons, things and events if we stripped them totally of their symbolic dimensions. Our only alternative – given our capacity for symbolization and for multidimensional, truly "time articulated", sequential behaviour (be that behaviour perception or response) – to a truly involved broad reaction to reality would be a side-slipping, a derailment into purely symbolic, dreamlike mentation; in short, into schizophrenic delusion.

Summing up, man's great capacity for segmentalization, for functional specificity, enables him to get fully involved with persons, things and time only by means of his complementary capacity to make reality highly multidimensional. This, in turn, permits a richer, broader, more fully involved response to reality, by means of a perception of, and response to, each item of reality, both as concrete and as symbolic.

If this capacity to ascribe also a symbolic meaning to external stimuli and to our own acts were lost, people would either become computers, of the *idiot savant* type, or, as is more likely, would lose all capacity to apprehend reality as real and external and would lapse exclusively into symbolic thinking – in which a toilet utterly ceases to be an hygienic device and is seen as only a throne, or as the entrance to a labyrinth in which dwells a dragon to whom daily faecal sacrifices must be offered (Devereux, 1978, Ch. 3).

I therefore see in fantasy – one facet or subdivision of which is the symbol – the chief guarantor of the capacity of that complex, segmentalization-prone being, Man, to remain in full contact with reality and therefore also with himself, in all his plenitude. In the anthropological perspective, the guarantor of fantasy is reality. In the psychological-psychoanalytic perspective, the guarantor of reality is fantasy. This is one of the many reasons inducing me to assert, in opposition to Whitehead, that Nature is, of necessity, open to the mind. As to Einstein's dictum, that the only miraculous thing about Nature is our capacity to comprehend it, I would add that the mind's capacity to comprehend itself is, if possible, even more miraculous – provided one defines as "miraculous" the existence of regularities, rather than the occurrence of exceptions to it.

References

DEVEREUX, GEORGE (1955). *A Study of Abortion in Primitive Societies*. Julian Press, New York. (Rev. ed. 1976, International Universities Press, New York.)

DEVEREUX, GEORGE (1966). Transference, screen memory and the temporal ego. *Journal of Nervous and Mental Disease*, **143**, 318–323.

DEVEREUX, GEORGE (1967). *From Anxiety to Method in the Behavioral Sciences*. Mouton, Paris and The Hague.

DEVEREUX, GEORGE (1970). *Essais d'Ethnopsychiatrie Générale*. Gallimard, Paris. (3rd ed. 1977.) (English translation in press, University of Chicago Press, Chicago, Illinois.)

DEVEREUX, GEORGE (1972). *Ethnopsychanalyse Complémentariste*. Flammarion, Paris. (English translation: *Ethnopsychoanalysis: Psychoanalysis and Anthropology as Complementary Frames of Reference* (1978). University of California Press, Berkeley, California.)

DEVEREUX, GEORGE (1973). Le fragment d'eschyle 62 Nauck[2]. Ce qu'y signifie ΧΛΟΥΝΗΣ *Revue des Etudes Grecques*, **86**, 277–284.

DEVEREUX, GEORGE (1975). Time: history versus chronicle; socialization as cultural experience. *Ethos*, **3,** 281–292. (Also in *Ethnopsychoanalysis* (1978), Chapter 11.)

DEVEREUX, GEORGE (1976). *Dreams in Greek Tragedy: An Ethno-Psycho-Analytic Study*. University of California Press, Berkeley, California.

DEVEREUX, GEORGE (1978). *Ethnopsychoanalysis: Psychoanalysis and Anthropology as Complementary Frames of Reference*. University of California Press, Berkeley, California.

FIRTH, RAYMOND (1973). *Symbols, Public and Private*. George Allen and Unwin, London.

FREUD, SIGMUND (1921). *Group Psychology and the Analysis of the Ego*. Standard Edition, vol. 18 (1955), pp 69–143. Hogarth Press, London.

LA BARRE, WESTON (1970). *The Ghost Dance: The Origins of Religion*. Doubleday, Garden City, New York.

SHUTE, NEVIL (1944). *Pastoral*. Heinemann, London.

Pythagoras in America

Claude Lévi-Strauss

TO RENDER TO George Devereux homage to his measure, one would have to prove oneself at once ethnologist, Hellenist and psychoanalyst, to be able, like him, to do research simultaneously in these three disciplines and even to discover transitions and links between the three. This I shall not attempt to do but will content myself with presenting here some remarks on a problem which transcends my competence and which I do not pretend to solve; but it offers at least the advantage of being situated at the conjunction of the first two of these domains and, in the opinion of some, also of the third. The problem concerns the special place which people – remote from each other in time and in space – assign to the seeds of this or that plant of the family *Leguminosae*, subfamily *Papilionaceae*.

The recent studies of Marcel Detienne (1970; 1972, pp. 96–100, pp. 110–114) sum up the controversies to which, ever since antiquity, Pythagorean traditions have given rise, and of which his studies offer a brilliant interpretation. However, the ethnologist cannot but pay attention to the recurrence of the selfsame beliefs and rites not only in the ancient world and outside the school of Pythagoras, but also, in a more general way, in the Old World and, as I intend to show here, in the New. For the comparative ethnologist, the views propounded by the Pythagoreans on the subject of beans (broad beans, *faba*) thus represent a particular example of probably earlier ideas and practices, whose geographical distribution seems considerably greater than an enquiry limited to the ancient world would suggest. Nor is that all: for, even in the ancient world, beans were the object of diametrically opposed beliefs.

In Greece, not only the Pythagoreans but also Orphic traditions and the Eleusinian rites proscribed beans. According to various sources, foremost that of Plutarch, this prohibition was the rule for whoever wished to lead a life of purity. Outside Greece, according to Herodotus, the Egyptian priests enjoined themselves neither to eat beans nor even to look at them; in Rome, the Flamen Dialis could neither eat this vegetable nor utter its name. On the other hand, still in the ancient world, there were also occasions on which the eating of beans was peremptorily prescribed. In Attica boiled beans were eaten during the feast called Pyanopsia; the Romans sacrified beans to various deities as well as to the dead during the Parentalia, the Feralia and the Lemuria. According to Pliny (XVIII, xxx), they put beans – as luck-bringers – amongst objects sold at public auctions.

Thus, though the Pythagoreans execrated beans, in some circumstances the opposite view prevailed. That the former attitude was, in fact, the more frequent of the two is made evident by one of Pliny's comments. After noting that the Pythagoreans forbade beans because they served as an abode for the souls of the deceased, he adds, "For that reason . . . beans are employed in memorial sacrifices to dead relatives", which explains why (he continues) "There is also a special religious sanctity attached to the bean; at all events it is the custom to bring home from the harvest a bean by way of an auspice, this being consequently called [the brought-back bean]" *(referiva, refriva)*.

The short survey just made shows that the Pythagorean prohibition was but one aspect, amongst others, of the attitude of the ancients towards beans. It is not possible to account for this attitude by looking only at its negative aspect. If an interpretation is to seem plausible, it would be necessary to find a single principle which would render comprehensible why, according to the context, beans inspired horror or respect; why eating them was now forbidden, now recommended; why, in a word, in one sense or another, beans had, in the eyes of the ancients, the character of a highly charged term.

One finds in America something like an echo of these beliefs, though there they do not concern the broad bean *(faba)*, which is a Eurasian plant, but the New World legume which most resembles it: the true (American) bean. The Pawnee, agricultural Indians of Missouri, tell in their version of a myth which corresponds to the myth of Orpheus and Eurydice and which is very widespread in North America, that, after having torn his young wife from the world of the dead, the hero stopped at the place of a supernatural protectress, whom he had already visited on his outward journey. She gave him red beans which, she said, he should cause the people of his village to eat, "so that they would receive power to communicate with the dead spirits". According to a variant of this myth, these same red beans would serve, on the contrary, for bewitching the living (Dorsey, 1906, p. 413, p. 537).

This episode brings to mind the Lemuria, as described by Ovid (V, 436 ff.). Each paterfamilias, his mouth full of black beans, went through his house spitting them out behind him: ". . . the shade is thought to gather the beans, and to follow unseen behind . . . and [he] asks the shade to go out of his house." Equally reminiscent of the American rite is the Setsubun, a mobile feast celebrated in Japan just before the coming of spring: "Beans are scattered about the house on the evening of this day in order to scare away demons." (Chamberlain, 1905, p. 161.) Thus, be it in order to establish or to interrupt communications with the beyond, the seeds of the *Papilionaceae* play a role in the thought of very diverse peoples. One can even broaden the paradigm if, beside the *Papilionaceae*, one makes a place also for plants of the family *Fumariaceae*, genus *Dicentra*, which the Onondaga Indians believed to be the food of the dead and called "ghost or spirit corn" (Beauchamp, 1898, p. 199). The fruit of these wild plants, cousins of the Bleeding Heart of our gardens, *Dicentra spectabilis*, is a longish pod filled with seeds which, when ripe, splits open right down to its base, thus resembling the haricot bean.

Do the mythical views of American Indians help to understand the role of intermediary between the living and the dead which these Indians assign at times to the bean and to fruits with a similar appearance? In America, the bean and the maize are often viewed as a sexed pair, but it so happens that, from one tribe to another, the sex ascribed respectively to each plant is reversed. For the Iroquois, maize is male and the bean female. They planted the bean very close to the maize when the stalk of the latter was about fifteen centimetres high, and let them grow up together – the rigid stalk of the maize plant served as a support and the beanstalk wrapped itself around it. By contrast, the squash extends its vine along the ground and seems to flee from the nearest maize plant. That is why, according to myth, Maize married "the Maid Bean" in preference to her rival (the squash) (Beauchamp, 1898, pp. 196–197).

But the Tutelo, who belong to the Sioux linguistic family, even though they lived in contact with the Iroquois (and, be it noted, perhaps precisely for that reason), took the opposite view: they made the maize female and the bean male, because, as they put it: "The men depend upon the women, as the beans cling on the corn [stalks] when growing." (Speck, 1942, p. 120.) The Iroquois symbolism reappears in Mexico and in Guatemala, where the Indians often plant maize and bean in the same hole (Pennington, 1969, p. 59; Vogt, 1969, p. 54). Both for the Chorti of Guatemala and for the people of the Mitla region in Mexico, the maize spirit is male and the bean spirit female (Wisdom, 1940, p. 402; Parsons, 1936, pp. 324–329). It cannot be asserted, however, that those American Indians who treat the bean as female, view – as do certain people of New Guinea (Berndt, 1962, p. 41, note 8) – Mother Earth as a kind of pod producing many seeds: New World myths concerning the origin of cultivated plants describe them as born from various parts of the body of a being who is sometimes female and sometimes male. To take only one or two examples – according to the Iroquois, the Huron, the Creek and the Cherokee – maize came from the breasts, from a thigh, from the stomach or from the vagina of a woman, and the bean came from her forelimbs (according to the Iroquois from the fingers), from the other thigh, or from her armpits. By contrast, the Kaingang of Southern Brazil chose for such purposes a male being: his penis became maize, his testicles beans, his head a squash (Ploetz and Métraux, 1930, p. 212).

This last system of correspondences evokes two others: one which resembles it, and one which, seemingly, contradicts it. In the fertility rites of ancient India a grain of barley symbolizes the penis, two beans the testicles (Indradeva, 1973, p. 37); but in Japanese mythology, the beans (*Soja* and *Phaseolus*) emerged from the genitalia of the goddess Ukemochi (Aston, 1896, vol. I, p. 33). Such divergences – of which it would be easy to give other examples – could be overcome if it were to be assumed that, of the sexual organs of the male, the penis, congruent with the stiff stalk of the maize and of cereals, is relatively more "male" than are the testicles. The opposition – common in America – between maize (male) and beans (female) would then follow from an implicit relationship of equivalence in terms of which the male principle stands to the female principle – with respect to sexuality – as the penis stands to the testicles with respect to masculinity.

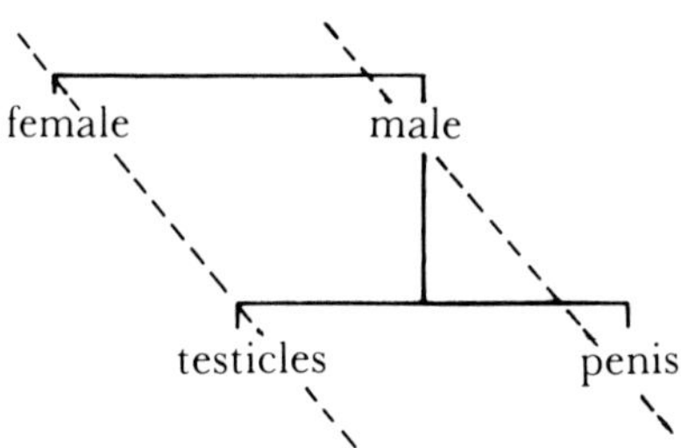

Though postulated for America, such a conception is directly verifiable in New Guinea, where various groups view the fruit of the coconut tree and that of the areca palm as a sexed pair, but each term of which is itself ambivalent, save only that a diachronic ambivalence amongst the Orokaiva (where each plant, originally endowed with one sex, subsequently acquires the opposite sex) appears as synchronic amongst the Tangu. Nonetheless, and in spite of the geographical distance between these two groups, coconuts symbolize for both of them, at one and the same time, breasts of women and testicles (Schwimmer, 1973, p. 169; Burridge, 1969, p. 190). Areca nuts, at first male and then female, according to the Orokaiva (Schwimmer, 1973, pp. 168–170), symbolize simultaneously for the Tangu both testicles and nubile young girls (Burridge, 1969, pp. 251, 306). Thus, data of this type indicate clearly that the testicles, the least ostensibly male part of the male organ, occupy in mythical representations from several regions of the world an ambiguous position between opposite categories.

These findings bring one back to Greece and to the controversies, which have been going on since antiquity, over the food prohibitions of the Pythagoreans. Diogenes Laertius (VIII, 34) records that Aristotle took into account, as one explanation among several others, the similarity between beans and testicles. Aulus Gellius went even further: he wrote, "Kúamous *hoc in loco testiculos significare dicunt*" (IV, xi), denying that the prohibition ascribed to Pythagoras and enunciated by Empedocles concerned food. He cited Aristoxenus in order to prove that beans were one of the favourite dishes of Pythagoras – a good example, be it noted in passing, of the ambivalence of beans, here centred upon the person of the founder. A modern author glosses the Greek name of this legume: "*Kúamoi* [beans] . . . eggs, vessels of seed, of generation, and connected with *kueîn*" (Onians, 1954, p. 112), which means "to swell, to be pregnant"– a surprising convergence of views between the ancient Greeks and the Tangu. As a matter of fact, George Devereux himself tells me that the ancient Greeks saw a connection between the broad bean *(faba)* and nubile girls; the same word, *kúamos*, denotes both that vegetable and the swelling of the breasts at the onset of puberty. Furthermore, in an important paper, Devereux (1968) has disclosed the unconscious equation prevailing in the minds of some patients between testicles and breasts.

If one dared to suggest that – as we hypothesized for America and were able to verify for New Guinea – the testicles are recognized in a fairly general way as a mediating term between opposite sexual categories, it would seem less strange that in the alimentary register, corresponding to the category of life, beans, symbols of the testicles, should also be – in contradistinction to cereals – relatively closer to the opposite category, that is to say, to the category of death. Between these two formalisms, in fact, a clear-cut homology may be observed:

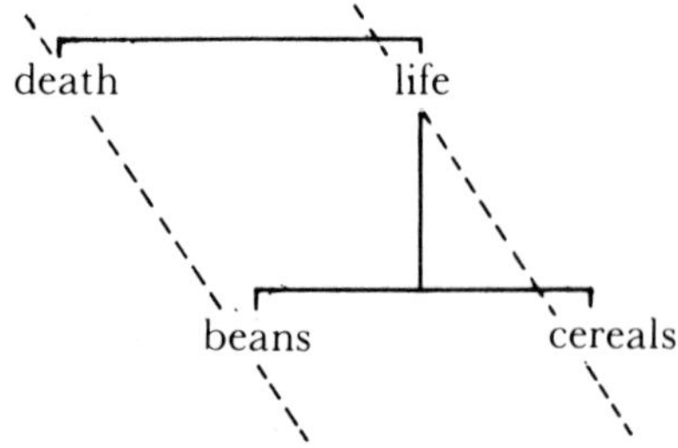

Hence, perhaps, the ambiguous position of beans between life and death upon which Detienne (1970, p. 153) so strongly insists and which, either in the same or in different cultures, predisposes beans to be given, according to circumstances, either a positive or negative connotation, as intermediaries charged either with the task of opening communication between the two worlds or, on the other hand, of interrupting it.

It may be added that the same ambiguity is manifest also on the culinary level. Beans, which the Romans believed to be the oldest cultivated plant, may be eaten raw when young; otherwise they can be eaten only when boiled in water or previously soaked. Herodotus (II,

37) takes care to distinguish between the two ways of eating beans, by emphasizing that Egyptian priests neither chew them raw nor eat them boiled. On the other hand, the earliest way of preparing cereals might have been to parch the grains on the fire, in the manner of "popcorn" (Braidwood, 1953, pp. 515–526). In contradistinction to cereals, which a quick roasting renders edible, the *Leguminosae*, oscillating between the categories "the raw" and "the boiled" (which is also, as I have shown elsewhere, the category of the rotten) would thus be situated on the side of nature and of death.[1]

Let it not be forgotten, however, that these brief reflections took their point of departure from American data, and that they cannot be incorporated into one's material without reservations. For the value of the Americanist contribution will remain uncertain as long as the problem created by the friezes of Mochica ceramics which sometimes represent half human, half bean personages (Hissink, 1951) remains unsolved. For the time being, and despite the efforts of the exegetists, it is possible that these motifs have not yielded up, as yet, all their secrets.

[1] It is true, however, that in the above-mentioned Japanese rite (p. 35) each paterfamilias scatters roasted soybeans. According to information obtained in Japan, roasting soybeans is not part of the normal cuisine. It is therefore tempting to assume that soybeans so prepared and destined for the inhabitants of the beyond (described in ancient Japanese mythology as the world of the rotten) might have, precisely because they are different from the normal diet, an added appeal.

References

ASTON, W. G. (1896). *Nihongi, Chronicles of Japan from the Earliest Times to A.D. 697* (translation, W. G. Aston). 2 volumes. Transactions and Proceedings of the Japan Society, London, Supplement I. Kegan Paul, Trench, Trübner and Co. Ltd, London.

BEAUCHAMP, W. M. (1898). Indian corn stories and customs. *Journal of American Folk-Lore*, **11**, no. 42, 195–202.

BERNDT, R. M. (1962). *Excess and Restraint: Social Control among a New Guinea Mountain People*. University of Chicago Press, Chicago, Illinois.

BRAIDWOOD, R. J. *et al.* (1953). Symposium: Did man once live by beer alone? *American Anthropologist*, **55**, 515–526.

BURRIDGE, K. O. L. (1969). *Tangu Traditions: A Study of the Way of Life, Mythology, and Developing Experience of a New Guinea People*. Clarendon Press, Oxford.

CHAMBERLAIN, B. H. (1905). *Things Japanese*. John Murray, London.

DETIENNE, MARCEL (1970). La cuisine de Pythagore. *Archives de Sociologie des Religions*, no. 29, 141–162.

DETIENNE, MARCEL (1972). *Les Jardins d'Adonis*. Gallimard, Paris.

DEVEREUX, GEORGE (1968). The realistic basis of fantasy. *Journal of the Hillside Hospital*, **17**, no. 1, 13–20.

DIOGENES LAERTIUS (1950). *Lives of Eminent Philosophers* (translation, R. D. Hicks). 2 volumes. Loeb Classical Library. Heinemann, London, and Harvard University Press, Cambridge, Massachusetts.

DORSEY, G. A. (1906). *The Pawnee; Mythology* (Part I). The Carnegie Institution of Washington, Washington, D.C.

GELLIUS, AULUS (1927). *The Attic Nights of Aulus Gellius* (translation J. C. Rolfe). Loeb Classical Library. Heinemann, London, and Harvard University Press, Cambridge, Massachusetts.

HERODOTUS (1942). The Persian Wars (translation G. Rawlinson). In *The Greek Historians* (Ed. F. R. B. Godolphin), vol. 1, pp. 1–563. Random House, New York.

HISSINK, K. (1951). Motive der Mochica-Keramik. *Paideuma. Mitteilungen zur Kulturkunde*, **5**, no. 3, 115–135.

INDRADEVA, SHRIRAMA (1973). La genèse de la civilisation Indienne à travers les Grhya-Sūtra. *Diogène*, **84**, 28–43.

ONIANS, R. B. (1954). *The Origins of European Thought*. Cambridge University Press, Cambridge.

OVID (1951). *Fasti* (translation Sir J. G. Frazer). Loeb Classical Library. Heinemann, London, and Harvard University Press, Cambridge, Massachusetts.

PARSONS, E. C. (1936). *Mitla: Town of the Souls*. University of Chicago Press, Chicago, Illinois.

PENNINGTON, C. W. (1969). *The Tepehuan of Chihuahua. Their Material Culture.* University of Utah Press, Salt Lake City.

PLINY (1950). *Natural History* (Libri XVII–XIX) (translation H. Rackham), vol. 5. Loeb Classical Library. Heinemann, London, and Harvard University Press, Cambridge, Massachusetts.

PLOETZ, H. and MÉTRAUX, A. (1930). La civilisation matérielle et la vie religieuse des Indiens Žé du Brésil Méridional et Oriental. *Revista del Instituto de Etnología de la Universidad Nacional de Tucumán*, **1,** no. 1, 107–238.

PLUTARCH (1936). The Roman questions. In *Moralia*, vol. 4, pp. 1–171 (translation F. C. Babbitt). Loeb Classical Library. Heinemann, London, and Harvard University Press, Cambridge, Massachusetts.

SCHWIMMER, E. (1973). *Exchange in the Social Structure of the Orokaiva.* Hurst, London.

SPECK, F. G. (1942). *The Tutelo Spirit Adoption Ceremony.* Pennsylvania Historical Commission, Harrisburg, Pennsylvania.

VOGT, E. Z. (1969). *Zinacantan. A Maya Community in the Highlands of Chiapas.* Harvard University Press, Cambridge, Massachusetts.

WISDOM, C. (1940). *The Chorti Indians of Guatemala.* University of Chicago Press, Chicago, Illinois.

The Influence of Methods of Observation on Theory, with Particular Reference to the Work of George Devereux and Margaret Lowenfeld

Margaret Mead

THROUGHOUT THE PERIOD that I have been privileged to know George Devereux, to read his published work, to listen to his presentations and discuss his work with him, I have been as preoccupied as he with the relationships among our growing sophistication as human scientists, the period in which we live and the demands that are made upon us for participation, in our relationships to colleagues and to the peoples among whom we work. Devereux has, however, been an active therapist, concerned with the treatment of individuals, and I have been primarily concerned with applied anthropology, especially in the modification of institutional structure and the building of new structures suitable for the changing state of interdependence which has now become world wide (Schwartz, 1976).

One problem that has concerned us both is the way our scientific findings can be communicated to others who have not themselves undergone the particular set of apprenticeship experiences that have made us cultural anthropologists and that make psychoanalysts, psychoanalysts. Interestingly enough, it has been at the Menninger

Foundation in Topeka, Kansas, USA, that both George Devereux and I have wrestled with many of these questions. This has been partly because of a series of historical accidents that have made the psychoanalytic community in Topeka rather unusually receptive to those trained in other disciplines, and partly because of Karl Menninger's special humane interest in American Indians and other aboriginal American peoples.

It was at Topeka that George Devereux conducted the first fully reported account of psychotherapy of an American Indian (Devereux, 1951). It was at Topeka, after participating for three months in a therapeutic community organized along psychoanalytic lines, that I came, I believe, to a deeper understanding of Freudian theory, the kind of understanding that I have been trained to derive from field experience in a group sharing the same culture (Mead, 1963). Both Devereux and I have been concerned with communication, recognizing that scientific enquiry depends upon making the findings of a particular discipline available to members of other disciplines, without their having to go through an apprenticeship experience, and that the physical sciences have developed as the findings of one discipline could be expressed in forms that were communicable, replicable or testable in other ways.

Both those of us in cultural anthropology, with its emphasis on detailed participatory field work, and those in psychoanalysis, that depends on the complete analytic experience, have been severely hampered in our efforts to communicate our findings to others. Our disciplines have become more refined and sophisticated but, nevertheless, the appreciation of these advances is still primarily limited to our own colleagues. Any anthropologist well trained in his discipline can understand and use the work of another ethnographer or linguist, simply by matching his own field experience against the material presented and deciding whether the fellow anthropologist is to be trusted or not. But traditionally, in both field anthropology and psychoanalysis, the full appreciation of any finding has depended upon *experience* rather than upon our ability to present our data in a form that could be examined (Bateson, 1941).

We have struggled with this problem in different ways, owing to the different character of our methods of work. Cultural anthropologists depend primarily on multi-sensory observation of interactive groups, with their own position, towards them and among them, fully specified. Psychoanalysts depend upon private dyadic relationships, in a setting primarily defined as having a therapeutic goal, in which the interchange is verbal, the paralinguistic materials are primarily in an auditory mode (hesitations, repetitions, pauses, emphases), and the interaction, although very complex in terms of levels expressed by the patients and observed in themselves, by the analysts, are still linear in type. In neither case have we had instruments which made it possible to give full access to colleagues in other disciplines, without asking them to repeat the actual experience. Furthermore, as the psychoanalytic process is verbal and linear, any complete repetition on tape or in transcription takes as long as the original event. The anthropological field experience is multi-sensory and unsusceptible to the types of linear expression used in verbal accounts (Foerstel, 1977).

Devereux's speed of note-taking, as illustrated in the reproduction of an interview in *Reality and Dream* (1951), might lead today's students to think that the interview had been tape recorded. Anthropologists of the period before the development of film and tape depended either upon verbal reports of informants which could be reproduced as interlinear texts or on a reconstruction of events based on notes which were necessarily highly selective and fragmentary. Neither record – that of the note-taking psychoanalyst or that of the note-taking field anthropologist – is anything like a full representation of the actual events, to which the field worker and the psychoanalyst are responding as whole persons.

Devereux responded to the need to articulate the way in which the therapist worked by publishing his notes, his interpretative comments and his test protocols. In *Reality and Dream* (1951) and in his later work, *A Study of Abortion in Primitive Societies* (1955), he was careful to provide the actual quotations from the works from which the data from the Human Relations Area Files, and other sources, were taken, so that readers could judge for themselves the nature of the fragmented and unsatisfactory material on which his cross-cultural survey was based, explicitly stated to be a substitute for analyses in depth as none were available. Later, in *From Anxiety to Method in the Behavioral Sciences* (1967), he elaborates the details of behaviour which he feels document the way in which various types of irrationality corrupt the appropriate objective neutrality of scientific judgement.

In his new introduction to the revised edition of *Reality and Dream* (1969) he makes his basic position about method even more explicit.

In preparation for my extended preface for that edition (Mead, 1969) we were able to sharpen some of the points on which we differed; I believe the original difference – whether, and in what ways, preoedipal experience contributed to the basic ethnic personality – is directly related to the methods of psychoanalysis and field work that are primarily oriented to psychoanalytic treatment of adults. Both of these methods are closely related to the problem which I wish to discuss here, and also to the way materials of cultural anthropology and psychoanalysis are to be made available for inspection and use by the uninitiated.

Devereux insisted that the cultural characteristics that he identified in the Plains Indian patient whom he treated in Topeka were postoedipally established and that this finding could be generalized to other areas, whereas I maintained that while his particular finding might be true of very recently assembled cultures – like those of the North American Plains, in which disparate groups entered the new culture after their personalities had been formed in different tribal cultures – this could not be said to be true of cultures with a longer tradition. There, the personality was formed, I believed, much earlier, through multi-sensory, preverbal and nonverbal interactive and environmental experiences (Mead, 1964).

Here the argument turns subtly on the relationship between Devereux's method of analysis – through words and unrecorded, auditory paralinguistic phenomena – and field work based on the verbal accounts given by informants, and protocols based on tests which rely heavily on words (Rorschach and Thematic Apperception Test). When words are the principal data on which the scientist bases his analysis, the post-oedipal involvement, including the reworking of earlier pregenital themes into a post-oedipal form, is salient. Whether or not the principal formation of the ethnic personality is oedipal – at the time that the personality of the child is being formed – it will appear in its oedipal form in a classical type of psychoanalysis which depends on adequate verbal communication.

From the mid 1930s on, although our methods of work differed, Gregory Bateson and I (Mead and Bateson, 1976) struggled with the comparable problem of what kind of material we could collect that would provide for continued post-field analysis. I reorganize all of my observations as I go along, and type up my notes with analytical comments, day by day, so that each observation benefits – or suffers –

from a conscious recognition of what I have already learned. Gregory Bateson's procedure was to accumulate a large mass of raw observations, texts, and later film and still photographs, and analyse the whole corpus after the field work was over. He was therefore more acutely aware of the need to collect a body of material that would be more satisfactory than the material he had collected in his early 1928 and 1932–33 visits to the Iatmul, which was later used for developing themes he had not recognized in the field, in his analysis of the Naven ceremony (Bateson, 1936). Bits of myth, bits of kinship terminology, a small set of photographs, a few ceremonies – all had to be used meticulously, but with many gaps, comparable to the unsatisfactory nature of the materials that Devereux used in his volume on the already half acculturated Mohave (Devereux, 1961).

So, in 1936, we turned to instrumentation – cinematography and still cameras – to provide us with a body of material that could be analysed later, and by others, was independent of words, but not of course independent of verbal recording, without which photographic materials are contextless and uninterpretable. The problem we had to solve was how to make the stuff of field observations available. *Balinese Character* (Mead and Bateson, 1942), in which context-specific photographs are juxtaposed in combinations illustrating relationships between different behavioural contexts, was our first answer, complemented by films in which records of parent–child behaviour could be placed in sequences with ceremonial behaviour (Mead and Bateson, 1952) within a single culture, or to make contrasts between two cultures. We did not have sound then, but it is now possible to do synchronous sound recordings of stretches of highly intricate behaviour and unique events of great complexity, so that further analysis in the light of new theory can be made by others, who need not be anthropologists, nor need they have ever been to the fields from which the materials are drawn (Byers, 1972).

A comparable solution for psychoanalysis involves the use of a tape recorder to give an equally objective report of the utterances of analyst and analysand. But this is far more difficult to do, partly because of the demand for privacy in a therapeutic situation and partly because it is linear material and so both time-consuming and dependent upon the memory of anyone who attempts to analyse it. Transcriptions rob the material of the paralinguistic dimension, and are still time-consuming and linear, but they do allow for reference back and forth.

Straightforward transcriptions, such as those made by Abramson (1956), lack the element of countertransference which Devereux acknowledges to be of great importance. There is no way at present that an analyst can simultaneously record his own countertransference behaviour and the audible responses of the analysand, even if tape is used, without disturbing the primary therapeutic process.

I would like to turn next to some problematic aspects of the use of products like drawings, modellings and scenes. These methods can be used to give access to pregenital behaviour, as is done in the use of toys in child analysis, and they can be used to provide material which can be analysed subsequently by other scientists (Erikson, 1955). Although the difference between drawing tests, which I had begun to use in Manus in 1928 (Mead, 1932, 1946, 1978), and Rorschach tests that depended upon words to provide the data, was obvious, the methodological implications were not so clear. Lawrence K. Frank named such tests as "projective" (Frank, 1939, 1948), but for a time we tended to oppose them in favour of other sorts of tests like the Stanford Binet, which also depended on words but were more highly structured and "performance tests" in which behaviour rather than words was recorded.

Margaret Lowenfeld added another dimension when she developed "objective tests" in which the essential point was that the subject or patient left a *product* in the form of a mosaic pattern, or a dioramic representation of a "world" that could be reproduced and independently examined (Lowenfeld, in press). The analysis of a series of Rorschachs remains sequential and dependent upon a series of formal protocols, while a whole wall-full of mosaics from different members of the same culture or different periods in a patient's treatment can be taken in at once. Working with these materials, Margaret Lowenfeld emphasized aspects of the child's developing consciousness which had previously appeared only as reinterpreted residues in later verbal analyses, in puns, punning dreams, poetry and verbal associations. Working with her materials, she reached into the feeling for the self and the relationship of the self to the universe, in ways that were different from the traditional type of analysis which stressed affective relationships to others. She felt also that the therapist, acting cooperatively with the child who was building a world, was not involved in the transference–countertransference situation, although this was, of course, very variable in terms of the degree of activity of the therapist's behaviour while the child selected material for the world or built from the poleidoblocs or kaleidoblocs (Lowenfeld, 1954; Bowyer, 1970).

Where the "projective tests" utilized vague and ambiguous materials into which the subject could project aspects of his personality and then translate his resulting perceptions and constructs into words, Margaret Lowenfeld dealt with highly structured materials, standard colours and two- and three-dimensional shapes which have explicit mathematical relationships to one another. The miniatures used in building the dioramic worlds were small, three-dimensional figures, made to scale, so that only the moulded sand in the tray where the diorama was constructed and the arrangement of the figures was left entirely to the subject or patient (Mead, 1952). If we think of the several characteristics of unconscious thinking which research revealed as (1) material never available in conscious form, (2) models built upon relations between significant others, and (3) models built upon proprioceptive and exteroceptive responses to the own-body and the natural world, the use of the Lowenfeld materials contributes significantly to this latter component of human development.

Objective and projective tests provide materials from both field work and psychoanalysis (child or adult) in which some of the subtleties can be shared with others. The interpretation of the tests becomes the language of communication among those from other disciplines who use them, and to whom a further understanding can be made available. It is still a somewhat esoteric language, far less neutral and objective than a table, a chart, an equation or a curve, but the fact that the results can be communicated independently of interpretations previously given is important. The circumstance that words are not needed also means that the results of objective tests are more suitable than projective tests in crossing cultural lines between countries which are developing their own version of the discipline of culture and personality.

Furthermore, in cases where many of the cultural values are not only consciously inarticulate but virtually unarticulatable, as Anthony Forge has suggested in his analysis of the Abelam of Papua New Guinea (Forge, 1967), objective tests which involve products, especially drawings and other productions by people whose perceptions are being explored, are invaluable. They may also be used to probe and communicate a people's responses to a deepseated cultural pattern, such as the Iatmul's preference for a complex type of symmetry and complementarity which makes them reject the Rorschach as too symmetrically simple (Métraux, 1976).

The question of the importance of instrumentation in making anthropological field work and psychoanalytic processes available can be approached from another angle. I believe that it is a mistake to say that there is only one origin of science in the observations of fairly regular phenomena like the tides or the constancies displayed by the sun and the moon. Not only is the study of these heavenly bodies and cosmological processes less anxiety producing, as Devereux notes (1967), and amenable to objective and impersonal investigation, but their observation, as it developed into astronomy, mathematics and physics, has relied more and more on the construction of instruments for precise measurement which made the correction for observer bias more possible. The kind of science that many people identify as true science or real science – of which physics is the model – has ultimately given us the instruments with which we can deal with the human sciences which not only cannot, but should not, be purged from human involvement. If we recognize that there have been two sources of science – in the sense of verifiable metacultural knowledge of the universe in which we live – one the observation of the heavenly bodies, and the other the ability to communicate our shared feelings and perceptions to our fellow human beings, we do not need to make a scale from the most to the least scientific operations, but simply realize that different behaviours are appropriate to each end of the spectrum. Instrumentation is the bond which can transform observations which have the least amount of anxiety and those which depend heavily on knowledge gained from observation of countertransference into a coherent whole (Mead, 1976). It would be almost impossible for anyone trained in the physical sciences, who had not been psychoanalysed, to understand Devereux's statement that it is through the countertransference that the behavioural scientist gets the only reliable information.

I do not think this statement of Devereux's holds any longer, now that we have video, film, tape and still photography on the one hand, and projective – and even more, objective – tests, on the other. Where Devereux has depended very heavily on the paraphernalia of philosophy and logic, it is now possible to depend upon multi-sensory recordings. Nor should the inclusion of these other forms of instrumentation be something which he – who, in his work with his American Indian patient, also used a variety of both projective and objective tests – should find unacceptable. For, together with his insistence upon rationality and an articulate relationship to the real world, he also has a fine, passionate grasp of the values that have accompanied our human condition. He never for one moment has attempted to introduce premature quantification or scientizing into work with human beings. Passion and vividness are essential parts of his work.

> *Case 53:* If one wishes to study the idea of the luxating penis ethnologically, one must view as a single universe of discourse a Tupari practice, a Mohave joke, a Zoroastrian myth, an Eskimo lie, the South Chinese and Indonesian koro neurosis, a tale from "Les Cent Nouvelles Nouvelles", a semi-pornographic Ancien Régime anecdote, the act of a German psychotic, the dream of a neurotic American woman, the paresthesias of a borderline Bostonian, the fantasy of a Midwestern obsessive, etc. (Devereux, 1954, 1957). Only a distributions map which records *all* of these *manifestations* of the *same idea* can be *anthropologically* meaningful – and the preparation of such a map requires that man be taken cognizance of in *all* his bodily and psychic reality. [Devereux, 1967, p. 90.]

Returning to the original point of disagreement between Devereux and myself, I believe the question of at what period in childhood the ethnic personality is laid down is still importantly related to method. Perhaps the use of words, appropriate to oedipal and post-oedipal stages in psychoanalysis, and characteristic of cultures which have a shallow time depth or are in rapid transition, may indeed be the most appropriate medium when we are considering the thin layer of homogeneity which has been established over an original heterogeneity of experience in pregenital terms. Then, in discussing modern attempts to produce a new kind of personality – as the Nazis and the Soviets both tried to do (Erikson, 1950; Mead, 1951; Bateson, 1953) – the implications of this late introjection of cultural forms should be taken into account. Age at which the new, or alien, culture is experienced by patients and by children would become most significant in attempting to understand the formation of personality in a rapidly changing world. It may even be that such characteristics as harshness towards women may accompany such oedipal period introductions to the prevailing culture, or that what we now characterize as oriental mysticism may be an attribute of longer periods of stability and homogeneity within which pregenital and oedipal methods of introjecting the culture are better blended.

References

ABRAMSON, HAROLD (1956). *The Patient Speaks*. Vantage Press, New York.

BATESON, GREGORY (1936). *Naven*. Stanford University Press, Stanford, California.

BATESON, GREGORY (1941). Experiments in thinking about observed ethnological material. *Philosophy of Science*, **8**, 53–68.

BATESON, GREGORY (1953). An analysis of the Nazi film Hitlerjunge Quex. In *The Study of Culture at a Distance* (Eds Margaret Mead and Rhoda Métraux), pp. 302–316. University of Chicago Press, Chicago, Illinois.

BOWYER, RUTH (1970). *The Lowenfeld World Technique: Studies in Personality* (with a Foreword by Margaret Lowenfeld). Pergamon Press, New York.

BYERS P.E. (1972). From biological rhythm to cultural pattern: a study of minimal units. Ph.D. dissertation, Columbia University.

DEVEREUX, GEORGE (1951). *Reality and Dream: Psychotherapy of a Plains Indian*. International Universities Press, New York. (2nd rev. ed. 1969. Doubleday, New York.)

DEVEREUX, GEORGE (1954). Primitive genital mutilations in a neurotic's dream. *Journal of the American Psychoanalytic Association*, **2**, 483–493.

DEVEREUX, GEORGE (1955). *A Study of Abortion in Primitive Societies*. Julian Press, New York. (2nd rev. ed. 1976. International Universities Press, New York.)

DEVEREUX, GEORGE (1956). Normal and abnormal: the key problem of psychiatric anthropology. In *Some Uses of Anthropology: Theoretical and Applied*, pp. 23–48. Washington Anthropological Society, Washington, D.C.

DEVEREUX, GEORGE (1957). Psychoanalysis as anthropological field work. *Transactions of the New York Academy of Sciences*, Series 2, **19**, 457–472.

DEVEREUX, GEORGE (1961). *Mohave Ethnopsychiatry and Suicide: The Psychiatric Knowledge and the Psychic Disturbances of an Indian Tribe* (Bureau of American Ethnology Bulletin No. 175). U.S. Government Printing Office, Washington, D.C.

DEVEREUX, GEORGE (1967). *From Anxiety to Method in the Behavioral Sciences*. Mouton, The Hague.

ERIKSON, ERIK (1950). The legend of Maxim Gorky's youth. In *Childhood and Society*, pp. 316–358. Imago Publishing Co., London. (Rev. ed. 1963, pp. 359–402, Norton, New York.)

ERIKSON, ERIK (1955). Sex differences in the play configurations of American adolescents. In *Childhood in Contemporary Cultures* (Eds Margaret Mead and Martha Wolfenstein), pp. 324–341. University of Chicago Press, Chicago, Illinois.

FOERSTEL, LENORA SHARGO (1977). Cultural influences on perception. *Studies in the Anthropology of Visual Communication*, **4**, no. 1, 7–51.

FORGE, ANTHONY (1967). The Abelam artist. In *Social Organization: Essays Presented to Raymond Firth* (Ed. Maurice Freedman), pp. 65–84. Aldine, Chicago, Illinois.

FRANK, L. K. (1939). Projective methods for the study of personality. *Journal of Psychology*, **8**, 389–413.

FRANK, L. K. (1948). *Projective Methods*. Thomas, Springfield, Illinois.

LOWENFELD, MARGARET (1954). *The Lowenfeld Mosaic Test*. Newman Neame, London.

LOWENFELD, MARGARET (in Press). *The World Technique*. ICP Press, London.

MEAD, MARGARET (1932). An investigation of the thought of primitive children, with special reference to animism. *Journal of the Royal Anthropological Institute*, **62**, 173–190.

MEAD, MARGARET (1946). Research on primitive children. In *Manual of Child Psychology* (Ed. Leonard Carmichael), pp. 667–706. Wiley, New York.

MEAD, MARGARET (1951). *Soviet Attitudes Toward Authority*. McGraw-Hill, New York.

MEAD, MARGARET (1952). Some relationships between social anthropology and psychiatry. In *Dynamic Psychiatry* (Eds Franz Alexander and Helen Ross), pp. 401–448. University of Chicago Press, Chicago, Illinois.

MEAD, MARGARET (1963). *Totem and Taboo* reconsidered with respect. *Bulletin of the Menninger Clinic*, **27**, no. 4, 185–199.

MEAD, MARGARET (1964). *Continuities in Cultural Evolution*. Yale University Press, New Haven, Connecticut.

MEAD, MARGARET (1969). Preface. In *Reality and Dream: Psychotherapy of a Plains Indian* (George Devereux), (2nd revised edition), pp. xi–xx. Doubleday, New York.

MEAD, MARGARET (1975). A note on the evocative character of the Rorschach test. In *Toward a Discovery of the Person: The First Bruno Klopfer Memorial Symposium and Carl G. Jung Centennial Symposium* (Ed. Robert Davis), pp. 62–67. The Society for Personality Assessment, Burbank, California.

MEAD, MARGARET (1976). Towards a human science. *Science*, **191** (4230), 903–909.

MEAD, MARGARET (1978). The evocation of psychologically relevant responses in ethnological field work. In *The Making of Psychological Anthropology* (Ed. George D. Spindler). University of California Press, Berkeley, California.

MEAD, MARGARET and BATESON, GREGORY (1942). *Balinese Character: A Photographic Analysis*. (Special Publications of The New York Academy of

Sciences, vol. 2) (reissued 1962). The New York Academy of Sciences, New York.

MEAD, MARGARET and BATESON, GREGORY (1952). *Character Formation in Different Cultures: A Balinese Family* (17-min. film), *Bathing Babies in Three Cultures* (9-min. film), *Childhood Rivalry in Bali and New Guinea* (20-min. film), *First Days in the Life of a New Guinea Baby* (19-min film), *Karba's First Years* (20-min. film). (16 mm., black and white, sound.) Distributed by New York University Film Library, New York and British Universities Film Council, London.

MEAD, MARGARET and BATESON, GREGORY (1976). For God's Sake, Margaret: Conversation with Gregory Bateson and Margaret Mead. Interviewed by Stewart Brand. *CoEvolution Quarterly*, **10** (summer), 32–44.

MÉTRAUX, RHODA (1976). Eidos and change: continuity in process, discontinuity in product. In *Socialization as Cultural Communication: Development of a Theme in the Work of Margaret Mead* (Ed. Theodore Schwartz), pp. 201–216. University of California Press, Berkeley, California.

SCHWARTZ, THEODORE (1976). Introduction to *Socialization as Cultural Communication: Development of a Theme in the Work of Margaret Mead*, pp. vii–xviii. University of California Press, Berkeley, California.

Species-Specific Biology, Magic, and Religion

Weston La Barre

GEORGE DEVEREUX IS universally acknowledged to be the ranking world authority in psychoanalytic anthropology. One has understandable pleasure in empathy with an admired mentor, and a perhaps forgivable pride in long mutual friendship with him, for these are ego-incomes that come naturally from admiration and friendship. George Devereux and I have known one another in a variety of circumstances – at the Menninger Clinic, in parachute school, and in intelligence service in China – now spread over nearly forty years. In honouring my colleague and friend, it is my intention to demonstrate the continued value of Freud's biology-based psychology in generating new insights into man. Nor may we forget that in this we stand on the shoulders of generations of giants: Freud, Róheim and, most notably here, Devereux.

To explain the omnipresent differences between magic and religion, anthropologists have commonly sought objectivist external clues, for example, that magic is private and religion social. This view can scarcely be maintained when it is manifest that magic rituals are very often social (whether in context, content, function or intention) and that much of religion is ineffably private. Further, in objective ethnographic fact, magic and religion are not infrequently co-present and mixed. Since we lack any consensus regarding the objective efficacy of magic acts and religious behaviours, it would seem that distinctions between them must be sought elsewhere, viz. in differing subjective stances. No other explanation explains *why*, given the epistemological inadequacies of magic and religion, both are repeatedly resorted to in human societies. Only a species-specific Freudian biology serves to explain this elusive difference, as we shall now demonstrate.

Fifty years ago, cultural anthropologists were concerned to emphasize the exotic specificities of each society in order to attack culture-bound notions of what "human nature" consisted in and to criticize unproven Frazerian assumptions concerning "the psychological unity of mankind" – as though to "test the limits" of variability in human cultural behaviour (for example, Malinowski's critique of the oedipus complex). Twenty years ago, anthropologists sought to show, now on much better empirical grounds, just what were the pan-human characteristics generic to all mankind (for example, the nuclear family and the universal mother–son incest taboo). At the present time we are criticizing some of the overly sharp distinctions then made between human behaviour and that of infrahuman primates, some of whom now seem to be incipient hunters and at least occasional meat-eaters, to use tools and even at times to exhibit something like learned group-culture. My present purpose is to criticize certain extremes of this last position and to show that there do exist species-specific traits in some human institutions, namely magic and religion.

Recently, psychologists have stated that "elephants wave branches at the moon with what our observer might infer is superstitious reverence", and that golden hamsters are superstitious because they can be induced experimentally to show behaviours which the human observer can then judge are "irrational". These interpretations seem to me naive anthropomorphic projections, which show a poor sense of what magic and religion are really like. To refine understanding of these transitional animal/human traits, we would do better to contrast human with higher ape behaviours, rather than with those of elephants and golden hamsters.[1]

One striking difference is that higher anthropoids do not lachry-

[1] Ronald K. Siegel, "Religious Behavior in Animals and Man", MSS 1976, citing R. Carrington, *Elephants* (1959, Basic Books, New York) and I. Douglas-Hamilton and O. Douglas-Hamilton, *Among the Elephants* (1975, Viking Press, New York). Timothy Keith-Lucas, unpublished experimental work on golden hamsters at Duke University.

mate, whereas human babies, and indeed their later adult counterparts, do cry with lachrymation when they are physically or psychologically discomfited. Ashley Montagu[1] has suggested that, whereas infra-human primate babies are characteristically carried about clinging to the mother's fur, by contrast human babies are not, but are sometimes left physically separate while the mother is busy with other affairs. This means that when hungry or otherwise in pain the baby must cry loudly, and often at length, to summon the mother, with triumphant success, whereas the clinging ape baby need only seek the proximate pectoral source for sustenance.

Now, the cells responsible for the sense of smell die when they are dried out; and, in crying at length, the passage of large amounts of air over the nasal mucous membranes would tend to dry them out. Lachrymation, then, is at first not so much a form of communication (such as it may later become in compelling interindividual response) as it is a new adaptation of normally present eye lubrication to the additional task of repairing nasal membrane desiccation. This thesis is confirmed in the fact that we sometimes also "laugh until we cry" when the emotions involved are subjectively quite the opposite, but while the same physiological need for lachrymation remains identical, viz. from the passage of large amounts of air over the nasal membranes. Such species-specific differences have relevance to the uniqueness of magical behaviour and religious beliefs in man. Certainly the magic cry is *successful* for infants in summoning succour of their needs, in spite of such danger as would attend it without lachrymation. Hence we must assume that such complex behaviour is *adaptive* in the neotenous human.

No other theory than the present psychoanalytical one, we repeat, has ever attempted to show *why* – or even to note the presence of the problem – when magical and religious behaviours are so often disconfirmed by other later experience, they are nevertheless firmly, even fervently believed in and resorted to. A rigorously oriented human biology will explain this, and indeed much more. For all neotenous and largely non-instinctual human beings pass through phases of ontogenetic ego growth, during which each one of these behaviours is

[1] Ashley Montagu, "Natural Selection and the Origin and Evolution of Weeping in Man", *Science*, **130**, no. 3388, 4 December 1959, 1572–1573; "Natural Selection and the Origin and Evolution of Weeping in Man", *Journal of the American Medical Association*, **174**, 24 September 1960, 392–397; *The Human Revolution* (1967, Bantam Books, New York), pp. 98–102.

temporarily adaptive and relevant. But in each case, the limits of such phase-usefulness are reached each time a new *kind* of object adaptation is required of the maturing individual.

The big-brained human baby, in a sense prematurely born with respect to any instinct-guided adult-like adaptations, is well equipped for *experiencing*, but very poorly equipped for *direct accomplishment* of its biological wishes and needs. That is, the highly dependent and long dependent human being is a learning animal, such that personal psychological learning and cultural adaptations from the past experience of the group tend to replace rigidly but narrowly once-and-for-all adaptive animal instincts, and indeed much of culture tends to discipline and edit the expression of remaining raw animal impulses.

Functionally, the human foetus is omnipotent in his first womb environment, for in that phylogenetically perfected Eden all biological needs are equivalent to their instant accomplishment. Small wonder, then, that societies repeatedly fantasy some far-off original Eden in the infancy of man (it lay, rather, in the infancy of the individual), and that in the "cosmic consciousness" of mystics and pantheists the individual fantasies a oneness with the universe, as though organism and environment were still symbiotically one through some omnibenevolent placenta (that original universe was the womb). But at birth, cast rudely out of that Eden, the erstwhile foetus must learn a new oxygenation technique in breathing, new body-heat homeostasis, and a new mode of food intake. Fixation at non-breathing obeys Thanatos, as does marasmatic fixation at non-eating; only breathing and suckling obey Eros, each a new synthesis with an object, with oxygen in the extra-uterine world, and milk in the mother's breast.

It is significant than in Upanishadic attempts to rereach that Nirvana-like state of mystic desirelessness – "O thou jewel in the flower of the lotus!", the foetus in the womb (or perhaps more literally in Hindu thought, the male principle, spirit, ensconced in the female, materia) – the control of breathing should be the technique ritually used; or that hells awaiting the sinful are fiery or frozen, too hot or too cold for human comfort; or that in bargains with the supernatural, fastings and food taboos and food sacrifices should be so prominent. Of course it is true that all other mammals save the monotremes are womb-born and hence have the same need for new postnatal adaptations. However, these higher mammals are biologically more mature and better prepared for birth, whereas only humans have the extravagant discrepancy between large experiencing brains and protracted near-total dependence *on others* in their physically immature postnatal state. In this lie the roots of magic and religion.

In the contemporary trend to minimize animal/human differences, much is made of the possibility that, with considerable effort and manipulation, chimpanzees can be taught limited kinds of human speech and even symbolizing. Much of this may be simple conditioning in an intelligent ape; certainly ape cries in the wild appear to be semantically "closed", with precious little of what we could interpret as generative grammar. In any case, the quantitative difference between human symbolic behaviour and that of apes is so enormous as to mean that, in quantum leap, both culture and language have species-specific qualitative difference in humans.

Consider that, after years-long experience of infantile dependency, and of an impotence during which the magic cry successfully commands the presence of mother, the human individual then learns to talk – that is, by and large, all individuals in all human societies. Human speech is in quality a biologically unprecedented technique for precise interindividual communication. Consider also that after years-long experience of physical dependence and helplessness, the individual then at about the same time learns to walk. Both walking and talking, *especially after such long delays*, are enormously significant to the individual emotionally. Much of desire remains inchoately nonverbal throughout life. But one has only to observe the differences in ego-tonus between the babe-in-arms and the toddler to realize that talking and walking dramatically enhance relationship to the human and physical environments respectively.

And now consider the two nearly universal types of sympathetic magic – homeopathic or effigy magic, and contagious or exuvial magic. Effigy magic is based on the belief that as the wax image *symbolizes* the enemy, so malevolent damage done to the image will also damage the enemy, "like for like". When Adam names the animals paraded before him, the name magically *is* the animal – and Plato still believed that the word *creates* the thing. What godlike power the use of symbols now gives us! Similarly, learning to walk gives another powerful new adaptation, a real potency of the physical body in a larger real universe. Indeed, the emotive "reality" of the physical universe begins in an ability to *handle* it. Further, the ability to manipulate the physical environment is the basis of our whole "alloplastic" human evolution, the control and creation of things outside the genetic body and organism-skin.

Contagious magic believes that if we can obtain a part of the enemy's organism – his hair, blood, sputum, faeces, or other exuviae – we can then control his body part-for-whole. Thus, symbolic effigy magic over-extrapolates the real powers we learned from symbolizing in speech: the symbol is considered to *be* the thing. Likewise, contagious part-for-whole magic illegitimately over-extrapolates our personal experience of the nature of organism: the faeces and sputum are *no longer functionally part* of our enemy's organism, and they are never part of one's own.

Hence, while walking and talking *do* give us new powers, they do *not* preserve the omnipotence we once knew in the womb or in infantile management of matter, and think we still have in any discrepancy between wish and world. Old adaptations are seductive precisely because of their experienced power. We must sometimes *unlearn* old adaptations to make new ones. The magic of words has its limitations. At one time the magic cry did in fact summon mother and procure succour of needs, and magic words still seem miraculously to manipulate the human universe. But, alas, even the most powerfully abusive word magic will not control a stubbornly non-functioning internal combustion engine. The wise child learns that "Sticks and stones will break my bones, but words will never hurt me" – at the same time that he may still magically use them against others in symbolic effigy magic.

Hovering behind magic is Lady Luck, an inchoate but cherishing mother-figure, always ready to edit physical reality for her favoured one. And rubbing Alladin's lamp brings at least a vaguely anthropormorphic, male, magically omnipotent genii outside one, but still categorically owned. The magician pulls quasi-neural strings to which nothing is attached, certainly not the organism of his enemy, whether simulated or particulated. The mystic supposes some placental attachment still to an omnibenevolent environment, the religionist more specifically to the omnipotent others, his parental gods.

Thus, religion, the belief in spiritual beings, requires a more highly developed experience of individual identity, and then through our projection of *experienced subjectivity*, the emotional reality of other subjectivities around us. (Of course we can also over extrapolate this *anima* illegitimately to sun, moon and stars, streams, winds and whatever, because these move or are warm like ourselves.[1]) Intense experience of *subjective personality* and intense libidinal ties to loved *persons* are required, in order to suffer the death of others, or to imagine the possibility of one's own. I think cows do not know or fear death, in so far as they lack both intense personal subjectivity and intense libidinal ties. But death is surely one of the major preoccupations in world religions.

Religion and magic constitute not so much objective differences in the nature of any cosmic or social reality as they do differing *subjective attitudes* toward these extra-somatic not-self realities. Magic arrogantly *commands* impersonal external reality to obey the mana power of omnipotent wish. But religion *beseeches* person-like spirits or the ghosts of persons, parents and ancestors, omnipotently to accomplish our needs *for us*. Each of us knew this adaptive technique too in early childhood – and experienced the success of it. Thus, while not necessarily earlier in cultural history, in life-history the impersonal magical commanding, or projection and incorporating, of ambiguously placed mana represents an *earlier individual phase* of adaptive ego growth than does religion, a later-phase development which knows in emotional reality the existence of persons. (Hence there can be no historic "cultural evolution" of magic and religion, with spurious questions of which came first, and both may occur mixed at any point of time or complexity in cultures.)

Magic and religion are near-ubiquitous responses in human societies because they represent universally human experiences in individual ego-growth, but illegitimately extrapolated or regressed-to adaptations to new objects: persons and things. We must learn the

[1]"The last and logically irrefutable word of the pure intellectuality of the ego on the relationship to other objects is a solipsism, which cannot equate the reality of other living beings and the whole outside world of personal experience, and speaks of them as more or less living phantoms or projections. When Freud ascribed to the unconscious the same psychical nature which one traces as a quality of one's own conscious ego, he made a step that was only probable in logic but never demonstrable in the direction of positivism. I do not hesitate to compare this identification with those we recognize as the prerequisite of libidinal transference. They lead ultimately to a kind of personification or animistic conception of the entire world around us. All this is 'transcendent' viewed from the logical–intellectual standpoint. We ought to replace this mystic sounding word by the expression 'transference' or 'love', and courageously assert that the knowledge of a part, perhaps the most important part, of reality is not intellectual but only to be obtained *experientially* as conviction." (Sándor Ferenczi, "Contra-Indications to the 'Active' Psycho-Analytical Technique". In *Further Contributions to the Theory and Technique of Psycho-Analysis* (1926), p. 229. Hogarth Press, London.) This adds another generation to my genealogy-of-giants, for Sándor Ferenczi was Géza Róheim's analyst.

limitations of our hands and our mouths, organisms and symbols, if we would become chastened to a scientific stance, there with enormous new alloplastic potencies, since in surrendering still more narcissistic omnipotence we have accorded the object a new emotional reality and independence of the self. We buy adaptive potency each time the baby in us surrenders another fragment of its initial illusory omnipotence, and by abdicating godhood discovers the world, the objective dignity of other persons and things. In each case a long powerlessness is followed by real power. The gold of self is traded for love, the paper money of narcissism is exchanged for the nourishment of object-love.

Yet organisms dare not completely surrender the arrogant ownership and temerarious control of one part of the world, that within the organic skin. The perigenetic defences of germ plasm (Ferenczi) extend beyond the metazoan body even to the bounds of society and culture themselves (Róheim). Some narcissism is necessary for life: any organism must preserve its finicky homeostases, psychic or physiological, in order to remain an organism, with contingent power over skin-contained reality, however finite in space and time.

Thus when individuals and societies reach the limit of ego-adaptive techniques at each new threat to this remaining narcissism, in the face of new historic vicissitudes, they tend to regress to using earlier successful adaptive techniques. Each authentically new ego adaptation to environment enhances Eros, in ever-more-improbable and complex life; fixation or regression, Thanatos, the more-probable, death.

Shamans and their societies represent oedipal-regressive relationships, in which the paranoid shaman has the parental omnipotence or the magic power, and his clients a childlike dependence on him. Given Freudian ontogenesis of the self in the neotenous human animal, we need not suppose that, because of learned convictions, magical and religious stances are now adaptive in the new crisis cult. Nor do non-commonsensical beliefs, passing back and forth between shaman and society, pose any epistemological or group-fallacy problem, since all in the group have experienced these once useful power techniques, and both shaman and society wish to believe. The eerily supernatural omniscience and compelling power of charisma, streaming from the shaman like irresistible magnetic mana, is the exact measure of his appeal to his clients' conscious and unconscious wish-fantasies. He is so unerringly right because he so pinpoints these wishes. In personal or societal crises, promulgation of the shaman's new wish-messages is effective because, in crisis, the supernatural cult diffuses quite like secular culture in any other of its manifestations, and shaman and society regress together to ontogenetically earlier techniques of adaptation.

An animal without *prolonged infancy* in a *nuclear family* has no *experiential basis* for regressive belief in magic or religion. Elephantine waving of branches at the moon, whatever it is ethologically, is not ethnologically religious behaviour, and the conditioned irrationality of golden hamsters is not superstitious magic. Only long-dependent infants can invent magic. Only oedipal apes can have religion.

Coping with Destiny, among the Tallensi

Meyer Fortes

A BELIEF IN A principle usually glossed as Fate or Destiny, parallel in many particulars to analogous notions in the religions of classical antiquity and in such extant scriptural systems as Calvinistic Christianity, Islam, Buddhism and Hinduism, is a prominent feature of many West African religious systems. At the level of doctrine it postulates a supernatural or mystical determinacy in human affairs such that the whole course – or at least significant parts – of each individual's life is set, if not minutely pre-ordained, by pre-natal allocation, prescription or commitment. Whether it is beneficent or maleficent in the way it works out, at this level it is conceptualized as inescapable, irrevocable, and unknowable until it manifests itself. But there is another level, the level of practice, where dogma is translated into ritual action directed towards coping with the vicissitudes of daily life. And here we meet with a paradox, whether or not there are formulated doctrines or no more than the loosely phrased metaphysical or cosmological premisses that can be inferred from the practices of non-scriptual traditional religious systems.

Fate, which is in theory irresistible and irrevocable, is in practice taken to be controllable. This applies particularly, as one might expect, in the face of what presents as injurious or evil Destiny. And the prophylactic or defensive measures that may be resorted to are as customary and as sanctioned, as much part of the accepted complex of metaphysical and ritual beliefs and practices, as the notion of Fate itself. It is thus recognized that it is not in the nature of man to submit blindly to what purports to be mystically inevitable. Our Western science and medicine, our politics, cosmologies and moral or religious systems, testify even more imperiously to this than do the attempts of Hindus, Buddhists or West Africans to control by ritual means what they designate as Destiny. Amongst us the most uncompromising hereditarians are at one with the most convinced environmentalists in promoting medical, social and economic programmes of action to overcome the genetic defects or to develop the genetic assets they claim to demonstrate.

The contradiction between theory and practice, doctrine and action, I am talking about is conspicuously – I would almost say intrinsically – embedded in the complex of beliefs and practices relating to the notion of Destiny throughout West Africa. Twenty years ago, analysing the Tallensi variant of this complex, I described how Destiny is supposed to manifest itself for ill as well as for good in people's lives (Fortes, 1959). I cited examples of the kinds of circumstances that were apt to be diagnosed as manifestations of a maleficent or "bad" Predestiny, and referred briefly to the ritual procedures that are available for attempts to expunge it.

It is these procedures that I want to examine more closely in this essay. For they not only exemplify rejection of the irrevocability of Fate; they also exemplify fundamental Tallensi ritual concepts and patterns of action. What is undertaken is ostensibly to constrain Fate by specific ritual means. But this depends inseparably on setting in train a complex series of social arrangements that mobilize the jural and moral and economic participation of responsible and concerned kinsfolk and lineage relatives, affines and neighbours. This is simply a reflection of the fact that a Tallensi is a person strictly and solely by virtue of the status he or she is endowed with by kinship, descent, marriage and residence. The creature of flesh and bone and blood, equipped with capacities to think and feel, with its organic needs and appetites and its vulnerability to failure, disease, and death, is of significance to himself as well as to others only as he is encapsulated in his identity as a person (cf. Fortes, 1973). It is in relation to his career and fulfilment as a person that his Destiny impinges on his life; but it is a career that is inextricably embedded in the matrix of his social relationships. In a very real sense every individual's Destiny is part and parcel of the Destiny of his family and lineage.

The case of Sinkawol's (of Tenzugu-Kpata'ar) wife Soorbon is typical. When Soorbon's second baby died soon after its birth like her first, and to add to her distress she became crippled with an ulcerated leg, the young woman's despondency could not be assuaged. Though she could not bring herself to speak to him of her grief, Sinkawol was well aware of it and indeed felt with her. It would have been unbecoming for her to complain directly to her husband or her in-laws. But she could and did talk to Naghabil, her husband's classificatory "son" (and therefore hers, too, though he was older than both) who was also a "sister's son" of her natal lineage and who had therefore served as the customary intermediary (*poghasama*, the marriage witness) for her marriage. Naghabil, as was his duty, then relayed her pleas to his "fathers"– that is, to her husband (Sinkawol) and his "fathers".

> He told us [Sinkawol explained] that she was saying that we don't care for her. If we did we would take steps to fix [literally, to build, *me*] her Destiny [*Yin*]. See how she has given birth to one child after another, beautiful babies, and then her bad Predestiny comes and slays them, yet we are doing nothing to fix her Destiny. She had heard that her father has obtained the goat he must provide for his part of the ritual and it is only we who are holding back.

Thus reproached, Sinkawol's "fathers"– his proxy father Teezeen (actually his deceased father's brother) and the head of the family, Nyaangzum (his deceased father's father's brother) – gave leave for the process to be taken in hand. He himself, being still jurally and therefore ritually dependent on them, could not initiate any action in any ritual or jural matter concerning himself. This, it was explained to me, is his father's responsibility. Indeed, and this is a fact of importance, it is on the jurally defined fathers of the couple that the duty to decide about and organize the ritual falls.

Teezeen set aside the malted guinea corn for the beer that would be needed and sent Sinkawol off to market to buy the goat, the fowls, the guinea-fowls and the "things" *(laghat)* their side had been commanded by diviners to provide for the ritual performance. And at the same time they sent a message to inform Soorbon's father at Sii of their decision.

This was the prelude to the ritual procedure of "building" or fixing Soorbon's "bad Destiny" *(Yinbeog)* which I recorded in March 1937. Some months earlier I had attended a similar ceremony for Mansami, a young man from a Namoo lineage (Sinkawol's lineage is Hill Talis)[1] and I recorded several informants' accounts of the procedure – the first in July 1934 when I had no proper understanding of the Destiny syndrome. So I had plenty of evidence that the pattern is, as Tallensi claim, a standard one throughout the area.

I have in my earlier publication (Fortes, 1959, pp. 38–39) referred to the ritual of ridding a person of a bad Predestiny as "exorcism" but this is, strictly speaking, a misnomer. The *Oxford English Dictionary* defines "exorcism" as "The action of exorcising or expelling an evil spirit by adjuration, etc.", echoing, one suspects, the gospel stories of Christ driving out devils and unclean spirits and the long tradition of similar practices in Christendom right down to modern times. As a method of healing or of relieving suffering, exorcism has a place in many non-Western religious systems, both scriptural, as among some devotees of Buddhism,[2] and non-scriptural, as in the many African societies in which some form of spirit possession is regarded as the cause of illness and other afflictions and exorcism is resorted to as a prelude to initiation as a diviner or as a member of a cult group.[3]

But the very notion of spirit or demonic possession, or mediumship in any form, is totally alien to the prosaic Tallensi concept of human nature. It arouses scepticism and repugnance. Tallensi who have seen Ga or Akan priests and priestesses in such states are apt to scoff at them as imposters. It is unthinkable, for them, that the dead can return among the living by taking possession of a living person's body, and they have no nature divinities. The malevolent powers they attribute to certain kinds of rocks and trees are not thought of as spiritual but rather as magical animation (cf. Fortes and Mayer, 1966).

Specifically as regards Predestiny, there is no question of its being thought of as invading or possessing (as among the Ga and other African peoples dealt with in Beattie and Middleton, 1969) or (as for instance in the Hausa Bori Cult) as being mounted upon and driving its bearer (cf. Besmer, 1977) and therefore requiring expulsion for the

[1] This distinction is explained at length in *The Dynamics of Clanship among the Tallensi* (Fortes, 1945).

[2] As among the Sinhalese of Sri Lanka who practise elaborate forms of exorcism of demons supposed to cause sickness and afflictions (cf. Yalman, 1964).

[3] As described, for instance, in Field's *Religion and Medicine of the Gã People* (1937) and in the papers of Field and others in *Spirit Mediumship and Society in Africa* (Beattie and Middleton, 1969). See also the classical paper by Firth on spirit mediumship (1959).

sufferer's health to be restored. Fate, Destiny, Predestiny, beneficent or maleficent, under whichever aspect it emerges in a particular case, is associated with the head,[1] which is the seat of good luck *(zug-song)* or bad luck *(zug-beog)*, as if, knowledgeable informants say, it were perching or hovering *(yaghal)* on, over, or beside, that is outside, the head. This, of course, is a metaphorical way of referring to it as "hanging over" him or her in the same way as, say, a debt hangs over or follows a debtor. More exactly, Destiny is thought of as a component of a person's personhood. It is supposed to be chosen by himself or herself pre-natally (while he was still "with Heaven above") and therefore to be already effective from his birth. Destiny distinguishes and indeed creates him as an individual encapsulated in his social being but endowed with a personal variant of the normal career pattern for someone of his status, as individual as his physical appearance and personality yet, equally, like every other man or woman in his society. Even animals, both domestic and wild, I have heard it said, surely have each their Destiny, not only as distinguishing a cow from a sheep or goat, or an antelope from a crocodile or leopard, but also as determining what happens to an individual cow or sheep, antelope or crocodile, in its lifetime – in other words, as distinctive of its nature and species.

The essential point is that Destiny is conceived of as accruing and adhering to the individual from the outside, as it were, like his shadow (though this is not explicitly stated by the Tallensi), not as being inside his head or body – as are, for instance, thought *(puteen)* or anger *(suhkpeleg)* or sickness *(toog)* – and yet Destiny is chosen by the

[1] The association of Destiny with the head is common in West Africa. Of particular interest is the rich elaboration of this conception among the Yoruba of Nigeria. The individual's "fate and his luck", which are derived in part from his ancestral guardian soul, are associated with his head, Bascom tells us in his profound and authoritative study of the Ifa divination system. "Good things", he says, "come to a lucky person with little apparent effort, but an unlucky person is not only unfortunate in his own affairs; he also brings bad luck to his relatives and associates. A lucky person is called 'one who has a good head' or 'one who has a good ancestral guardian soul', whereas an unlucky person is one who has a bad head or ancestral guardian." (Bascom, 1969, p. 114.) I cite these Yoruba beliefs in particular to show that their obviously very similar Tallensi counterparts are representative of a wide range of West African cultures.

As to why the head is thus selected as the seat of luck and of fate, Tallensi offer no explanation. They do not regard the head as the organ of thought or of feeling – these are located in the abdomen and heart – but there are linguistic usages which imply that the head is the locus of conduct. What we should, in different contexts, describe as common sense, or wisdom, or sound judgement, or probity, is in Talni comprised in words like *yam*, associated with the head. There is no explicit or implicit association of the head with the phallus, as has been reported for other parts of the world.

individual though it must be awaited to manifest itself, as I have outlined in my analysis of 1959.

Given these ideas, it is consistent that Tallensi define the ritual of ridding a patient of a bad Predestiny as a ritual of "sweeping away", divesting the patient of his or her lot and casting it out to make way for its reversal.

More precisely, to make the sweeping away possible the abstract and intangible Predestiny must be recognized and then captured, so to speak, and materially fixed so that it can be ritually handled; and this is the essence of the ritual of "building" it. A good Destiny also has to be recognized and "built", but in this case it is embodied in a permanent shrine at which sacrifices and offerings are made by its beneficiary, always a male, since females do not have the jural autonomy to officiate directly in religious rituals.

This is not exorcism in the strict sense. Nor, incidentally, would it be appropriate to speak of "purging" an evil Predestiny, as is done, for instance, in the Zulu treatment of affliction by inducing vomiting of the "bad" internal stuff engendered by strife among kinsfolk by means of "black" medicines to make way for "good" internal stuff which restores amity, as is exhibited in vomiting induced by "white" medicine (cf. Ngubane, 1977). This type of internally located somatic representation of infringement and restoration of moral status is as alien to Tallensi conceptions of human nature as is its antithesis, the notion of spirit possession.

And there is one further and crucial point. The religious system of the Tallensi is dominated by their ancestor cult; and, as they have no specialist priests, the ritual activities and obligations of their ancestor cult are primarily family and lineage responsibilities. In their world view the ultimate power in the affairs of men, for good and for ill, for life and for death, and the ultimate sanctions of morality, rest with the ancestors. Thus, in the last resort, even Destiny falls under their jurisdiction; and this is the key to the possibility of bringing under ritual control and reversing the workings of an evil Predestiny.

Let us now go back to Sinkawol's wife, and let me begin with the explanation given by the head of Sinkawol's family, his proxy grandfather, Nyaangzum.

> Destiny is an old story among us, hence there is a known and customary way of dealing with it. When the young woman's first infant died, there was the customary divination to find the cause. They learnt from the diviner that it was her *Yin* [her

Destiny] which had killed the child. Before her birth she had declared that she did not want children. They were instructed to *veel* the *Yin*,

Veel is a reduced, placatory, almost token version of the "building" ritual, retaining only the most indicative elements. It serves as acknowledgement of the power of the "bad" Destiny which, previously concealed or dormant, had betrayed itself by causing the child's death and had made itself known in the divination. To accept, to submit, is the first and obligatory step in any procedure for coming to terms with any occult power or agency, be it ancestors, Earth or Destiny. Where *veel* mainly differs from the full ritual (Nyaangzum and others explained) is in the omission of the major sacrifices. It is of interest that a similar *veel* ritual is carried out as the first stage of setting up a divining shrine. Sometimes this is sufficient. The malign Destiny is mollified, "cools down" or relents *(maageremi)*, and the woman bears children who survive. In Soorbon's case the *veel* procedure failed. When her second baby died and she was laid up with an ulcerated leg divination revealed that her Destiny was still hostile and the decision was taken to "build" this evil Destiny.

To help follow the procedure, I list here the principals and the responsible parties.

1. The afflicted woman, Soorbon, and her husband, Sinkawol – the patients.
2. The marriage witness of this couple (or his representative), who must be a member by birth (a "son") of the husband's patrilineage and a "sister's son" to the wife's lineage (Naghabil).
3. The father and the lineage elders of the afflicted woman's lineage, as the responsible agents of her patrilineage.
4. The proxy father, Teezeen, and the family head, Nyaangzum, of her husband's family and other elders and members of his patrilineage, as the responsible agents of his patrilineage.
5. The womenfolk of the husband's home.
6. Women of the wife's natal home.

As I have already noted, the decision to proceed with the ritual was taken by Sinkawol's "father", Teezeen, with the concurrence of the head of the house, Nyaangzum, but only after consultation with diviners. Such decisions, though in fact arrived at for practical reasons, are phrased as acquiescence in diagnosis and prescription revealed by diviners as emanating from the ancestors. This is taken to imply a successful outcome if conscientiously followed. No important ritual activity is ever undertaken without such authorization by divination. Yet it is both characteristic and significant that in Tallensi ritual practice the whole sequence is standard. Ask any elder what would be the likely diagnosis in a case like that of Sinkawol's wife and he will say it is probably due to a bad Predestiny; and he will go on to describe the appropriate ritual procedures which, though customary, will be formally prescribed in divination and thus relieve the principals of ultimate responsibility for the event. This fits the general character of Tallensi ancestor worship as a system of beliefs and practices concerned with what I have elsewhere (Fortes, 1977) called externalized representation of conscience. This also reflects the essentially realistic Tallensi attitudes about human affairs. It is well understood and accepted that human affairs are always unpredictable. In terms of their religious beliefs this becomes an understanding that ancestors are not bound by the prayers and offerings they exact. They remain unpredictable, and therefore inferences about promises revealed by diviners are grounds of hope but never of certainty.

It is worth stopping for a moment to consider what types of affliction are apt to be attributed to an evil Predestiny. Tallensi do not regard these afflictions as forms of sickness. A wife who is childless as a result of successive miscarriages or successive child deaths or sterility is an almost certain candidate. The bad *Yin* is said to kill her children or to spoil her fertility. So is a mature man who has been unsuccessful in finding a wife and settling down to a stable family life (as was the case with Mansami), or who has failed, after several marriages, to keep a wife. In such cases the bad *Yin* is said to drive away the wife. These are the commonest and the stereotypical victims generally quoted as examples. Their plight is understandable. They have failed to achieve normal adulthood as reproductive members of their families and lineages. An anomalous failure or accident (for example, a youth climbing a tree to rob a beehive and falling to his death) or a lingering illness may be attributed to the victim's evil Predestiny. I have a record of a case in which a daughter's evil Predestiny was divined to endanger her mother's life if they remained together in the same house. Diviners prescribed that the child should be sent away to live with her mother's brother – rather conveniently, since there is always tension between the three families of her paternal family, her stepfather's and her mother's brothers, for possession of the child – and, similarly, I have a record of a case in which the death of an infant brother was attributed to the evil Predestiny of his immediately preceding brother – again perhaps consistent with the customary expectation that successive siblings of the same sex will be by nature rivalrous and mutually hostile, though loyal to each other in relation to outsiders.

This does not exhaust all the possibilities but it serves to indicate the general pattern. An evil Predestiny is apt to be diagnosed to account for a condition or a mode of conduct that, from the Tallensi point of view, runs unnaturally counter to the customary norms of personal development, social and familial relationships, and productive and reproductive efficacy. It is, in other words, apt to be diagnosed where the victim or those who have rightful control over him could logically be held to be, at bottom, himself or herself, responsible for his or her condition or conduct. In objective terms, it seems that a bad Predestiny is apt to be adduced in cases where there is a difficult or impossible moral dilemma to be resolved. Soorbon's husband could not, for example, repudiate her, though she was failing him in his most ardent hopes and wishes. Indeed, the standard formula, as Nyaangzum put it, is that the bearer of the evil Predestiny did himself or herself repudiate these norms – but pre-natally, before he or she became human by birth, and he or she is therefore exonerated in his or her human capacity – a formula which can be interpreted as shifting what would have been the guilt of deliberate choice to the plane of unconscious choice appositely displaced to work as if from the outside, diachronically as having originated pre-natally, synchronically as becoming conscious only at the time of its revelation.

Better to appreciate what is distinctive of the Tallensi Predestiny complex, let us look very briefly at some contrasting African schemes of belief. Among the Ashanti the plight of Sinkawol's wife would undoubtedly be attributed to the maleficent witchcraft of one of her closest maternal kinsfolk, her mother or a sister or a brother, as the cases cited by Field (1960) amply demonstrate. To redress the injury the accused must make public confession of her or his secret maleficence and do penance as prescribed by the priest of the witchfinding cult. Among the Ndembu her affliction would be attributed to a variety of occult powers, above all to the shades of the woman's female matrilineal forebears, who are deemed to be punishing her for neglect or some wrongdoing, and the cure consists of an extremely elaborate ritual of purification and magical restoration of the fertility of the woman and her husband (Turner, 1969). Among the Zulu, lineage sorcery would be blamed and treatment with protective medicines would be prescribed (Ngubane, 1977). And lastly, among the non-Muslim Hausa the trouble might be attributed to some form of spirit attack, and treatment is by initiation into a cult group through spirit possession (Last, 1976).

These few examples must suffice to bring out the point I wish to emphasize here. It is that, by contrast, Soorbon did not perceive herself as being persecuted and betrayed, nor did she blame herself for her plight, nor is there any implication of pollution in her circumstances; and this is how her husband and other members of her conjugal and, for that matter, her natal family looked at the situation – and it would be the same with anyone else who is found to be encumbered with a bad Predestiny. Being outside her, so to speak, to sweep it away is the appropriate treatment.

To return to the sweeping away ritual, the beer having been brewed at Soorbon's conjugal home and the other standard items prescribed by the diviners having been obtained, the first episode followed. Escorted by an elder, Bogharaam, and the marriage witness, Naghabil, of her husband's lineage, she was sent off to her father's home at Sii, about three miles away, with the beer, millet flour, fowls and guinea-fowls that would be required for the sacrifices there. I was not present, but received a very full account of the proceedings from Bogharaam. Soorbon's father sacrified one fowl to his long-dead father and another to his own divining ancestors, who were Soorbon's guardian ancestors. "He told them", Bogharaam said, "that she had no child and pleaded that they might permit her to conceive. He said that her Destiny was being blamed but they, the ancestors, were her guardians and must deal with this Destiny that was dogging her." After these domestic sacrifices, all went up to the house of the clan head. There, all the elders of Sii being assembled, the clan head offered a fowl and guinea-fowl provided by the visitors on the altar of the collective clan ancestors, the External Boghar,[1] with similar pleas for the woman to conceive, and sent them away with blessings promis-

[1]The shrine of the collective clan ancestors, later referred to as Tongnaab (cf. Fortes, 1945, Chapter 6).

ing that the ritual would be successful and that Soorbon would soon conceive.

That evening I asked Sinkawol what account he had received of his wife's visit to her paternal home. "Oh", he said, "they told me that all the fowls sacrificed had 'received'." This is the literal translation of the Talni term, *ba deeya.* It refers to the posture of a sacrificial fowl – and it is always and only the domestic fowl which is thus used – when it expires. If it dies on its back, wings outstretched, this is a propitious sign indicating that the offering has been accepted, and this augurs a successful outcome of the ritual. If it dies lying on its breast or on its side, this signifies rejection by the ancestors or other occult agencies to whom the offering was made. The usual interpretation, then, is that this is due to some fault of omission or commission on the part of the supplicants which must be put right before the ancestors can be expected to respond benevolently. Tallensi insist that the way the chicken expires is not under human control.[1] How could the presence and responsiveness of the perceptually inaccessible occult agencies be verified, or their benevolence ascertained other than by some such test which the Tallensi consider objective? At the same time, Tallensi well understand that there can never be a complete guarantee of success in matters of ritual since human affairs are, at bottom, unpredictable. As for details of the ritual at Soorbon's paternal home, Sinkawol was totally uninterested. The fowls had "received" and that was all that mattered; and this is a typical attitude in such circumstances.

It is significant that the ritual "building" process begins at the Destiny patient's father's house. Why thus, I asked the elders. Surely it was obvious, they replied. Was it not her father who begot her? It was as her father's daughter in the care of his ancestors and in fulfilment of his Destiny that she came into the world. Her Destiny, to which she was already committed before her birth, came down trailing along with her father's Destiny. It was as her father's daughter that she grew to womanhood and was endowed with fecundity. It was as her father's daughter that she acquired her basic social identity; and it was her father who gave her in marriage and thus transferred to her husband the sole right over her sexuality and procreative capacity.

[1] As a matter of interest, it is worth recording that during 1936–37 I instructed our cook to slaughter our almost daily chicken and throw it to the ground in the proper ritual way and to report whether or not it had "received". A hundred birds were thus slaughtered over a period of about four months and the results were forty-eight "received" and fifty-two "refused".

To be sure, the "building" ritual concerns her *performance* as wife and mother, not daughter, but it is the *capacity* for this that is at stake and to protect it the ritual must go back to its origins. Thus it becomes her father's responsibility to put things right. But it is important to add that this is a responsibility he has by reason of his jural status as father. There is no implication of his having to repair a conscious failure which he might have been able to avoid originally. He does not consider himself, nor is he considered to be, guilty through sins of commission or omission. Indeed, he is not even exclusively and solely responsible. The task is shared with his lineage elders and the ancestral help that is sought is that of the collective clan ancestors at their Boghar shrine. This, too, is a reflection of the premiss that a person is a person primarily by virtue of his or her lineage membership. He is responsible but, let me emphasize again, there is no question of guilt in this. The formula is that his daughter chose her own pre-natal Destiny, that is, when she was still "with Heaven above"– a state of affairs for which Tallensi have only an oblique explanation. They say that it has to do with the fact that sexual intercourse does not invariably lead to conception but only when Heaven above in some mysterious way permits it. The father's role is that of the duty-bound benevolent intercessor commending his offspring to his, and therefore her, ancestors.

In accordance with custom, her father had checked with diviners and was told to provide a white chicken, a white goat, white millet flour, and a white cowrie shell for the main ritual task. This took place, appropriately, at Soorbon's conjugal home or, as Tallensi would put it, her husband's home, where she was as wife and mother suffering the malice of her Destiny. It took place on the day after her propitious visit to her paternal home. It had naturally to be carried out jointly by the two parties with a stake in her wellbeing and fertility, her father and his lineage kin on the one side and her husband's father and his lineage kin on the other.

Preparations began in the morning, desultorily, as is usual among the Tallensi on such occasions. By mid-afternoon a group of Kpata'ar men, elders and others, were all assembled in front of the gateway of Teezeen's homestead impatiently awaiting the contingent from Sii. It was nearly sunset when they arrived, led by Kurug, an elder to whom her father had delegated the task of performing the ritual. They brought with them the goat, the chickens, and the other items prescribed as the Sii contribution to the rituals and, what was much more important, the *boghakyee*, the portable shrine of the clan ancestors which, Tallensi say, draws the ancestors themselves along to the scene of the ritual.

This is not the place to recount the whole course of the proceedings over the seven hours through which the ritual activities were spread. As is characteristic of occasions of this sort among the Tallensi, the proceedings began and were interspersed with arguments about differences of customary practice between the two parties and the episodes of ritual concentration alternated with a hubbub of general conversation and movement. I must limit myself to the critical ritual activities.

Let me first note, however, that these activities are always conducted by men – the only woman directly included is the patient, who is passive throughout. Partly this is because officiating in a ritual is a male prerogative and responsibility associated with men's status of jural majority which women can never attain. When women carry out a ritual activity it is always under the direction of men. But in this case what is also represented is the circumstance that the responsible parties are the two sets of "fathers". Appropriately, therefore, the proceedings take place in the male space out of doors and in the family head's *zong* room which houses the shrines of his earliest ancestors. This room is separated from the living quarters, which are ruled over by the wives and mothers, where the children are licitly produced and where everyday food is properly cooked. This is also symbolically appropriate, in that the bad Predestiny is dealt with outside to make way for admitting the good Destiny into the homestead, as we shall see.

The proceedings opened with a sacrifice in the *zong* room, symbolically, therefore, in the presence of the Kpata'ar ancestors, who would thus be both made aware of the occasion and enlisted on the side of the Sii group's efforts. A very short account of this episode, which took nearly an hour, is all I have space for, but it will suffice to show up the critical elements that recur throughout the ritual sequence. Kurug crawled in and placed the *boghakyee* on the floor and was followed by a dozen or so elders, some from each side. The patients were summoned and seated in a corner, legs stretched out and heads lowered in the customary posture of humility required of supplicants. Squatting over the *boghakyee*, Kurug sprinkled on it some millet flour from a calabash handed to him and, holding up a small dish of beer, called out, "Speak up now. Speak up and tell her it has come about."

"What do you mean 'speak up'?" protested Nyaangzum, the senior Kpata'ar elder. "It's the woman's Destiny you have come here to build and what is there to talk about?"– emphasizing, that is, that the circumstances were fully known to everybody present. But Kurug insisted. It was necessary for the ritual to be properly performed. Thereupon the Kpata'ar elder who had the previous day represented Teezeen and the lineage at Sii spoke up, addressing himself to the spokesman of the other side. It was a long, elaborate and rhetorical speech, as is usual on such occasions, studded with vivid figures of speech, fervent exhortations, and reiterated pleas. He told how "We of Kpata'ar" had sought the girl in marriage; how she had, as was hoped, borne children, which had died; how diviners had revealed that the cause was her evil Destiny. He concluded:

> That is why we informed you and asked you to come over, so that we could share our trouble. We prepared all the things we need for the ritual and now we ask you to do what is necessary so that the woman's Destiny may become cool and she may conceive a child, so that farms may be farmed and livestock bred and wellbeing abound.

"Thank you", said the Sii spokesman, and turning to Kurug he went on: "Kurug, listen. This is their story. We and these people of Tenzugu, we have had much to do with one another. Doesn't our kinship connect us? We went and married our wife and she bore us this child and she grew"– and he described how she had been given in marriage to the Kpata'ar people. "Men marry", he continued, "in order to have children." He dwelt on how her children had died and how diviners had declared that "when she was still with Heaven, she had spoken in an ugly way saying she did not want children, or a husband, or good farming, or livestock breeding", and concluded that "having been told all this, we have come to put things right and build this Destiny – here is this Destiny's red chicken, his beer, all his things, may he permit this chicken to be accepted and may he let the woman conceive."

These are the bare bones of a long, declamatory, much embroidered exhortation, listened to attentively and silently by all those present. It struck me then that this recapitulation of the history, circumstances, ritual prescriptions and hopeful expectations of the occasion, fully known as the details were to all present, had the effect of a formal presentation to Kurug of the equivalent of a material document. A similar procedure is followed in court cases. The responsible officiant cannot carry out his task if such a formal and public statement, concurred in by all participants, is not presented. This ensures that, as Tallensi put it, "we are all of one mind" and, what is more, that the ancestors of all participants are apprised and at hand.

Responding to this, Kurug clapped his hands over the *boghakyee* and, speaking in a loud and commanding tone and with many rhetorical flourishes and exhortations, addressed himself to the *boghakyee* as follows (again I summarize drastically):

> It is Tongnaab that I here take hold of, great brother of Bem, of Zubagah, and of all of us – Ancestor Tongnaab, hearken to me.[1] We married a wife, took her home, and there she bore a child, an only child, and the child grew up, became a woman, and then this son of Teezeen came and begged for her – and we, would we deny him? Are we two not one stock? Well then, the woman bears a child and it dies, bears again and it dies. So they went to diviners, and diviners declared [and his voice rose as if in dismay] that it was her Destiny, that she had said she wants no child, that her husband would not farm his farming, breed his livestock, that she would have no child, that she spoke thus when she was above with Heaven before she came down here.

And he went on to recount how they had first *veel* this Destiny, but to no avail, and that the diviners had then commanded them to "build it", prescribing the animals and other items required. He continued urgently:

> Tongnaab, Ancestor, here stands your goat, here is your beer and your chicken, grant that this Destiny may depart to the distant low land and disappear in the wilderness. It is Soorbon's Destiny which we are going to sweep away, so that offspring may come and farms be farmed and livestock be reared. Tongnaab, you are master of everything, you can calm everything that is disturbed. Grant that these two may be at ease, that children may be born, farms farmed, livestock reared and restful sleep slept. Grant that a houseful of people may be built and that their names may be praised.

And so he continued repeating in different locutions the insistent call that it was Soorbon's evil Destiny they were sweeping away, the ugly Destiny which she had assumed when she was still with Heaven above, and reiterating his pleas that it might be made to vanish and childbearing be restored "so that", he ended emphatically, "we may know that you really exist".

[1] Tongnaab is the generic title of all the External Boghars of the Hill Talis, to which cluster both Sii and Kpata'ar belong. It is the altar and sanctuary of all the clan ancestors of each of its adherent groups of clans. The other allusions are to adherent communities outside Taleland. The invocation is a summons to all the clan ancestors.

He poured some beer on the shrine calling out, "Here is your beer. Accept it and may it prompt you to accept your chicken too." And then, holding up the chicken, he added, "Here, take your red cockerel, grant that it is accepted at once and permit us to rejoice." He slaughtered the cockerel, dripped some blood on the *boghakyee* and, still invoking, threw it to the floor. It fluttered and died on its breast, "refused". A moment's consternation was followed by a hubbub of comment and a call for another cockerel. This was quickly produced and, invoking as before and ending urgently, "Tongnaab, Ancestor, accept this your chicken, accept it", he offered it and threw it down. It fluttered and died on its back, propitiously. "Good, good", shouted Kurug laughing, amid a burst of approval from those around.

Though I have omitted many details and have severely compressed the invocations, their significance is clear. The threefold repetition of the same, fully familiar story and the same urgent appeal might seem supererogatory to an obsessional degree. But this does not, in fact, signify an intention or hope of persuading the occult agencies invoked by the sheer weight of redundant repetition. The case is presented from different points of view by the two parties. The Kpata'ar spokesman addresses the Sii elders, soliciting the intercession and help which they alone are qualified and obliged to give and the theme is the concern of the husband's lineage that the woman should be set free to fulfil the primary purpose of marriage, which is the production of children. Note that, far from blaming her, the spokesman implies sympathy with her plight. The Sii elders, first through their spokesman and then directly through the officiating elder, Kurug, address their ancestors. The way their spokesman restates the Kpata'ar story amounts to accepting accountability (but not culpability) – incurred, to be sure, in good faith and unintentionally – for the crisis. The stress all through is on the woman's tribulations being due to her own prenatal vow, even though it was not a conscious and deliberate repudiation of the normal humanity which she now yearns for. She is not a sinner deserving retribution but rather a sufferer, almost unjustly so, pleading for relief. And the implication is that her father, and consequently the ancestors, have some responsibility for her plight since they must be concerned for the wellbeing of their descendants and have the superhuman power and authority to annul the pre-natal vow. Note also the repeated emphasis on the animals and "things" demanded by the Destiny and the ancestors through the diviners as having been conscientiously provided. These are offered not as a bribe but as earnest of the trust in the goodwill and powers of the ancestors and of submission to their authority.

The Sii ancestors thus having been enlisted, as their acceptance of the sacrificed cockerel signified, the company moved outside to the gateway for what is regarded as the crucial ritual phase. They sat down on two sides of a small heap of wet puddled mud. After some preliminaries, Kurug put the *boghakyee* down beside the heap next to a hoe blade and instructed the "sister's son" of Sii, the Kpata'ar marriage witness, Naghabil, to prepare four mud balls. Naghabil quickly rolled out four largish mud balls and laid them in a row beside the hoe blade. "Bring the things", called Kurug, squatting down and Sinkawol, squatting behind him, held out a handful of wriggling, grey grubs and the dried carcase of a white egret.[1] Kurug pressed one of the grubs into each mud ball and put the egret carcase down beside them. A youth came over with a handful of earth which he said was the "mousehole dust" he had been sent to fetch. Kurug sprinkled this over the mud balls, and told the patients to go and stand in the gateway, where they wedged themselves in uncomfortably. Then he called to the marriage witness, "Tell your 'fathers', the Kpata'ar people, to speak out." "What do you mean?" exclaimed Nyaangzum, protesting again that they had been through it all. But the Sii elders insisted it had to be so. Sighing, Nyaangzum addressed himself to the marriage witness and launched out on his speech, speaking as if it was all completely new to the company. No details were spared. The whole story of the woman's privation was repeated in the customary declamatory manner, ending with a rehearsal of the diviners' verdicts and of the call to her natal lineage –"so that we could be of one mind and they might sweep away the woman's evil Destiny, so that I might get some good farming and livestock and a child and build up my house". Naghabil thanked him and addressing the Sii people, said, "My uncles, you have heard, have you not?" A Sii elder repeated this to Kurug. "Indeed", came the answer and Kurug drew a handful of ebony leaves out of the *boghakyee*, picked up one of the mud balls with the hoe blade and placed it on the leaves in his hand and walked slowly to where the patients were standing impassively in the gateway a few yards away.

[1] Also known locally as a "tick-bird" from its habit of following cattle and perching on their backs to pick out the ticks that infest them.

Silence fell suddenly on the seated gathering and all eyes were fixed on the scene at the gateway. Raising the ball of wet mud and the ebony leaves towards the patients, Kurug addressed them in a loud, singsong voice, every phrase of his incantation being very distinctly enunciated – and being immediately repeated by the patients in the same singsong tone, but in so low a voice as to be almost inaudible.

"Yin Yoo! Yin Yoo! Yin Yoo!", called Kurug, summoning the Destiny as one would a distant person, each phrase being repeated by the patients.

> We have heard that Soorbon when she came into the world talked crazily, coming hither from high up Heaven, saying that she is going thence, but she will never clasp a child in her arms – she does not want any children – indeed she will have nothing to do with a man – for him to farm so that they may have food to eat – he will not have a farm – he will not rear livestock – never will he acquire livestock – nor ever will he go out to hunt, no, never go hunting – and we have gone round to diviners, consulting them, and the diviners revealed that Soorbon had declared that she does not wish for a child – she does not wish for a husband – she does not want a mother – she does not want a father – that is what the diviners revealed – it was her bad Destiny – they picked out Sabeg [to be the ritual officiant] and Sabeg deputed me – to come here, to cast it out – here is its beer – here stands its goat – a white goat – here is its chicken – and all its things are here – so it is that we have come here purposely to sweep it away.

At this point he lifted the mud ball and the leaves higher and made a sweeping gesture thrice[1] down the woman's abdomen and repeated this with her husband. Then he held up the mud ball and the leaves to the mouth of each and commanded, "Spit!" Each spat once on the mud ball and Kurug walked around to the back of the homestead and threw the mud ball away. He returned, took up the second mud ball in the same way as before and repeated the earlier procedure, though with some curtailment of the exhortation. 'Yin Yoo, Yin Yoo, Yin Yoo', he began, and repeated the invocation he had made previously. Again he "swept" the patients, made them spit on the mud ball and went off to throw it away (cf. Fig. 1).

A third time he repeated the whole procedure, though now with a much shortened exhortation – his voice sounding quite tired. When he stopped to pick up the fourth ball, a Sii elder leaned forward and pushed a (white) cowrie shell into it. Kurug took a fresh supply of leaves out of the *boghakyee* bag (the first lot had been thrown away with the last mud ball), and at the same time picked up the egret carcase. With the leaves and the dead bird in one hand and the hoe blade on

[1] He should have done this four times – four being the female ritual number. But such casualness is typical of Tallensi ritual attitudes.

which he was carrying the mud ball in the other, he again took up his position facing the patients.

He repeated the invocation, again much shortened, and as the patients repeated each phrase after him he waved the leaves and the dead bird in front of them. At the end he called in a louder voice, "Be

FIG. 1. Sweeping away Mansami's evil Destiny (cf. reference to Mansami, p. 67 above). The officiant "sweeps" the patient and his "wife" with the leaves of the *gaa* tree as he calls on the evil Destiny to descend. In this case, the patient being a man, the ritual took place during the daytime and I was therefore able to obtain some photographs, which was, of course, impossible in Soorbon's night-time treatment. Note that in this case the patient sits humbly on the ground outside the homestead side by side with the little girl who takes the role of the wife Mansami has failed to win. Note the white goat and the white chicken in the background.

it a white Destiny [*Yinpeeleg*] let it descend hither, or be it a red Destiny [*Yinziug*] let it descend hither, or be it a black Destiny [*Yinsableg*] let it descend hither"– the patients still repeating after him. Then he "swept down" the patients from head to foot with the leaves and the egret, held the mud ball out to them with the command to spit, and then said "take hold". Each placed a hand on the bunch of leaves and the dead bird he was holding and together they walked back to where the mud balls had first been placed and put the mud ball Kurug was carrying and the leaves and the dead bird down on the ground.

This done, the patients returned to the gateway. "Where is the chicken?" Kurug asked, and he was handed the white fowl with which he went up to the patients again. With the fowl he "swept" them down as before and then, opening out first one wing and then the other, told them, in turn, to spit under the wing (Fig. 2). He was just turning away when the Kpata'ar marriage witness called out, "You haven't cried out Red Destiny come down, White Destiny come down, Black Destiny come down." "Oh, I forgot", said Kurug and, turning

FIG. 2. Sweeping away Mansami's evil Destiny. The rite of "sweeping" the patients with the white chicken. The bird is presented wings spread out for the "wife" to spit under the wing.

back to face the patients, he held the chicken up towards the sky and called out, in a quavering voice, "Red Destiny come down, Black Destiny come down, White Destiny come down." He then returned to where the mud ball and the leaves and the egret had been placed. Squatting down, he put down beside the heap the *boghakyee* which he had been carrying slung over his shoulder all the time, and asked for the beer, against a background of conversation which was the more striking in contrast to the silence that had prevailed throughout the rites at the gateway.

Again there was an argument about procedure, the Sii elders insisting that the Kpata'ar elders should invoke their ancestors to stand by, the latter protesting that it was not their responsibility since it was the duty of the woman's paternal kin to perform the ritual. However, characteristically, they nevertheless yielded and Nyaangzum as head of Sinkawol's own branch of the lineage complied, followed by the heads of the two other branches.

Kurug meanwhile went on with his task. The beer for which he had called was brought to him in a large earthenware dish. It was not in fact real beer, but token or symbolic beer made of malted grain he had brought from Sii, coarsely ground and steeped in hot water by the women of the household. Kurug emptied this on to the heap made up of mud, ebony leaves and the dead bird, significantly without a prayer – as if to say this is not real beer or a real ancestral shrine, on which properly brewed beer accompanied with prayer would have to be poured, but only a symbolic, a make-believe shrine, built in order to bring down the evil Destiny to a manipulable material embodiment and due to be thrown away as no ancestral shrine can be.

Kurug then asked for the chicken to be handed to him again. Now the Sii spokesman addressed him, transmitting to him, as in the *zong* rite, the Kpata'ar story, in the same rhetorical style and in almost the same words as before. Squatting by the *boghakyee*, Kurug took a handful of millet flour from a small calabash dish and scattered it over the "shrine". Addressing the shrine in the same declamatory, almost demanding, tone as before, he began, "It is Tongnaab that I am taking hold of", and then came the Sii story of Soorbon's beginnings and of the crisis. Again the diviners' revelations –"Did they", he exclaimed, "perhaps offend a [dead] father? Or perhaps a more distant ancestor? But the father said he has no hand in it – the ancestors said they have no hand in it – it came out instead that it was the Destiny she had." The diviners' prescription that they should take the ancestral shrine, Tongnaab, to Kpata'ar to sweep away the Destiny and the conscientious provision of the various animals and "things" demanded were eloquently enumerated. Ancestor Tongnaab was invoked to put things right and to drive away the evil Destiny. "Tongnaab," he ended, "if you really exist grant that this Destiny may relent, that it may depart to the wasteland, that it may depart to the wild bush, grant that the woman may bear a child, that farming prosper, that livestock increase, and that the house be built up." He poured some beer on the *boghakyee* and then, holding up the chicken, called out, "Take your chicken, here is your chicken, a pure white one.'' He slaughtered it, dripped some blood over the *boghakyee*, and threw it down, crying out, "Accept your chicken, arise and accept your chicken.''

It was refused. There was a moment of silent dismay followed by an outburst of loud and anxious discussion. Had some preliminary ritual requirements been omitted? Another chicken was called for. Holding it up, Nyaangzum appealed for a clear sign of where the fault lay. There was a call for Teezeen in his capacity as custodian of the External Boghar and Earth shrines of Kpata'ar to appeal to them, which he did, pouring a libation of beer on the ground. Then the Sii spokesman invoked Tongnaab to intercede with whichever ancestor or other occult power on their side might be the impediment, promising to make amends later, and as Kurug slaughtered the chicken, Nyaangzum cried out, "If the Destiny has indeed come down may he permit the fowl to be accepted and we will tomorrow make amends for any fault on our side.'' Kurug dropped the chicken on the ground. It leapt in the air and landed on its back, to the loudly voiced relief of all at this sign that the Destiny had "descended'' to accept its "things''.

Now a couple of Kpata'ar youths slaughtered the white goat brought by the Sii people and took some of the blood in a dish for Kurug to drip on the *boghakyee* and the mud "shrine'', after which Kurug called for a large calabash full of flour mixed with beer to be handed to him. The patients sat down, legs outstretched, beside the mock "shrine''. Kurug took a mouthful of the liquid and, stooping, squirted it out four times on the *boghakyee* and the shrine, then made the woman first and Sinkawol second repeat this action. They went back to sit at the gateway and Kurug, after scraping some consecrated dry red mud, which he took from the *boghakyee*, into the liquid, carried the dish to the patients and made them each take a sip. More beer was added and they were offered a good drink and allowed to scoop out and eat some of the flour. This was the first food and drink they had had all day as they had been obliged to fast from dawn. The ritual was over for the time being and the visitors were invited into the homestead to partake of the lavish hospitality that had been prepared for them.

The concluding episode took place around midnight. I did not see it but had a full report from Sinkawol and others. Porridge had been cooked outside at the gateway and marked as of ritual significance by the use of an ebony stick to stir it instead of the normal stirring stick owned by women. Sinkawol told me:

> When they finished cooking the porridge they pulled the ebony-wood stirring stick out and scooped some porridge into a calabash dish. They scraped off the porridge stuck to the stirring stick and gave it to the officiant [Kurug] who plastered it on to the "Yin" shrine to seal it up, and gave some to me and my wife to eat. The officiant then put the ebony stick on the shrine and slung the *boghakyee* [which had been brought out for the rite] over his shoulder and escorted me and my wife into the house as far as the outer courtyard. This means bringing into the house the good Destiny. The woman's Destiny had been harsh and they threw off that Destiny and took the good Destiny to bring it into our home so that my wife may bear a child which will live. And then one of our sister's sons gathered up the shrine – the mud ball and all the things as well as the stirring stick – that's the evil Destiny – and went off some distance and threw it all away. When the officiant sealed up the "Yin" shrine he pronounced the same invocation as before, calling upon it to accept [the offering] so that the Destiny could be pacified and the evil Destiny depart utterly and so that farms may be farmed and livestock be reared and the woman may bear children and a house be built. He pours some beer on the shrine and then seals with the porridge.

The visiting Sii elders did not leave for home until the moon rose at about 2 a.m., nearly ten hours after their arrival. They had been royally regaled – as Nyaangzum commented next day: "If we had not treated them so well they would have gone home and scoffed at us and some would have said that we are poverty stricken, and others that we are only mean."

The next day I asked Sinkawol how he and his wife had felt at the time of the ritual and after. He described how he had been anxious all through, especially after the white fowl had "refused", and what a relief it was when the next chicken, brought in specifically to test whether or not the Destiny had "come down", was accepted. And he added that when it was all over he and his wife were extremely happy – *ti poor peeya pam*, he said, which literally translated means "our bellies were extremely whitened [with joy]". Now all would be well, he thought, and they would soon have a child.

Much significant detail had to be omitted in the foregoing account of the "sweeping away" ritual. But what I have recorded invites some exegetical comment. Let me begin then by noting again the quasi-externality attributed to Soorbon's evil Predestiny. It is defined as being external to her conscious, socially embedded self; developmentally as having been chosen in a pre-existent state and contemporaneously in respect to her current existence. The invocations that accompany the sacrifices and libations repeatedly emphasize this.

Let me risk an interpretation. Soorbon's plight is perceived by others and experienced by herself as an unnatural commitment in which she is trapped. For no woman voluntarily repudiates motherhood, the most ardently desired and indeed lived for crown of life for her: and no normal person voluntarily repudiates parents and siblings, husband or wife or the normal sources of a family's livelihood, its farming and its livestock rearing and other male productive pursuits. Yet there it is. Why should a woman's so much desired children die one after the other? It would be unthinkable by Tallensi norms for her husband or any of his kin or her own kin to wish it. Perhaps, in some obscure and incomprehensible way, she herself brought it to pass. She could never know this directly let alone admit it; nor is it possible, given Tallensi family ideals and moral norms, for her to be accused of this. It comes out into the open, as Tallensi put it, as an incontestable revelation of the ancestors transmitted through the authoritative medium of divination. And it is the more acceptable because it is transposed by customary, hence socially legitimate, evaluation into an external compulsion, exonerating the sufferer from any implication of guilt.

Would it be too far fetched to think of the evil Predestiny as a projected representation of perhaps feared and self-recriminatory impulses? I will not venture to suggest more than this. For if one tries to discuss her problems with a woman like Soorbon one elicits a confession of grief and despondency, but also a statement of the conventional evaluation in terms of Predestiny. At all events it is evident that the attribution of externality to the evil Destiny amounts to defining it as detachable and therefore susceptible to being "swept away".

Speculative as this interpretation is, it does, I think, throw light on the ritual process. It is worth recalling that the patient is not thrown back on herself, or her husband, to overcome the oppression of which she is the victim. For, as I pointed out earlier, she exists as a social and moral person only in virtue of her relationships with kinsfolk conferred by marriage. Her tribulations are theirs too and her struggle is absorbed into their response to her plight. It is significant that the treatment consists in mobilizing paternal duty and benevolence (the good father accepting accountability, if not responsibility, for her condition) and exercising their rightful claims on the goodwill of ritually transposed fathers and forefathers on behalf of their "daughter". The cure consists in restoring the hope and self-esteem with which she entered into marriage.

What of the procedures in contradistinction to the actors? Invoking and enlisting the mystical intervention of the ancestors at the outset reflects the general principle that all human affairs are under their ultimate jurisdiction. I have remarked earlier on the length, the rhetorical elaboration and especially the apparently redundant reiteration of all the information relating to the patient's plight and of the pleas for redress for her. As I noted earlier, the main reason for the exchanges preceding them and for the form of these prayers is to ensure full participation and mutual accountability of all present to one another and to the ancestors.

I have elsewhere (1975) described Tallensi prayer as a cathartic exercise and this aspect is prominent also in the way the invocations to the ancestors are offered in the present context. What cannot be overemphasized is that the ancestors are believed, one might almost say are felt, to be mystically present. The rhetoric and repetitions convey an insistence on being heard and understood, and a concern to ensure that no relevant information is left out. The liturgies of scriptural religions follow the same lines for they, too, are addressed to occult powers and agencies whose response to prayer cannot be directly known. So the "red" cockerel – red here standing for any mixtures of brown or orange or similarly coloured plumage – is offered not as a sacrifice to persuade the ancestors but as a vehicle of appeal to test their responsiveness.

The offering of a red cockerel is standard procedure in this episode of the ritual though it was represented as having been commanded by diviners. Tallensi sacrificial animals fall into three large colour clusters: the white (which includes all light colours), the red (which covers another broad range of red-tinted colours), and the black (which includes all dark colours, for example, green and dark blue). A red chicken is a common sacrifice to occult agencies invoked to repel or crush a mystical source of enmity such as is implied in the case of an evil Destiny – red being the colour of anger.

Colour symbolism enters also into the ritual directed at the Destiny itself. Expert informants assured me that an evil Predestiny has been known to demand a "red" or a "black" chicken or goat for the sweeping away ritual, but in the two cases I witnessed and in others I was told about the demand proved invariably to be for a white goat and a white fowl. White stands for light, calmness, coolness, benignity, for what is propitious in general. In the present case the ritual of ridding the patient of her malign Destiny is, as it were, suffused with whiteness and the Destiny itself is tempted with white offerings to come down to take its "things" and go. Furthermore, the participants, and in particular the patients, having fasted all day and so having symbolically cleared themselves of their preoccupations,[1] eat and especially drink of the white offerings: the beer and white flour sanctified by having been used in libation; the ritually marked porridge; and portions of the flesh of the sacrificed chickens and of the goat. This communion aspect is much emphasized as an essential act in the appropriation by the patient and her husband of the good Destiny that is assumed to take the place of the expelled evil Destiny.

As regards the most dramatic episode, when the evil Predestiny is actually swept away, the symbolism is almost self-evident. Again the excess, the overdetermination of the magical effectors, is noteworthy. Words, though indispensable, are evidently not enough. Consider the Destiny's "things". Nyaangzum gave me the conventional explanation which I also received from other elders on this and on other occasions. All the "things" he said were "revealed" by divination. What do they mean? The mousehole dust was demanded by the Destiny, he explained, because "there are always mice in a woman's sleeping room and when a woman gives birth there the mice flee and get away". I asked if perhaps the idea was to hide away the evil Destiny in a mousehole, but he rejected this. "What!" he exclaimed, "drive out an evil Destiny and let it come back into the sleeping room?" No, the point, as I understood it, was that the mousehole dust signifies an empty mousehole and consequently the flight of the mice which would herald the hoped-for birth of a child. As for the white egret, Nyaangzum continued, "these birds disappear completely when the rainy season (which is the propitious season for a Destiny-building ritual) comes. We don't see even a single one then and we don't know where they go to – perhaps to your distant land!" Swallows are sometimes demanded, he added, though they don't disappear completely, and sometimes other birds that are very rare in the rainy season.

This item, then, images the Destiny as being carried off, as the invocations phrase it, to such far away places as the remotest wilderness. The magical intention is clear from the use of a dead egret.

[1] My interpretation. This fasting, the elders explained, is obligatory by custom. When the patients fast, they said, the bad Destiny is also deprived of food and drink. For as one is, so is one's Destiny. This is an added spur to it to come and take its "things" and the offerings and depart.

Indeed, I was assured, if it was impossible to obtain a whole bird, a wing or even a single feather would suffice. Similarly, the invocations explain the "earth dog" *(tengn-baa)*. This small grey grub, Nyaangzum explained, "burrows into the earth" and has to be dug out. The Destiny is summoned, by the implied authority of the ancestors vouchsafed through the *boghakyee*, to descend into the mud balls of the mock shrine like the "earth dogs" that are "burrowed" into it – in order, as the cowrie shell expresses it, to engender the coolness of a mind at peace.

Next the ebony tree leaves and stirring stick. The ebony *(gaa)* tree is believed to be a dangerous or evil tree, liable to be magically animated and then to injure or even kill people. This is well known but I was never able to elicit a reasoned explanation from even the best informed of my friends and it would lead me too far afield, in the present context, to explore further the beliefs about "good" and "bad" trees and the properties that might give rise to such ideas. In the "sweeping away" ritual the leaves are taken to be imbued with the power of the *boghakyee*. In this situation it is "bad" power since it aims at driving out the "bad" Destiny, like driving out like. In contrast, the red clay which is also taken from the *boghakyee* and crushed to be added to the beer given to the patient and her husband, is the vehicle – quite literally internalized, to replace the expelled evil. Ebony leaves and the consecrated red clay are used in similar ways in the rituals of initiating Talis youths into the Boghar cult.

The "sweeping" which is accompanied by the summons to the Destiny to descend and take its "things" is self-explanatory. What the imagery comes to is that the Destiny shall descend and adhere to the patient and her husband so that it can be swept off them into the mock shrine made up of the balls of mud. It thus becomes manipulable in a concrete way and can be literally carried away from the homestead and thrown away. I was unable to obtain an explanation of the spitting rites. A similar action is required of initiants into the Boghar cult in a rite which pledges them to absolute secrecy on pain of death for betrayal. But a possible interpretation suggests itself from a consideration of the significance of the mouth as the organ of speech.

The Tallensi do not have a belief in the "evil eye". The equivalent for them is the "evil mouth". Envious or threatening words and curses, especially if spoken by kinship seniors, can injure or even kill and, conversely, spoken blessings can do good. It will be recollected that an evil Predestiny arises because the sufferer spoke "crazily" or in an "ugly way" pre-natally. It is as if the patient turned her "evil mouth" against herself. The spitting and squirting rites would appear then as gestures of renouncing the pre-natal evil mouth, giving it back, as it were, to the Destiny. This is most evident with the sacrifice of the white fowl. It is offered to the Destiny, through the ancestors, with pleas for the Destiny to come and take its "things" and depart. But what is critical is that it should be accepted; and if it is refused additional birds will be offered until the sign of acceptance is vouchsafed. For this is taken to show that the Destiny has descended to take its "things" and depart. It is in short a "scape-fowl". The goat has similar attributes but it is offered primarily as a gift, as if to recompense the Destiny for descending to take its "things" and departing. The distribution of the meat is typical and is explicitly regarded as demonstrating the amity felt by the participants for one another and their common concern for the ritual to succeed.

I asked some of the elders why the patient's Destiny was being summoned as if from a great distance and in the sky, seeing that the Destiny is also spoken of as if it were close to, hovering over, her. Laughing at what they regarded as my *naïveté*, they answered: "We can't see Destiny. We think it comes from Heaven. But how do we know where it really is? That is why we call upon it to come from wherever it may be." Not knowing what it looks like accounts also for the invocation by colours. The implication is not that it might be white or red or black. These colour terms are used metaphorically to imply all conceivable modes of existence the Destiny may have; and the emphasis is on the Destiny's externality in relation to the patient.

At the end, the last section of the Destiny's mock shrine is "sealed" with the porridge and offered to the Destiny as if it were customary hospitality to a guest. It is finally carried away by a "sister's son" who throws it away, preferably in an uncultivated area some distance from the homestead. He calls out "Yin Yoo, Yin Yoo, Yin Yoo, come and receive your things and take them all away. Go down into a river with them, not into a pool; hide them in a hole in a rock, not in a tree hole." When he returns he is rewarded with a dish of porridge and some of the goat meat. On the earlier occasion, when I took part in the ritual of sweeping away Mansami's evil Predestiny, it turned out that there was no "sister's son", even in the widest classificatory sense, among the participants. Thereupon a boy was sent off to the neighbouring clan area about a mile away to explain the situation and request the help of a young man who was known to be a "sister's son" of Mansami's lineage. In about half an hour he arrived, duly performed the ritual service requested of him, took a token mouthful of the dish of porridge placed before him and excused himself. "This is the custom", explained the head of Mansami's lineage.

> Have we not besought the Destiny to depart from us and leave us and once you have said so would you thereafter again touch it with a hand? No. We flatter and ingratiate ourselves with the Destiny, so that he might have pity on us and let us rest, so we give him the things he wants and cook this food for him to take all and go quickly to his own place.

The point, he elaborated, was that the whole lineage is implicated in this action on behalf of one of its members and having been decontaminated, as it were, by the ritual, it would be tantamount to bringing back the evil Destiny if they were to be in contact again with the shrine and the "things" that now contain it. As with the marriage witness, a "sister's son" is by matri-kinship on the patient's side and therefore to be trusted to care for his well-being, but by patri-descent excluded from participating in the corporate responsibility for him and therefore, as a quasi-outsider, immune to the evil Destiny.

What, it may well be asked, would have been the expectations and hopes left with Sinkawol and his wife – and their kin on both sides – by the apparently successful removal of her evil Predestiny? I have already mentioned Sinkawol's relief and expectations. His wife too spoke of her relief and hopes, as did the lineage elders. But the Tallensi have far too pragmatic a philosophy of life to expect certainty in the fulfilment of such hopes, even though they are engendered by successful ritual action. The hazards of daily existence remain, reflecting, as they would put it, constant possibilities of intervention in their lives by ancestors and other occult agencies. It has been known, Teezeen once remarked to me, for an evil Predestiny to return as if from a tactical retreat. Tallensi religious beliefs and ritual practices, paradoxical as it may seem to us, serve them effectively as a means of coming to terms with the realities of individual and social life.[1]

[1] I am indebted to a grant from the Leverhulme Foundation for secretarial assistance in the preparation of this paper.

References

BASCOM, WILLIAM (1969). *Ifa Divination: Communication between Gods and Men in West Africa.* Indiana University Press, Bloomington, Indiana.

BEATTIE, JOHN and MIDDLETON, JOHN (1969). *Spirit Mediumship and Society in Africa.* Routledge and Kegan Paul, London.

BESMER, FREMONT E. (1977). Initiation into the *Bori* cult: a case study in Ningi Town. *Africa,* **47,** 1–13.

FIELD, M. J. (1937). *Religion and Medicine of the Gã People.* Oxford University Press, London.

FIELD, M. J. (1960). *Search for Security: An Ethno-psychiatric Study of Rural Ghana.* Faber and Faber, London.

FIRTH, RAYMOND (1959). Problem and assumption in an anthropological study of religion. *Journal of the Royal Anthropological Institute,* **89,** 129–148.

FORTES, MEYER (1945). *The Dynamics of Clanship among the Tallensi, Being the First Part of an Analysis of the Social Structure of a Trans-Volta Tribe.* Oxford University Press, London.

FORTES, MEYER (1959). *Oedipus and Job in West African Religion.* Cambridge University Press, Cambridge.

FORTES, MEYER (1973). On the concept of the person among the Tallensi. In *La Notion de Personne en Afrique Noire,* No. 544. Colloques Internationaux du Centre National de la Recherche Scientifique, Paris.

FORTES, MEYER (1975). Tallensi prayer. In *Studies in Social Anthropology: Essays in Memory of E. E. Evans-Pritchard* (Eds J. H. M. Beattie and R. G. Lienhardt), pp. 132–148. Clarendon Press, Oxford.

FORTES, MEYER (1977). Custom and conscience in anthropological perspective. *The International Review of Psycho-Analysis,* **4,** 127–154.

FORTES, MEYER and MAYER, DORIS Y. (1966). Psychosis and Social Change among the Tallensi of Northern Ghana. *Cahiers d'Etudes Africaines,* **6,** no. 21, 5–40. (Also in *Psychiatry in a Changing Society* (1969) (Eds S. H. Foulkes and G. Stewart Prince), pp. 33–73. Tavistock, London.)

LAST, MURRAY (1976). The presentation of sickness in a community of non-Muslim Hausa. In *Social Anthropology and Medicine* (ASA Monograph no. 13) (Ed. J. L. Loudon), pp. 104–149. Academic Press, London and New York.

NGUBANE, HARRIET (1977). *Body and Mind in Zulu Medicine: An Ethnography of Health and Disease in Nyuswa-Zulu Thought and Practice.* Academic Press, London and New York.

TURNER, VICTOR W. (1969). *The Ritual Process: Structure and Anti-Structure.* Aldine, Chicago, Illinois.

YALMAN, N. (1964). The structure of Sinhalese healing rituals. In *Religion in South Asia* (Ed. Edward B. Harper), pp. 115–150. University of Washington Press, Seattle.

Prevented Successions: A Commentary upon a Kuranko Narrative

Michael Jackson

> A comparative study . . . of the kinds of individuals which writers in various periods have chosen for their heroes often provides a useful clue to the attitudes and preoccupations of each age, for a man's interest always centres, consciously or unconsciously, round what seems to him the most important and still unsolved problem. The hero and his story are simultaneously a stating and a solving of the problem.
>
> W. H. AUDEN

ONE OF THE CHARACTERISTICS of a myth or folk-tale is that it occasions thoughts, feelings, associations, and recollections which carry far beyond the narrative itself. Yet these subjective, concrete and idiosyncratic elements are pruned out or played down in both myths and myth analyses. Devereux has suggested that this is because a myth or folk-tale becomes widely accepted only when concrete incidents are generalized, superfluous details omitted, the narrative fitted into the conventional mould of narrative technique, and the basic plot "ground down to its universally valid nucleus" (1948, p. 238). In order that it be generally available, a narrative must seem to transcend the private worlds of the myth-maker and the myth-teller. And in order that it convey with authority the official meaning assigned to it, a narrative must always retain a conventional camouflage of impersonality.

The problem of myth analysis is comparable to the problem of myth making, for, in both cases, the "made thing" must facilitate or mediate a dialectic between subjective particularities and conventional or universal meanings. The myth-maker or narrator must organize and represent subjective, idiosyncratic elements of his own life in ways which enable others to discover their own meanings in his work. The myth analyst must establish a similar rapport: between his own response to a narrative and the meanings it has for people in another society.

The difficulty of myth analysis is one of avoiding a reduction of the meaning of the myth to particular subjective realities, whether of a narrator, an informant, or of oneself. At the same time one must avoid a reduction of subjective realizations to conventional authorized meanings. We cannot expect to develop an inductive science of mythology. Professional and personal predilections will always influence the mode of analysis. And one cannot tell the same tale twice. The art of myth analysis is to make a virtue out of these conditions. The concerns and interests of the analyst and the ways in which a narrative varies from context to context and from person to person should be regarded as means for attaining new syntheses rather than as obstacles to attaining a set goal. In this way the myth analysis becomes like the myth, continually transcending the conditions that fostered it. Lévi-Strauss speaks of this process in a famous passage:

> . . . it is in the last resort immaterial whether . . . the thought processes of the South American Indians take shape through the medium of my thought, or whether mine take place through the medium of theirs. What matters is that the human mind, regardless of the identity of those who happen to be giving it expression, should display an increasingly intelligible structure as a result of the doubly reflexive forward movement of two thought processes acting one upon the other, either of which can in turn provide the spark or tinder whose conjunction will shed light on both. [1970, p. 13.]

This paper begins with an analysis of a Kuranko narrative and an examination of the ways in which the narrative treats, and perhaps resolves, various problems associated with intergenerational succession. The analysis leads to a consideration of the nucleus of more or less universal elements, at the level of latent content and of structure,[1] present in the Kuranko narrative. I then explore, somewhat specu-

[1] Devereux has referred to the "double invariance" of a myth: the invariance of its latent content, and of its structure. The logical relationship between these two invariances (or explanations of invariance) is that of Heisenbergian complementarity (Devereux, 1970, p. 1229).

latively, the significance of physical imagery in myths concerning the births of heroes. The progression of the argument, from particular ethnographical problems to more abstract, speculative concerns, and back to particular problems again, is influenced by the narratives which it seemed appropriate to consider in this essay. It is my view that myths and folk-tales are essentially like this and serve this purpose. They occasion and mediate a transcendent contemplation of the world, the better to return with altered experience to the mundane and particular situation from which one took one's departure.

The Kuranko narrative: "The origins of rivalry among half-brothers"

A certain chief had two wives. These two women became pregnant at almost the same time. So they gave birth on the same day. Both babies were male. Before this time the chief had appointed two *finabas*, one to each wife, so that they would announce the births to him as soon as they occurred.

The *finaba* appointed to the first wife went to announce the birth of her child to the chief. When he arrived at the chief's house he found the chief eating. Instead of delivering the message and informing the chief that his son was born, the *finaba* sat down and accepted an invitation to partake of the food. The second wife also sent her *finaba* to tell the chief about the birth of her child. He went and found everyone eating. He was invited to eat. But he said, "I was sent to deliver a message first: your wife has given birth to a baby boy." Then the chief said, "Good, that is the child to whom I shall give my father's name." So that child was named after the chief's father. Thus the second child became the first.

Then the first wife's *finaba* said, "Oh chief, I came to deliver the same message: your wife has given birth to a baby boy." But by then it was too late. So the first child became the second.

Now, before the birth of these children the diviner had told the chief that one of his sons would prove eminently capable of succeeding him. The children lived together. But the first wife was never content. She was always unhappy about the position of the second son who had been proclaimed the first. During this time the children were growing up and receiving instruction in the same household.

There came a time when the second son (who had been proclaimed the first) began to walk. The first son could only crawl. This went on for several years. The mother of the first son (who had been proclaimed the second) began telling her son that God had perceived his inadequacy and so had made the boy's father proclaim him second. "Now look at my co-wife's child, he goes about gathering wood and doing everything for his mother, but here you are, lame and unable to do a thing for me. And every time I have to send your brother on errands for me, his mother tells me that she is not responsible that my own child is lame."

The woman continued to upbraid her child. But his was no ordinary lameness. The reason for it was that on the very day he walked his father would die. But as a result of his mother's persistent nagging he got up on to his knees and went to a monkey-bread tree, seized it, shook it, and uprooted it. He brought the entire tree trunk and laid it at his mother's door. He then told his mother's *finaba* to go and tell his father to send him the iron bow. They brought the iron bow. When he drew back the bow it broke. He sent for another one. The same thing happened. Then he announced that he would go himself. He stood up. His mother sang:

Yata tamanda, Yata tamanda, keliya le kake,
Yata tamanda; bi yo, bi yo, bi yo, ma bi nyornye.
(Yata walked, Yata walked, envy made
Yata walk; today oh, today oh, today oh, there has never been a day like today.)

As soon as Yata stood up a serious illness befell his father. So the boy sat down. But his mother was laughing at him, taunting him. So he finally stood up, walked straight to his father and took his father's gown and cap and put them on. As he walked away his father died.

Because of his tremendous strength he became ruler. But the other wife was jealous and urged her son to go away rather than be ruled by the proclaimed younger brother. The second son who had been proclaimed first went away. He never ceased to be resentful of his brother's position. Since that time this rivalry between brothers has existed. Up to the present time brothers of the same father but of different mothers are rivals and competitors.

Ethnographical background

The Kuranko occupy the region of the western and north-western Guinea Highlands. Of a total population of over 125,000 some 90,000 live in Sierra Leone. The Kuranko are a Mande-speaking people, recognizing their origins in "Mande", and closely related to the Malinke of Upper Guinea. My field research among the Kuranko (Sierra Leone, 1969–70 and 1972) included the collection and study of oral narratives. Narratives are generally categorized, either as *kuma kore* (lit. "word old/senior/venerable") or as *tilei*. The first category includes clan traditions and "myths" (which are considered to be a legacy of the ancestors and thus "true"), while the second category includes "folk-tales" (which are admittedly fictional although concerned with "things that really happen"). The narrative about Yata is categorized as *tilei*.

I have published elsewhere accounts of Kuranko kinship and social structure; here I will simply draw attention to those facts which are directly relevant to understanding the Yata narrative.[1]

1. Succession (including succession to chieftaincy) generally follows the principle of primogeniture, although in practice an eldest son will be passed over in favour of a younger brother or even father's younger brother if he is not capable of shouldering the responsibilities of the office.[2] The eldest son's assumption of his father's position formally takes place *after* the father's death. The assumption is signified by the son inheriting and donning his father's cap and gown. "Positions", say the Kuranko, "are like garments".

2. A man's immediate successor is normally the first-born son of his first ("senior") wife. According to Kuranko naming custom, the first-born son takes the father's father's name; the second-born is named from the mother's side (usually after the mother's father). The successor is thus identified with the patriline, while the second-born is identified with the jurally insignificant matriline.

Conventionally, the relationship between a man and his eldest son is characterized by formality, restraint, and latent antagonisms. The father's high expectations of his heir are often felt to be burdensome and unrealistic. The father adopts a critical, disdainful attitude towards his heir, particularly in public. Many

[1] See particularly Jackson (1974, 1975, 1977a, 1977b, and in press).

[2] Among the Kuranko there are usually several claimants and competitors for chiefly office; personal ability is the decisive factor in election (cf. Southwold's study (1966) of the importance of personality factors in the selection of successors to the Buganda king).

Kuranko see this behaviour as a necessary pretence, as a way of deflecting attention away from the privileged position of the heir and thus avoiding envy among the heir's younger brothers. But many elder sons do not perceive the artifice of their father's belittling and reserved manner; particularly when young, their experience is of paternal rejection.

3. Although a man's fate and fortune are largely determined by his patrilineal forebears and by his membership of his patrilineage, the ancestral blessings are mediated by a man's mother. Thus, a diviner will often explain a man's misfortune as being a consequence of disrespect shown by the mother towards her husband. Good fortune is typically and readily attributed to the proper conduct of a man's mother. Partly as a consequence of these ideas, women tend to blame themselves for misfortunes suffered by their children. But, since the blessings of the patrilineal ancestors are a kind of scarce resource competed for by a man's several wives (each of whom strives for the prosperity of her own children), a woman may be inclined to blame a co-wife (whose children are well favoured) for the failures and misfortunes of her own children. From this tension and latent antagonism among co-wives, the Kuranko derive the usual explanation for the rivalry among half-brothers (sons of the same father but of different mothers). The resentments of junior siblings are equated with the resentments of junior wives. The authoritarian, selfish behaviour of "elder brother" or of "senior wife" constitutes one of the commonest *leitmotifs* in Kuranko folk-tales.

The relationship between half-brothers or ortho-cousins is known as *fadenye* (lit. "father's children-ship"), and the term *fadenye* may be applied in describing any deep-seated rivalry or feud among people. It is thus directly comparable with the Bambara *fadena* (Griaule, 1973, p. 12) and the Malinke *fadenya* (Hopkins, 1971, p. 100).

4. Kuranko society is composed of four major estates: the rulers; non-ruling "commoner" clans; traditionally Muslim clans; the occupational and hereditary groups with whom rulers may not marry. The latter grouping is known as the *nyemakale*. It includes the xylophonists and praise-singers (*jeli*s) and the bardic keepers of the chiefly traditions and genealogies (*fina*s). Ranked lowest in the social hierarchy, *fina*s (the terms *finaba* and *jeliba* refer to *fina* men and *jeli* men; *ba* meaning "big") are in the service of rulers whose

patronage they enjoy. Apocryphal stories abound in the ruling families, attributing all the catastrophes of the warrior past to the caprice and cunning of *finas* and *jelis* who exceeded their servile roles, initiated rash projects and, by reminding chiefs of their courageous forebears, connived to encourage rulers on disastrous courses of action.

Yata and Sundiata: the Manding connections

The Yata narrative was related to me in English by my field assistant, Noah Bokari Marah, in Kabala, July 1970. At that time neither Noah nor I was aware of the resemblances and possible connections between the Kuranko narrative (to which Noah gave the aetiological subtitle) and the well-known Mande epic of Sundiata.

The hero, Yata, whose name is mentioned only in the refrain his mother sings when he gets up and walks for the first time, is undoubtedly Sundiata, although this name and epic are scarcely known among the Kuranko in Sierra Leone. Among the Kuranko in Guinea, "the name Sundiata is vaguely known but his legend is practically ignored" (Person, 1973, p. 207, footnote). The hero of Kuranko epics is invariably the ancestor of the hunters, Mande Fa Bori, but his name is never linked to Sundiata as it is in the "Mandingo" epic (Niane, 1965). The sole version of the Sundiata epic which I heard among the Kuranko was related to me by a *jeliba*, widely travelled in Guinea. This version, narrated by Yeli Fode Gibate in Kabala, August 1970, was given as an explanation of the origins of the xylophone and of praise-singing. I shall hereafter refer to this version as "the Gibate version". Those passages which are relevant to the subject of this essay are abstracted below.

The ancestor of the Mansare was called Mande Sundiata . . .

He first demonstrated his powers of witchcraft[1] against his mother. His mother conceived him but she remained pregnant for four million, four hundred and forty years, four months and four days. During this time Mande Sundiata would leave his mother's belly at night. He would go into the bush and hunt. He was a great hunter. At dawn he would return to town and leave the animals there. Then he would return to his mother's belly. At night his mother would look at her

[1] Witchcraft=*suwa'ye*. In this context it is a metaphor for Sundiata's extraordinary powers.

belly but see nothing; but during the day her belly would be swollen. This confused her. She went to a diviner and said, "By day I am pregnant, by night I am not." And she said, "Every morning people find dead animals in the town." The diviner said, "You must prepare rice-flour [*dege*] for sacrifice and offer it to four elderly women. There is something in your belly that will conquer and command the entire world." Sundiata was the first chief in this world.

The woman carried out the diviner's instructions. Then the elderly women told her that when she next woke at night and found her belly empty she should take a mortar and place it on her sleeping mat. They also told her to cover the mortar with her bed sheet and then leave that place and sleep elsewhere. They said, "By the grace of God you will give birth to your child tomorrow; that child is older than its own mother."

That night Mande Sundiata left his mother's belly. When she saw that he had gone she did just as the old women had told her: she took the mortar and covered it with her bed sheet, went and slept elsewhere. Very early in the morning, at cock-crow, Mande Sundiata returned. He wanted to re-enter his mother's belly but the mortar prevented him from doing so. He knocked his head against the mortar and cried out. Then everyone exclaimed, "Oh, Mande Musukoro has delivered her child." Mande Sundiata was crying like a baby. But when the people came to see him they found that he had teeth. Although he cried like a baby he was a grown man. Everyone gathered round. A chicken was killed and cooked. The baby, Mande Sundiata, ate it all. Everyone was astounded. The wise men came and said, "You should not be worried, this is no mere baby, this is something great."

When other boys went to gather leaves, Mande Sundiata would go too, crawling like a baby to gather leaves for his mother. When the senior hunters came to town with meat for sale, Mande Sundiata would disappear. When he went into the bush he would be a grown man, but when he came back to town he would be like a baby again. So when they speak of Mande Sundiata, they are not speaking of an ordinary man. He was a *nyenne*.[1]

[1] The reference to Sundiata as a *nyenne* ("spirit of the wild") is metaphorical, a way of emphasizing his extraordinary powers and his anomalous position (like the *nyenne*, half-way between the world of man and the world of animals).

The narrative continues with a description of how Mande Sundiata went on living a double life: a child by day, a supreme hunter by night. The townspeople never suspected that Mande Sundiata was the provider of their abundant meat supplies. On one journey into the bush, Mande Sundiata steals the xylophone from the spirits of the wild (the *nyenne*), shooting and killing them. Then Sira Kaarta takes up the xylophone and becomes Sundiata's praise-singer. He gives Sundiata the title *keita*, the Kuranko folk-etymology of which is "property-taker" (from *ke*, "property"). The Kuranko also say that Sundiata means "heart-burner", from *sūn* ("heart") and *ya* ("dry" or "searing"). According to Yeli Fode, another praise name of Sundiata is Sumaworo, said to derive from *sume* ("elephantiasis of the scrotum") and *woro* ("calf of the leg").[1]

> His name is made up from his deeds. They named him for what he did. Sundiata, because he could strike fear into people's hearts. Keita, because he could seize anyone's property. Mande Sumaworo, because when he became angry he would make others so afraid that they would be afflicted by elephantiasis of the testicles. These were the words with which Sira Kaarta praised Sundiata. [Yeli Fode Gibate, from his 1970 narrative.]

One of the most lengthy and detailed versions of the Sundiata epic is that of Djeli Mamoudou Kouyaté, recorded and published by D. T. Niane (translated from the French, 1965). In order to indicate similarities and differences between the Kuranko narratives and the "Mandingo" epic recorded by Niane, a synopsis of the events preceding Sundiata's exile is presented below. I shall hereafter refer to this as "the Niane version".

Sundiata's father, Maghan Kon Fatta, has three wives: the first, Sassouma Bérété, mother of the heir and future king, Dankaran Touman, and his sister, Nana Triban; the second, Sogolon Kedjou, mother of Sundiata and his two sisters, Sogolon Kolonkan and Sogolon Djamarou; the third, Namandje, mother of Manding Bory (or Manding Bakary), best friend and half-brother of Sundiata.

A soothsayer informs the king that his true heir is not yet born, even though Dankaran, his eldest son, is eight years old at this time. The soothsayer foretells the coming of a hideous and humpbacked woman whom the king must marry, for she "will be the mother of him who

[1] In the Niane version, Soumaoro Kanté is a powerful sorcerer-king whom Sundiata fights and finally defeats in his conquest and unification of Mali. The significance of the reference to the calf of the leg *(woro)* is discussed in a later section of this paper.

will make the name of Mali immortal for ever" (Niane, 1965, p. 6).

The king marries, as predicted, but his wife – Sogolon Kedjou – repulses his advances. To his griot *(jeliba)* the king confesses his inability to possess Sogolon; furthermore, he doubts that she is a human being since "during the night her body became covered with long hairs", so striking fear into his heart. But the "wraith" which possesses Sogolon is finally subdued, and she conceives the king's child.

The king's first wife – Sassouma – becomes envious and afraid of Sogolon whose son, it has been predicted, will rule over her own. Sassouma uses sorcery in a vain attempt to kill Sogolon.

Sundiata is born and named (Sundiata is a contraction, according to the narrator, of Sogolon and the boy's name – Djata). His development is slow and difficult. At three years of age he still cannot walk or stand. Sassouma, whose own son is now eleven, derives a malicious pleasure from the adversity of her co-wife's child. She taunts the child for being retarded and "stiff legged". At seven years of age Sundiata still cannot walk or stand.

The king dies and Dankaran succeeds him. Sassouma continues to persecute Sogolon and her backward child. Sogolon weeps because of the public ridicule she must endure.

> Sogolon's son was spoken of with nothing but irony and scorn. People had seen one-eyed kings, one-armed kings, and lame kings, but a stiff-legged king had never been heard tell of. No matter how great the destiny promised for Mari Djata might be, the throne could not be given to someone who had no power in his legs. . . . Such were the remarks that Sogolon heard every day. [Niane, 1965, p. 18.]

One day Sogolon happens to be short of condiments and she asks Sassouma for some baobab leaf. Sassouma points out that her son picked the leaves for her; she laughs derisively at Sogolon and mocks the uselessness of her son, Sundiata. Humiliated and enraged, Sogolon strikes her son with a piece of wood, blaming him for her misfortunes and for the insults she has suffered. Sundiata then declares, "I am going to walk today." He sends to his father's smiths to have them make the heaviest possible iron rod. In order to wipe out the insult she has suffered, Sogolon asks that Sundiata bring the entire baobab tree (not just the leaves) to her house.

The iron rod is forged. A praise-singer cries, "Today is a day like any other, but it will see what no other day has seen." The iron rod is brought to Sundiata. Sitting up and then standing with the aid of the iron rod, he bends it into the shape of a bow. Sogolon sings the praise of God who has given her son the use of his legs. Sundiata then uproots the baobab and takes it to the door of his mother's house.

Quickly, people begin to compare Sogolon with her senior co-wife, Sassouma.

> It was because the former had been an exemplary wife and mother that God had granted strength to her son's legs for, it was said, the more a wife loves and respects her husband and the more she suffers for her child, the more valorous will the child be one day. Each is the child of his mother; the child is worth no more than the mother is worth. It was not astonishing that the king Dankaran Touman was so colourless, for his mother had never shown the slightest respect to her husband and never, in the presence of the late king, did she show that humility which every wife should show before her husband. People recalled her scenes of jealousy and the spiteful remarks she circulated about her co-wife and her child. [Niane, 1965, p. 22.]

Sassouma now attempts to kill Sundiata by witchcraft. Sogolon, fearing for the safety of her son's vulnerable half-brother, Manding Bory, and her daughters, decides to take her family into exile.

Other versions of the epic, treated in an essay by Pageard (1961), supply details which are also found in the Kuranko narratives. According to one of these versions (hereafter referred to as the Pageard version), which Pageard collected in Segou:

> Soundiata, the eldest of these [that is, Sogolon's] children, could not walk before the age of seventeen. When he got up for the first time, it was to avenge the honour of his mother and he had to lean against a huge iron bar which gave way. It was on that occasion that the father of the KOUYATE griots (Dionkouma Doga) and Soundiata's two half-sisters, SOGOLON (KOLONGA) and SOGOLON (SOGONA) invented the song beginning with "Soundiata was able to get up to-day". [Pageard, 1961, p. 56.]

Pageard also stresses that Sundiata's voluntary exile was "justified to the extent that it prevents a brotherly struggle and everyone knows the strength of the 'fadenya' (a rivalry between sons born of the same father but of different mothers) in the Manding country" (1961, p. 63).

Finally, it is worth noting a synoptic account of Sundiata's birth, given by Bird (1971). In this account (hereafter referred to as the Bird version), details of Sundiata's birth are much more similar to those in the Yata narrative.

After Fasaku Magan's marriage to Sogolon, both women become pregnant and both give birth on the same day. Saman Berete's son, Dankaran Tuman, is the first born, but Sunjata's birth is announced first to the king. He joyfully proclaims Sunjata his heir over the protest of Saman Berete. Saman Berete has a spell cast on Sunjata as a result of which he is paralyzed for nine years. The spell is eventually broken and Sunjata walks, giving rise to a magnificent series of songs. [Bird, 1971, p. 21.]

It is outside the scope of this paper to attempt a scholarly comparative study of the several versions of the Sundiata epic which I have referred to or summarized above. Rather than investigate the sources, history, and diffusion of the epic among the Mande-speaking peoples of the West Sudan, I wish to use these versions, first, to establish for the Yata narrative a wider historical and cultural context,[1] second, to highlight certain *leit-motifs* which are characteristic of these narratives and of hero myths throughout the world. For example, all these narratives include problematic episodes associated with the hero's conception, gestation, birth, or maturation: prolonged infancy (reluctance to walk) in the Yata narrative and the Niane, Pageard, and Bird versions; delayed and difficult conception in the Niane version; prolonged gestation (reluctance to be born) in the Gibate version. Other themes include: the artificial reversal of proper birth-order position (the Yata narrative, the Bird version); the correlation of tensions and rivalries within a generation with tensions and rivalries between the generations; the anomalous attributes of the hero, often established through physical imagery pertaining to weakness and strength, precocity and backwardness. I propose to elucidate the ways in which these motifs may be regarded as variations on a single theme and approaches to a common problem, the significance of which may prove to be transcultural.[2]

The Yata narrative: an analysis

First, it is important to note that the *finaba*'s failure to transmit the message from the chief's senior wife to the chief brings about an am-

[1] The Yata narrative could be regarded as a surviving fragment of the Sundiata epic, now become a mere village tale existing at a lower level of mythological thought (Lévi-Strauss, 1970, p. 333). Bird notes that some episodes of the Sundiata epic are often omitted or abridged in narration (1971, p. 21). Perhaps, as in the case of so many myths, the "complete" version is a fiction, or a product of the context of recording.

[2] My method of analysis is derived from and inspired by the structural approach of Lévi-Strauss. I have, however, placed greater emphasis on content, applying several of the ideas and insights of Devereux.

biguous situation. The proper status distinction between the two sons is reversed, but the superior ability of the rightful heir, although at first camouflaged, remains intact. Second, the *finaba*'s error is that he allows his appetite for food (personal gratification) to deflect him from his social duty as a message-bearer.

Myths from throughout Africa attribute the breakdown of social unity and continuity to a failure to communicate a message. Death and affliction have their origins in a message garbled or information incorrectly transmitted (Abrahamsson, 1951). In the Yata narrative, the *finaba*'s error has two secondary consequences. First, since the rightful heir is named second in line of succession, the delayed transmission of the message has the effect of *increasing the distance* between the chief and his senior wife's son. This momentarily obscures a contradiction which arises from the fact that although the birth of a son guarantees the continuity of the lineage it also presages the displacement of the incumbent. Social continuity must be maintained despite the discontinuous nature of individual life. But this continuity is often jeopardized, (1) by the resistance of the incumbent to the idea that he can and must be replaced, (2) by the heir's reluctance to accede. The second consequence of the *finaba*'s error in delaying transmission of the message is that the *distance is decreased* between the two brothers. Instead of becoming unequivocally status differentiated, the senior wife's child becomes the junior (but will claim the chieftaincy by right *and* by virtue of superior ability) while the junior wife's child becomes the senior (but will fail to claim the chieftaincy because of his inferior birthright *and* inferior ability).

This analysis suggests that the nascent conflict between a chief and his heir is resolved fictionally by a kind of displacement: the conflict comes to be focused upon the relationship between first and second sons. This "displacement" (which in a structural analysis would be termed a "transformation") has been noted by Rank in his study of hero myths: "The duplication of the fathers (or the grandfathers) by a brother may be continued in the next generation, and concern the hero himself, thus leading to the *brother myths* . . ." (1959, p. 90). Herskovits (1958, pp. 88–89) has also referred to this transformation/displacement in Dahomean narratives where intergenerational conflicts are often transmuted by intragenerational ones. Among the Kuranko it is in fact often asserted that a father's feigned rejection and overbearing criticism of his eldest son is an attempt to disguise the actual line of succession. The father's delegation of authority to the eldest son over the latter's younger brothers is interpreted similarly: as a way of deflecting attention and envy away from the privileged relationship between father and eldest son. Both stratagems are seen as ways of preventing *fadenye*.

Other transformations in the narrative must now be examined, particularly since the father's role is played down and the mothers' roles played up. Indeed, in all versions of the Sundiata epic which we have examined, Sundiata's father is peripheral and inconspicuous. Let us first contrast two crucial episodes:

1. The senior wife's *finaba* delays transmitting a message. As a consequence the status distinction between the chief's two sons is reversed, and a great distance exists between the chief and the rightful heir.
2. The senior wife berates her son because of his backwardness. As a consequence the status distinction between the chief and his eldest son is reversed since, as soon as Yata walks his father dies (and Yata becomes chief).

The first episode involves male–male oppositions while the second involves female–male oppositions. They are linked by virtue of the fact that both *finaba*s and women occupy marginal, mediatory, message-bearing positions. When they exceed the passive, mediatory functions ascribed to them, calamity follows.[1] The second episode is thus a transformation of the first, but while it reiterates the same moral stricture (message-bearers should not be message-senders) it has the effect of displacing blame from the *finaba* on to the senior wife. The narrative thus leads to the conclusion that she is ultimately responsible for the chief's death. She goaded her son into walking, although her son was reluctant to show his powers lest his father die. Once again, an intergenerational conflict (mother–son) is transmuted by an intragenerational one (wife–husband). In the Niane version the conflict between senior and junior co-wives is emphasized far more.

The preceding analysis establishes the basic transformational pattern of the narrative: intergenerational (parent–child) conflicts are transformed into (or displaced on to) intragenerational (sibling) con-

[1] The most obvious Kuranko examples, in which self-interest and self-willedness eclipse duty and passivity, are: the wife as witch (see Jackson, 1975), and the mother as lover (recreative versus procreative sexuality) (see Jackson, 1977b).

flicts, and the source of conflict is located in male–female rather than male–male relationships. The displacement of tension and conflict away from "central", "vertical" relationships towards "peripheral", "lateral" relationships is as characteristic of day-to-day Kuranko explanations as it is of Kuranko fictional schemes. The pattern is typical enough in traditional African societies[1] to justify a digression to discuss the relationships between institutionalized and fictionalized variations of it.

Aspects of succession

The Freudian concept of displacement implies that emotional stress is deflected from the important to the less important. In Abraham's words, "The least important is substituted for the most important and is transposed into the focal point of interest." (1909, p. 188.) Freud himself referred to this process as "the inversion of all values". In the narratives discussed so far, displacements of the following kinds are typical:

father–son → elder brother–younger brother
(vertical → lateral)
elder brother–younger brother → half-brother–half-brother
(central → peripheral)
half-brother–half-brother → co-wife–co-wife
(male–male → female–female)

The question now arises: given the basic transformational pattern of the Yata narrative, why should intragenerational and male–female relationships be considered less important than intergenerational and male–male relationships? At this point we must look at some of the problems associated with vertical systems of agnatic succession in Africa.

[1] Among the Lugbara, witchcraft accusations within the minimal lineage are of two kinds: a son against his father, "brother" against "brother". Apart from indicating the tension and repressed hostility that often exist between father and son, the pattern of witchcraft accusations indicates a trend towards displacement. Thus, accusations between "men of equal generation, 'brothers', tend to occur at later stages in the cycle of development of a lineage". "Accusations by a son against a father . . . occur mainly during the earlier stages." (Middleton, 1960, p. 227.) It should also be noted here that the love–hate relationship between father and son is sometimes exacerbated when senior sons compete with the father for the affections of his junior wives. This is the case among the Dinka (see Deng, 1974, p. 175).

In his superb study of succession to high office, Jack Goody refers to what he calls the "Prince Hal complex".

> Where office passes between close agnates of adjacent generations, there is a potential heightening of tension within a relationship that usually carries the burden of the whole process of socialization. To the ordinary conflicts between father and son are added those arising out of the transmission of office; this is one of the problems Shakespeare sees in the uneasy relationship between Henry IV and Prince Hal . . . [Goody, 1966a, p. 34.]

One "solution" to this problem is exemplified by the custom of the "banished heir" (ibid.). For example, even though Mossi custom decreed that the eldest son of the previous incumbent be made Mogho Naba, the heir lived away from the palace with his mother's kin, guarded and educated by palace servants. If his father was on the throne at Ouagadougou when the boy reached ten, he was formally installed as chief of the Djiba district, the traditional seat of the Crown Prince (Skinner, 1964, p. 45). Strict formality obtained between the ruler and his sons. Skinner observes that "the Mogho Naba was not expected to enjoy seeing his son and heir, because of the Mossi father's traditional anxiety regarding those individuals who would profit most from his death" (1964, p. 48). Younger sons were also given district chieftainships or assignments away from Ouagadougou. In the Mossi case, it is noteworthy that although the most capable person (in the royal minimal lineage) acceded to power, the emphasis placed upon the *principle* of primogeniture was considerable. This is equally true of the Kuranko, and it is worth remarking the striking similarity between the following Mossi "folk rumour" reported by Skinner and the Yata narrative (Kuranko). A more direct similarity is with the Bird version (Mande).

> If the child was a boy, the ruler or Crown Prince was notified immediately, because the important privileges of a first-born hinged upon this notification. Since several wives of the Mogho Naba might be pregnant at the same time and errors might be made about the onset and duration of pregnancy, primogeniture had to be established immediately to forestall dynastic conflicts. For example, it is commonly believed that the present Doulougou Naba was born several days before Mogho Naba Sagha II (1942–57) but was deprived of the *nam* ["the power first possessed by the ancient founders, which is described by the Mossi as 'that force of God which enables one man to control another' " (Skinner, 1964, p. 13)] because the messenger who brought the news of his birth reached Mogho Naba Kom after the messenger who announced Sagha's birth. [Skinner, 1964, p. 45.]

Another "solution" to the Prince Hal problem is to avoid or delay making public the identity of the heir. The Swazi (who also sometimes "banish the heir") are quite explicit about the value of this strategy. "The heir's position is coveted, and ambition for the power and wealth it brings often leads to strife – strife in the homestead between father and sons, between brothers, between co-wives, between women and their husbands . . ." (Kuper, 1947, p. 89.) Identical ramifications are traced out in the narratives we have referred to.

Goody also refers to a "basic alternative" (and thus a kind of solution) to the problems inherent in the vertical system, namely a "horizontal or fraternal one" (1966a, p. 35).[1] He points out that by including brothers among the eligibles there is less strain on the father–son relationship; "a wider range of kin acquires a direct interest in the throne; and you have older office-holders and shorter reigns" (ibid.). For example, although the Kuranko place considerable ideological emphasis on the principle of primogeniture, actual successions involve manipulations of both vertical and lateral possibilities in order to elect to office the most capable individual. Informants admit that the attributes of leadership are not always found in the heir and that both brothers and sons of an incumbent regard themselves as potential successors.

Finally, it should be noted that a system of rotating or circulating succession has the effect of shifting political conflicts away from the domestic domain and shifting the tensions of intergenerational succession on to distant rather than close relationships (Goody, 1966a, p. 39; 1966b, p. 165).

All the institutional and "official" solutions summarized above have parallels in the narrative schemes earlier discussed. These parallels can be elucidated as follows:

Institution	*Narrative scheme*
1. Banishing the heir; avoidance relationship between incumbent and heir.	1. "Distancing" the heir by reversing the status distinction between first-born and second-born sons.

[1] I have argued elsewhere (Jackson, 1977b) that laterally structured cult associations among the Kuranko offset and eclipse tensions and conflicts within the vertically structured descent field. Neumann has also suggested that the "horizontal organization of age groups obviates personal conflict in the sense of a hostile father–son relationship, because the terms 'father' and 'son' connote group characteristics and not personal relations. . . . Conflicts, so far as they exist at all, are between the age groups and have a collective and archetypal, rather than a personal and individual, character." (Neumann, 1954, p. 141.)

Institution	*Narrative scheme*
2. The identity of the heir is masked or uncertain.	2. The heir's development is retarded; there is uncertainty about his capability to accede.
3. Increasing the number of eligibles to include brothers.	3. Succession does not conform to the ideal pattern (primogeniture); in the Niane and Bird versions Sundiata is the second-born.
4. Circulating succession; conflicts shifted away from close to distant kin.	4. Displacement of conflicts from father–son to brother–brother to half-brother–half-brother.

The relationships and transformations between imagined and actualized solutions to recurrent social problems demand further study. But my intention here is only to demonstrate a general tendency to displace conflict and tension away from the father–son relationship on to functionally less important relationships, particularly when a rule of primogeniture exists.

This frequently implies a discrepancy between the ideal rule and actual practice (see Goody, 1966b; Southwold, 1966). The significance of "good character" as a factor in Swazi succession may be given as an example. "Occasionally an outstanding son has won for himself such affection that he is appointed with his own mother over a child whose mother is of nobler birth. *But this is not put forward as a general principle* by any family council" (Kuper, 1947, p. 103, my emphasis). The "fundamental principle" underlying the selection of an heir is that power is inherited from men but transmitted through women, whose rank determines the choice of successor (Kuper, 1947, p. 91).[1] Quite clearly, bending the rules is necessary in order to have the most capable person accede to power. Genetically, it is improbable that the nominal heir will always be the cleverest, strongest, most eloquent person around. The discrepancy which often arises between a determinate principle (such as primogeniture) and indeterminacy in practice is, I have argued elsewhere, made good through fictional devices which contrive the semblance of a "fit" between high *ability*

[1] The Swazi expression is *Nkosi ngunina* (a ruler (is ruled) by his mother) (Kuper, 1947, p. 91). Similar maxims are used among the Kuranko: "The child is the book of its mother"; "A person's destiny is in his mother's hands".

and high *status*.[1] For example, in many Kuranko narratives a weak chief is deposed or killed[2] by a strong and precocious son. The plot thus confirms the Kuranko ideal: that a chief should also be strong and clever.

I want to turn now to a consideration of some of the ontogenetic aspects of the customs and narratives which have already been referred to. As an introduction I will remark certain parallels between the Kuranko narratives and the Greek myth of the birth of Heracles.

Heracles

The circumstances of the conception, gestation, and birth of Heracles bear remarkable resemblances, both in detail and at the level of formal organization, to the Yata narrative. The genealogy and synopsis in Fig. 1 (from Kerényi, 1959) will assist further exposition.

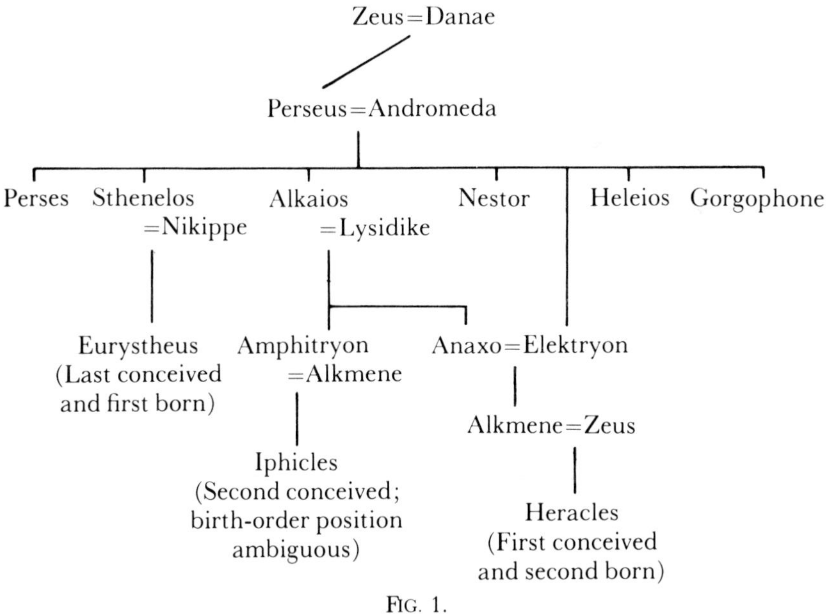

FIG. 1.

[1] For a complete exposition see Jackson (in press).

[2] For example, among the Furiiru (Kivu province, Zaire), when the king is too sick or old to embody the ideals of kingship (unifier, increaser, and peacemaker in the land) he is ritually and secretly disposed of (usually by strangulation) by the very ritual experts who enthroned him (Biebuyck, 1973, p. 71).

It will be recalled that Zeus impersonated Amphitryon on his wedding night. Zeus slept with Alkmene, and the night was of the length of three. Heracles, child of this union, was thus called *triselenos* ("child of the triple moon"). Later, during this same artificially prolonged night (some versions say the following day), Amphitryon returns and Alkmene conceives his child, Heracles' twin brother Iphicles. Nine months later Zeus boasts about the imminent birth of his son, who would rule the House of Perseus. Hera makes him promise that any prince born before nightfall to the House of Perseus should be High King. Hera now hastens the birth of Nikippe's son, Eurystheus, and artificially delays the birth of Heracles. When Heracles appeared, "one hour too late, he was found to have a twin named Iphicles, Amphitryon's son and the younger by a night. But some say that Heracles, not Iphicles, was the younger by a night; and others, that the twins were begotten on the same night, and born together . . ." (Graves, 1955, vol. 2, p. 86).

The parallels between the myth of the birth of Heracles and the Yata narrative should be now clear:

Heracles	*Yata*
First conceived, second born (thus seeming to have lost his right to rule the House of Perseus).	First born, proclaimed second (thus seeming to have lost his right to succeed to his father's position).
Artificially delayed birth.	Artificially delayed growth.
Great physical strength (contrasted with his brother's greater power: Eurystheus, whose name means "the widely powerful", becomes king).	Great physical strength (contrasted with his brother's superior position).

Both myths may be considered as examples of contrived ultimogeniture, since both heroes are deprived of their rightful status as firstborn. The person artificially made younger/junior ultimately succeeds to a high position (Heracles becomes a god) because of his superior strength and ability. Devereux has drawn attention to this theme in his study of the relationships between the Heracles myth and myths of the founding of the Scythian royal dynasty. In the Scythian myth proper (as distinct from the version of the Pontic Greeks[1]), the first inhabitant of Scythia was Targitaos (or Targitaus). Targitaos = Heracles. Targitaos fathered three sons: Lipoxais, Arpoxais, and the youngest, Kolaxais. Four golden objects fell from the sky: a chariot, a yoke, a war-axe, and a cup. The oldest sons were unable to take hold of the objects, but Kolaxais the youngest picked them up and became the founder of the *senior* royal dynastic line. The objects subsequently became the insignia of Scythian royalty (Devereux, 1972, pp. 263–264). Summarizing the Heracles myth, Devereux stresses certain key episodes and themes:

> L'important, ici, c'est que ce mythe explique comment l'enfant qui était le *dernier* à être *engendré*, mais qui *allait naître* le *premier* (après une grossesse de sept mois seulement) put *devenir roi* – un roi cruel et lâche, qui tyrannisait celui qui, quoique *engendré* le *premier, était né après lui*, la grossesse de sa mère ayant été artificiellement prolongée. Dans cette tradition, un miracle malveillant confère au cadet (biologique) les droits de l'aînesse (dynastique). En d'autres termes, la succession s'effectue conformément au *principe de l'ultimogéniture, frauduleusement déguisée en primogéniture.* [1972, pp. 268–269.]

Ontogenetic approaches

The general theme which the narratives and institutions discussed in the preceding pages have in common is the delaying or disguising of the rightful succession. From this point of view, the *retarded birth* of Heracles has the same significance as the *retarded maturation* of Yata. A device with similar significance – the artificial prolonging of a pregnancy – does not occur in the Yata narrative but it is present in several other Kuranko narratives including the "Gibate version" abstracted in this paper. Another device, again with similar significance, and present in the Heracles myth and the "Niane version", is difficulty in conceiving. These devices (or "mythemes") for delaying or disguising the rightful succession can, of course, be compared with various customs earlier discussed: banishing the heir; suppressing the name of the heir; avoidance relationship between father and eldest son in societies practising primogeniture. What has been institutionalized in one society may be found in the fictions of another, and vice versa.

[1] Herodotus gives three versions, "the Scythian and the Pontic Greek, which are mythological, and a third (c.II seq.), which he adopts as resting on the authority of both nations (12.3), and which he partially confirms by quoting Aristeas (c.13), who differs only as to the race which drove the Scyths into their new country". (How and Wells, 1964, vol. 1, p. 304.)

In myth and in social reality, the strategems of the father attempting to resist or deny his inevitable displacement and supercession are familiar from cultures throughout the world. The Hindu myth of the birth of Krishna relates how Kamsa, wicked king of the Bhojas and Satvatas, hears a prophecy that the eighth child born of his cousin Devaki will kill him. He orders that the offspring of Devaki be killed at birth and Devaki isolated. Vishnu decides to place himself in the eighth embryo. Krishna's elder brother (the seventh embryo) – Balarama – is transferred before birth from Devaki's womb to the womb of Rohini. Kamsa thinks that a miscarriage has occurred. Both Balarama and Krishna are then transferred to the house of Yasoda, the wife of Kamsa's cowherd.

> When the time of the pregnancy was complete, after eight months, the two women, Devakī and Yaśodā, brought forth children together. On the night when the lord Kṛṣṇa was born to Devakī . . . on that same night Yaśodā, wife of the cow-herd Nanda, brought forth a daughter. Yaśodā and Devakī had become pregnant at the same time, and so when Devakī gave birth to Viṣṇu, Yaśodā gave birth to a daughter. [O'Flaherty, 1975, pp. 211–212.]

Subsequently the two children are exchanged. Kamsa kills his "daughter" who later swears gruesome vengeance upon him. In the myth of the birth of Krishna, the parents of children born at the same time exchange their offspring; in the Yata narrative, children born at the same time change their positions. In both cases, these events can be interpreted as attempts to prevent or delay the displacement of the king/chief.

Among the Nyanga of Kivu, Zaire, the birth of the culture hero Mwindo is similarly unusual. The hero's mother is the preferred wife of a chief. Her pregnancy continues long after her six co-wives (who conceived at the same time) have delivered infant girls. The chief, Shemwindo, has vowed to kill any wife who gives birth to a male child. During the prolonged pregnancy, the unborn child helps his mother by fetching firewood, water and vegetables. When finally born, he emerges through the middle finger. His father, the chief, attempts to spear him to death, but fails. He orders the child to be buried alive. The child, Mwindo, born laughing and speaking (and so often referred to as "The little-one-just-born-he-walked"), threatens retaliation against his father: suffering, diminution of status, "excessive emotional experience", weakening, and death (Biebuyck and Mateene, 1969, pp. 53–57). This narrative has an exact counterpart in a

Kuranko narrative – the story of Gbentoworo – but most elements are also found in the Gibate version of the Sundiata epic.

Greek mythology abounds with comparable examples of a high-born father trying to prevent the birth of a child who, it has been prophesied, will usurp, succeed, or kill him: Ouranos and his off-spring; Kronos and his children[1]; Acrisius and his son Perseus; Priam and Paris; Laius and Oedipus. Kirk notes, in his discussion of the displacement of elders theme in Greek myth, that it was "the thrusting ambition of the young, rather than the necessity for replacing the hopelessly old, that was the prime force" (1973, p. 199). Kirk also notes that these myths may be projections of the "frustrated resentment of old age" (ibid.).

The Yata narrative is, however, complementary to the kinds of narratives referred to above, since the rightful heir prevents his own growing up; the chief plays no direct part in preventing the succession. A complete account of this mythological complex thus demands attention to the viewpoints of both the senior and junior generation. The point brings us to a consideration of Rank's study of this complex (1959), and to a consideration of Oedipus-type myths in general.

The myth of the birth of the hero

Rank stresses the importance of the detachment of the growing individual from the authority of the parents. Achieving this independence is difficult and painful. Many children do not want to grow up and relinquish identifications with the parents who are a source of faith, security, and succour. The child's earliest desires to get free of parental authority are expressed in daydreams which denigrate the real father and "substitute" a noble and perfect one.

> The entire endeavour to replace the real father by a more distinguished one is merely the expression of the child's longing for the vanished happy time, when his father still appeared to be the strongest and greatest man, and the mother seemed the dearest and most beautiful woman. [Rank, 1959, p. 71.]

[1] It is noteworthy that in many societies the succession is compared with the act of eating. Among the Ila "to succeed a person is *Kudyaizhina* (to eat the name), the successor is called *Mudyezhina* ('Eater of the name') and actually adopts the deceased's name" (Miller, 1928, p. 222). Among the Mossi, the expression "eat the *nam*" means to "accede to power" (Skinner, 1964, p. 36), and similar expressions are noted by Kuper for the Swazi (1947, p. 88).

As for hero myths, they are ways in which adult men relive their infantile revolt against the father – the "first heroic act" (Rank, 1959, p. 84).

> The fictitious romance is the excuse, as it were, for the hostile feelings which the child harbors against his father, and which in this fiction are projected against the father . . . The child simply gets rid of the father in the neurotic romance, while in the myth the father endeavours to lose the child. [Rank, 1959, p. 72.]

Rank's ontogenetic approach to hero myths is admirable, but several criticisms must be made. First, Rank overemphasizes the role of relived infantile experiences, that is, the viewpoint of the junior generation. Adult experiences are thus reduced to infantile ones. The truth is that intergenerational conflicts and tensions are experienced differently by members of junior *and* senior generations. That one viewpoint rather than the other is played up in a narrative may be arbitrary. Although the Yata narrative works from the viewpoints of the sons and wives of the chief, other comparable Kuranko narratives work from the viewpoint of the chief.[1] But whichever viewpoint is adopted, it remains true that the father's desire to retain omnipotent control and the heir's desire to remain a child have the *same social consequences*: a prevention of succession and a breakdown of lineage or social continuity. It is noteworthy that a reluctance to *surrender or assume* a position of authority in the family or lineage has the *same social consequences* as a reluctance to surrender sisters and daughters to another lineage in marriage. The latter is, of course, a widespread theme in myth and folklore (Acrisius and Danae; Aleos and Auge; Indo-European tales in which almost impossible conditions attach to the winning of the King's daughter). Prevented succession leads to a breakdown of continuity *within* a lineage; prevented marriage leads to a breakdown in the alliance networks *between* lineages. This comparability on the structural plane may help explain why oedipal and incestuous themes are frequently found together in myths concerned with the interrelationships of the moral and social orders.

Second, the ambivalence and contention of the father–son relationship in some societies is not universal. In many Polynesian societies, for example, diffuseness of the paternal role and the widespread prac-

[1] When one considers the personality and interests of the narrator, then the viewpoint adopted is far less arbitrary. Unfortunately space precludes a discussion of the impact of the personality of the narrator on the Yata narrative.

tice of adoption and fosterage mean that "the" father is perceived as peripheral and is not held responsible for a child's problems, or idealized, or blamed (Levy (Tahiti), 1973, pp. 457–466; Kawharu (New Zealand Maori), personal communication; Lessa (Ulithi), 1956, p. 68). Thus, the father–son relationship tends to be peripheral in the myths from these societies. Fraternal conflicts and tensions are, by contrast, played up, as in the well-known and widespread Maui myths. It would be absurd to claim that the "brother myths" are displacements of repressed conflicts between father and son, especially since versions of the Maui myth do exist which stress filial rather than fraternal tensions. Versions from Rennell and Bellona (Polynesian Outlier Islands in the Solomons) consistently emphasize Maui's conflict with his father 'Ataganga, from whose excrement he was born (Elbert and Monberg, 1965, pp. 109–136). Similar Oedipus-type myths are known in other areas of Micronesia and Lessa concludes that "the presence of the tale type is mostly the result of diffusion and not of some psychological mechanism inspiring people independently to create it" (1956, p. 71). In other words, the content of a myth is *often* contingent (cf. Lévi-Strauss, 1963, p. 208).

Third, Rank fails to consider all the details in the narratives, and he fails to recognize structural differences among texts which are similar in some details. One result of this piecemeal approach is that all relationships within the "atom of kinship" (Lévi-Strauss, 1963, p. 48) are not taken into account. For instance, Rank only alludes to the wife/mother as a means of supporting the classic psychoanalytic view that the basis of the oedipus complex is sexual (1959, p. 77). It will be remembered that in the Yata narrative an impasse is reached when Yata refuses to grow up and displace his father. This impasse is broken when the mother's humiliation and anger causes the child to get up and walk. The mother occupies a crucial mediatory role both in the narrative and in Kuranko social life: she enables continuity. The transformations which occur in the narrative thus involve several kinship relationships, none of which can be reduced to any other one.

Fourth, to claim, as Rank does, that adults create myths "by means of retrograde childhood fantasies" (1959, p. 84) ignores (scotomizes) the *complementary* character of the oedipus complex by placing all responsibility for it on the child or on the junior generation (cf. Devereux, 1953, p. 132). It is the complementarity of the father's reluctance to be displaced and the son's reluctance to grow up which I now want to explore further.

Retardation: phylogenetic and clinical aspects

Several examples of the mythical child–adult have been referred to already: the Nyanga culture hero Mwindo, Sundiata (especially in the Gibate version), Maui (the youngest of five brothers but the most able), Heracles (the infant with the strength of a man), Krishna the "infant god" (Kinsley, 1975, p. 13). These heroes display great precocity *and* various infantilisms. The anomalous character is nicely summarized by O'Flaherty, referring to the mythology of Krishna the baby: the mythology "plays constantly upon the contrast between appearance and reality – the apparently tiny mortal (the dwarf, the infant, the individual soul) which occasionally reveals its true nature as the infinite immortal (the giant, the god, the universal godhead)" (1975, p. 214). These infantilisms may be interpreted variously: as devices to foster and emphasize the value of caring behaviour (Eibl-Eibesfeldt, 1975, pp. 490–491); as images of foetalization in human evolution (Dobzhansky, 1971, pp. 195–196); as fantasied regression (Rank, 1959, p. 84); as ways of establishing the hero as a mediator between childhood and adulthood. Only the last interpretation emphasizes the coalescence in the one person of childlike and adult characteristics.

Undoubtedly, different values attach to the same mytheme in different societies and for different individuals. In the Yata narrative, however, I suggest that the hero's spurious retardation is a consequence or expression of excessive filial piety. His conviction that his father will die on the day he walks is a projection of his fear that his own growing strength implies his father's growing weakness. Yet it is imperative that Yata "forget" his father in order that he "become" him. Because of the failed message, the distance between Yata and his father is greater than it would be ordinarily. This allows Yata to remain a child for longer than usual, to delay his detachment from his parents. His procrastination is, moreover, associated in his mind with keeping his father, the chief, alive and in office. This attitude is remarkably similar to that of a psychiatric patient whose retrospective insights into the sources and rationalizations of his own infantilisms are discussed by Devereux.

The patient commented:

> If I remain a child forever, if my very existence continues to depend on the presence of my parents, I can arrest the progress of time. By staying a child, I prevent my

parents from becoming old and dying. If I am a dependent child, they simply have neither the right, nor even the possibility, of deserting me by dying. [Devereux, 1964, p. 185.]

Devereux cites a parallel case from Chinese sources, originally given as an exemplary case of filial piety.

> "Lao Lai-tsu was a man of the country of Ch'u. When he was 70 years old, his parents were still alive. His filial piety was very strong. Constantly clothed in a medley of garments [like children], when he carried drink to his parents, he pretended to stumble on arriving at the hall, then remained lying on the ground, uttering cries after the manner of little children." Or else, *"with the object of rejuvenating his old parents*, he remained before them playing with his long sleeves, or amusing himself with chickens." [Devereux, 1964, p. 185.]

Resemblances clearly exist among exemplary tales, narrative and mythological schemes, clinical cases, and individual biographies.[1] In all these instances, conflicting imperatives and contradictory identifications are displayed. These may be summarized as follows:

1. If the continuity of the lineage is to be assured, the father must accept the inevitability of his own death and displacement, and the son must assume the responsibilities of the paternal role. This social imperative is often in conflict with subjective factors: the father's reluctance to be superseded, the son's reluctance to come of age and assume his adult responsibilities.
2. A son can only realize his own identity by establishing his independence from his father. This change of identification and this independence are difficult and require "more or less sanctioned intermediary periods between childhood and adulthood, often characterized by a combination of prolonged immaturity and provoked precocity" (Erikson, 1968, p. 156). This "psychosocial moratorium", as Erikson terms it, is characterized by a delay of adult commitments and by selected permissiveness. Such is the period of initiation in Kuranko society, and adolescence in Western societies. And everywhere, images of death and birth accompany this transformation of identity. As Winnicott expresses it, "If the child is

[1] Two of the best clinical biographies, which are relevant here, are Freud's account of parricide in Dostoevsky (Freud, 1928) and Erikson's account of William James's relationship with his father (1968, pp. 150–155). In both cases, the son's ambivalence towards the father leads to a form of self-immobilization: in the case of Dostoevsky "neurotic epilepsy", in the case of William James "delayed maturation".

to become adult, then this move is achieved over the dead body of an adult" (1974, p. 170). However, this existential imperative is often in conflict with subjective factors: the father's reluctance to allow the son to grow up and prove himself, the son's reluctance to abandon dependence upon and identification with the father.

These double-bind situations lead to the development of ambivalent attitudes. The hero frequently embodies this ambivalence as the "child-adult", although other derivative images may be noted:

- Youngest of several brothers, yet the most able (Maui; Kolaxais).
- A baby confined to the domestic world by day, yet by night, in the bush, a great hunter (Sundiata in the Gibate version).
- Apparently weak and retarded, yet actually strong and precocious (Yata; Sundiata in the Niane, Pageard, and Bird versions).
- Human, yet a god (Heracles).
- Babbles and cries like a baby, yet has teeth at birth and eats solid food (Sundiata in the Gibate version).
- Stiff-legged, yet potentially strong and fleet-footed (Sundiata in the Niane version).

The hero is thus variously made to mediate between conflicting imperatives and different worlds. He facilitates the fictional resolution of recurrent problems arising from a contradiction between social necessity and personal inclination. That the heroic tale records the crises and binds involved in achieving a mature identity ("second birth") makes explicable the hero's bizarre parentage: both human and divine, both human and animal, from one parent only. My point is that ambivalent attitudes are expressed and worked through in terms of physical images associated with the heroic figure. It is the nature of this physical imagery that I wish now to consider.[1]

Physical imagery

In the Yata narrative the Kuranko word used to describe Yata's retarded development is *namara*. Ordinarily the word means "lame"

[1] The various coalesced images that are used in order to establish the ambiguous and equivocal character of the hero–mediator are discussed by Lévi-Strauss (1963, chapter II) and Leach (1973).

or "limping"; here it connotes "inability to walk". I regard Yata's lameness as far more than a physical image of his psychosocial immaturity. It signifies, in my view, the hero's ambivalence, for he desires simultaneously to remain a child (so preserving his father's life and position) *and* realize his potential away from his natal family (so achieving status and authority equal to his father). These contradictory imperatives immobilize him.[1]

The frequency with which hero myths from cultures throughout the world incorporate references to limping and to the legs as loci of power, has often been referred to. Lévi-Strauss has noted that limping, as a mythological and ritual sign, is "everywhere associated with seasonal change" (1973, p. 463). He observes that a normal gait is a symbolic representation of the periodicity of the seasons; limping is a "diagrammatic expression" of a desired imbalance – a desire for more rain or less rain, for a longer summer or shorter winter etc. (1973, p. 464). In an earlier study, Lévi-Strauss commented upon the "universal characteristic of men born from the Earth that at the moment they emerge from the depth they either cannot walk or they walk clumsily" (1963, p. 215). He cites Pueblo Indian and Kwakiutl parallels to Oedipus ("swollen-foot") in order to establish the connection between ambulatory difficulties (particularly lameness in one leg) and a doctrine of autochthonous origins (only one parent). Although there are myths from Africa which would be susceptible to these kinds of interpretation,[2] Yata's lameness has little to do with either seasonality or parentage. But it is an image (a "diagrammatic expression") nevertheless of a desired imbalance with regard to the succession of generations. The slow-maturing, stiff-legged hero signifies prevented or delayed succession. And his sudden maturation, signified by suppleness and strength, presages his father's death. In a version of the Maui myth from Rennell and Bellona, the son's vengeful killing of his father, 'Ataganga, is preceded by the following incident:

> 'Ataganga defecated, and a child fell out therefrom. He raised [it], and the child grew up. He called [him] Mautikitiki. 'Ataganga looked at Mautikitiki; [he] was stiff, the body members were not pliant. And he told [Mautikitiki] to climb into a tree and jump down from it. And [Mautikitiki] fell down and his legs and arms broke, and so his arms and legs became pliant. [Elbert and Monberg, 1965, p. 113.]

[1] I think here of the visual paradox contained in the figures of the pre-Hellenic *kouri*, androgynous and striding in perpetual fixity.

[2] For example the Sonjo culture hero, Khambageu (Gray, 1965).

The Icelandic saga hero, Grettir, we are told, was "not of quick growth in his childhood" and fumbled feminine tasks (Magnusson and Morris, 1869, p. 28). And the Trobriand Island mythological hero, Tokosikuna of Digumenu, is initially crippled, lame (according to one version he has no hands or feet), and very ugly (Malinowski, 1972, p. 308). These examples of partially immobilized heroes are paralleled by narratives in which the father tries to hobble or otherwise immobilize his son in order to prevent the succession. The example of Laius who pierced Oedipus' feet with a nail (and, according to some versions, bound the feet) before abandoning the baby on Mount Cithaeron is perhaps the best-known of these narratives.

The notion that strength, power, and potency reside in the leg is almost universal. The Riddle of the Sphinx itself refers to the legs and to walking as a dramatic way of signifying the ages of man. But what is important in the present context of discussion is that immobilization may be connected not only with preventing succession but with preventing the "second birth" by which the son becomes detached from his father and initiated into the wider male community. Bunker and Lewin have traced out the philological and "unconscious" connections among such words as "knee", "know", "generate", "generation", and suggest that the leg (particularly the knee) is a kind of "male womb" of the "second birth" (1965, p. 364).[1] Onians has made an intensive study of similar connections in Roman and Greek thought, and shows how suppleness and fluidity in the legs connoted potency and strength (1973, chapters 4 and 5). It is also noteworthy that the pre-Socratic terms for the sense-organs ("the body") were *melea* and *guia*, that is, "limbs" (Popper, 1969, p. 410). Onians also cites traditions of generation from the legs. A Masai narrative, recorded by Hollis, tells of an old man who has no wife and lives alone; his knee becomes swollen and eight months later, thinking it to be a boil, he lances it and two children emerge (Onians, 1973, p. 179). A Sonjo myth relates how the culture hero Khambageu was born from his father's swollen leg (he had no mother) (Gray, 1965, p. 56). And a comparable Kuranko narrative tells how the hero Gbentoworo (his name derives from *woro*: "calf of the leg") is miraculously conceived in the calf of his mother's leg; he remains there for more than seven years until one day a splinter of wood lances open his mother's leg and he

[1] Commenting on the Greek "preoccupation with the knee", Devereux equates it with "penis" (1970, p. 1231).

emerges as a mature, strong, though small-statured person. In a Vera Cruz version of the Mayan Popol Vuh epic, maize is represented by a "clever little fellow called Homshuk" whom an elderly couple find hatched from an egg. He comes to maturity in seven days, successfully avoids his foster-father's attempt to kill him (and then his foster-mother's attempt to avenge her husband's death), and assumes the title "He who sprouts at the knees; He who flowers" (Burland *et al.*, 1970, pp. 192–193).

The left–right asymmetry of the hands (which is genetically determined and related to cerebral asymmetry) has long been exploited to articulate symbolically and to justify various socially produced asymmetries (see Needham, 1973). The symbolic significance of the legs, of walking, of the limbs and joints is no less important although it has been scarcely explored.

Man evolved in the Pliocene, bipedal and well adapted to open plains living. Dexterity, physical agility, fleet-footedness, and suppleness of limb must have had survival value and supplied, on the intellectual plane, some of man's first images and metaphors for socially adaptive behaviour. Long after the evolution of semi-permanent settlement and sedentary habits, physical mobility and agility continued to serve as images of culturally valued traits: quickness of mind, strength of purpose, flexibility and vitality of thought. Infirmity, lameness, dragging the feet, and physical imbalance served, similarly, as images of social breakdown and discontinuity. Among nomadic and semi-nomadic peoples, physical immobilization (particularly of the aged) meant abandonment and death.[1] A Kuranko clan myth which I have published elsewhere (Jackson, 1974) refers to the period when the ancestors of two clans were journeying together from Mande towards Sierra Leone. When one ancestor was halted by an impassable river (his companion could change into a crocodile and thus cross over), the other cut off his calf and gave it roasted to the first so that he would not perish of hunger. The significance of this self-sacrifice is appreciated only when one realizes that mobility meant survival, both for the individual ancestor and for his lineage.

Having suggested a basis, both real and metaphorical, for the

[1] As among the Eskimo. Bronowski paints a moving portrait of this desertion among the nomadic Bakhtari: "What happens to the old when they cannot cross the last river? Nothing. They stay behind to die. . . . The man accepts the nomad custom; he has come to the end of his journey, and there is no place at the end." (1973, p. 64.)

connections between *physical immobilization* and *social discontinuity*, I want to consider briefly the "problem of time". The key concepts which have emerged in this essay can be set out and interrelated as follows:

Social continuity (images of physical strength, agility and potency) implies the *progress of time* which implies the *succession of generations* which implies *individual mortality*.

Social discontinuity (images of physical weakness, retardation and delayed birth) implies the *arrest of the progress of time* which implies *no succession of generations* which implies *individual immortality*.

Preventing succession – either by the father hindering the birth or development of his son, or by the son hindering his own development – can be understood as an attempt to annul time. So too can the themes of *difficulty in conceiving* and *prevented marriage* which I have referred to earlier. In the Yata narrative, circumstance allows Yata to prolong his childhood, to postpone realizing his potential. This "psychosocial moratorium" implies a double-bind. If the precocious hero reveals his nascent identity, then his father will die. If he continues to camouflage his identity, then a false and incompetent heir will assume his father's position. This impasse is broken, as I have shown, as a result of the mother's behaviour which obliges Yata to get up and walk. The mother thus enables time to pass again. The son displaces the father, the chief is strong, the continuity of the lineage is assured.

The narrative suggests a profound contradiction between biographical time (which is irreversible) and social time (which is reversible). It emphasizes the need for the intergenerational transmission of power and knowledge over the desires of individuals who want to arrest the passage of time. Individual growing up (even though the second birth leads to a death) is thus the most important precondition for *social* continuity.

Conclusions

My approach to the Yata narrative has not pretended objectivity; nor have I confined my elucidation of the narrative to the Kuranko cultural milieu. I began by pointing out that any person's response to a myth or folk-tale is influenced by his or her "subsidiary awareness" (Polanyi, 1969). My own response, influenced by my experience of living among the Kuranko, by my personal and cultural background, could never, therefore, overlap exactly with any other person's response, Kuranko or otherwise. This is because each person's "subsidiary knowledge" is a unique and always changing configuration. Only at the level of "focal awareness" could my response coincide with the orthodox Kuranko response to the narrative. And here there is no disagreement: the Yata narrative is concerned with the origins (ontogenetic and folk-historical) of the relationship of rivalry between half-brothers *(fadenye)*. Yet to let the matter rest there would be to ignore details of the narrative structure and evade the challenge which the narrative offers: to explore and account for the responses it occasions.

My style of exposition has been deliberately discursive and digressive. I have hoped thereby to avoid trivializing the narrative or reducing it to some single determining factor. At the same time I have endeavoured to demonstrate the importance of analysing a narrative at the level of both content (manifest and latent) and structure.

Although structuralist and psychoanalytic models imply different aims and interests, there are intriguing similarities between the structural operations of "transformation", "mediation", "resolution", and the psychological operations (or "defence mechanisms") of "displacement", "representation" (or "symbolic disguise"), "scotomization" and "projection". Moreover, both methods search for a "truth" underlying the manifest content, and both approaches stress the manner in which the mechanisms of myth serve to resolve problems and contradictions. The rigour of the structuralist method, with its insistence on considering *all* details in *relation* to one another and avoiding *a priori* assumptions about the value of signs, was a corrective to the excesses of many psychoanalytical interpretations. But if the psychological content of a myth is ignored or regarded as contingent, then structural analysis limits itself unnecessarily. This need to explore the total context of a narrative – social, historical, personal – brings us to another aspect of this essay.

The devices and strategems elucidated in the Yata narrative have parallels in numerous other myths (both in Mande and elsewhere in the world), in exemplary or moral tales, in individual fantasies, in social institutions, and even in various historical epochs.[1] The world of a myth is not, and cannot be, set apart from other worlds. It is involved in a continuing dialectic with them, and this dialectic is not the mere function of Mind communing with itself for it is informed by the unending quest for the resolution of universal human problems.

References

ABRAHAM, KARL (1909). Dreams and myths: a study in folk-psychology. In *Clinical Papers and Essays on Psycho-Analysis* (1955), pp. 153–209. Hogarth Press, London.

ABRAHAMSSON, H. (1951). *The Origin of Death.* Studia Ethnographica Upsaliensia no. 3, Upsala.

AUDEN, W. H. (1951). *The Enchafèd Flood,* p. 83. Faber and Faber, London.

BIEBUYCK, D. (1973). *Lega Culture.* University of California Press, Berkeley, California.

BIEBUYCK, D. and MATEENE K. C. (Editors and translators) (1969). *The Mwindo Epic from the Banyanga (Congo Republic).* University of California Press, Berkeley, California.

BIRD, C. S. (1971). Oral art in the Mande. In *Papers on the Manding* (Ed. C. T. Hodge), pp. 15–25. Mouton, The Hague.

BRONOWSKI, J. (1973). *The Ascent of Man.* British Broadcasting Corporation, London.

BUNKER, H. A. and LEWIN, B. D. (1965). A psychoanalytic notation on the root *GN, KN, CN.* In *Psychoanalysis and Culture* (Eds G. B. Wilbur and W. Muensterberger), pp. 363–367. International Universities Press, New York.

BURLAND, C., NICHOLSON, I. and OSBORNE, H. (1970). *Mythology of the Americas.* Hamlyn, London.

DENG, F. MADING (1974). *Dinka Folktales.* Holmes and Meier, New York and London.

De MAUSE, L. (1974). The evolution of childhood. In *The History of Childhood* (Ed. L. De Mause), pp. 1–73. The Psychohistory Press, New York.

DEVEREUX, G. (1948). Mohave coyote tales. *Journal of American Folklore,* **61,** 233–255.

[1] For example, *killing or attempting to kill* the rival and heir corresponds historically to what de Mause calls the "infanticidal mode" of parent–child relations (antiquity to fourth century A.D.), while *contriving to set a distance between* ruler and heir by disguising the latter's identity or banishing him corresponds to the "abandonment mode" (fourth to thirteenth century A.D.) (de Mause, 1974, p. 51).

DEVEREUX, G. (1953). Why Oedipus killed Laius: a note on the complementary Oedipus complex in Greek drama. *The International Journal of Psycho-Analysis*, **34,** 132–141.

DEVEREUX, G. (1964). An ethnopsychiatric note on property-destruction in cargo cults. *Man*, **64,** 184–185.

DEVEREUX, G. (1970). La naissance d'Aphrodite. In *Echanges et Communications* (Eds J. Pouillon and P. Maranda), vol. 2, pp. 1229–1252. Mouton, The Hague.

DEVEREUX, G. (1972). Quelques traces de la succession par ultimogéniture en Scythie. *Inter Nord*, no. 12, 262–270.

DOBZHANSKY, T. (1971). *Mankind Evolving*. Yale University Press, New Haven.

EIBL-EIBESFELDT, I. (1975). *Ethology: The Biology of Behavior* (2nd ed.). Holt, Rinehart and Winston, New York.

ELBERT, S. H. and MONBERG, T. (1965). *From the Two Canoes: Oral Traditions of Rennell and Bellona Islands*. University of Hawaii Press, Honolulu.

ERIKSON, E. H. (1968). *Identity: Youth and Crisis*. Faber and Faber, London.

FREUD, SIGMUND (1928). *Dostoevsky and Parricide*. Standard Edition, vol. 21 (1961), pp. 173–196. Hogarth Press, London.

GOODY, J. (1966a). Introduction. In *Succession to High Office* (Ed. J. Goody), pp. 1–56. Cambridge University Press, Cambridge.

GOODY, J. (1966b). Circulating succession among the Gonja. In *Succession to High Office* (Ed. J. Goody), pp. 142–176. Cambridge University Press, Cambridge.

GRAVES, ROBERT (1955). *The Greek Myths*. 2 vols. Penguin Books, Harmondsworth.

GRAY, R. F. (1965). Some parallels in Sonjo and Christian mythology. In *African Systems of Thought* (Eds M. Fortes and G. Dieterlen). Oxford University Press, London.

GRIAULE, M. (1973). The mother's brother in the Western Sudan. In *French Perspectives in African Studies* (Ed. P. Alexandre), pp. 11–25. Oxford University Press, London.

HERSKOVITS, M. J. (1958). *Dahomean Narrative*. Northwestern University Press, Evanston, Illinois.

HOPKINS, N. S. (1971). Mandinka social organization. In *Papers on the Manding* (Ed. C. T. Hodge), pp. 99–128. Mouton, The Hague.

HOW, W. W. and WELLS, J. (1964). *A Commentary on Herodotus*. 2 vols. Clarendon Press, Oxford.

JACKSON, MICHAEL (1974). The structure and significance of Kuranko clanship. *Africa*, **44,** 397–415.

JACKSON, MICHAEL (1975). Structure and event: witchcraft confession among the Kuranko. *Man*, **10,** 387–403.

JACKSON, MICHAEL (1977a). Sacrifice and social structure among the Kuranko. *Africa*, **47**, 41–49 and 123–139.

JACKSON, MICHAEL (1977b). *The Kuranko: Dimensions of Social Reality in a West African Society*. C. Hurst, London.

JACKSON, MICHAEL (in press). Dogmas and fictions of birth-order position. In *Yearbook of Symbolic Anthropology*. McGill-Queen's University Press, Montreal.

KAWHARU, I. H. (1976). Personal communication.

KERÉNYI, K. (1959). *The Heroes of the Greeks*. Thames and Hudson, London.

KINSLEY, D. R. (1975). *The Sword and the Flute*. University of California Press, Berkeley, California.

KIRK, G. S. (1973). *Myth: Its Meaning and Functions in Ancient and Other Cultures*. Cambridge University Press, Cambridge.

KUPER, HILDA (1947). *An African Aristocracy: Rank Among the Swazi*. Oxford University Press, London.

LEACH, E. R. (1973). Structuralism in social anthropology. In *Structuralism: an Introduction* (Ed. D. Robey), pp. 37–56. Clarendon Press, Oxford.

LESSA, W. A. (1956). Oedipus-type tales in Oceania. *Journal of American Folklore*, **69**, 63–73.

LÉVI-STRAUSS, CLAUDE (1963). *Structural Anthropology*. Basic Books, New York.

LÉVI-STRAUSS, CLAUDE (1970). *The Raw and the Cooked*. Jonathan Cape, London.

LÉVI-STRAUSS, CLAUDE (1973). *From Honey to Ashes*. Jonathan Cape, London.

LEVY, R. I. (1973). *Tahitians: Mind and Experience in the Society Islands*. Chicago University Press, Chicago, Illinois.

MAGNUSSON, E. and MORRIS, W. (1869). *Grettis Saga*. F. S. Ellis, London.

MALINOWSKI, BRONISLAW (1972). *Argonauts of the Western Pacific*. Routledge and Kegan Paul, London.

MIDDLETON, J. (1960). *Lugbara Religion: Ritual and Authority among an East African People*. Oxford University Press, London.

MILLER, N. (1928). *The Child in Primitive Society*. Kegan Paul, Trench and Trubner, London.

NEEDHAM, R. (Ed.) (1973). *Right and Left: Essays on Dual Symbolic Classification*. Chicago University Press, Chicago, Illinois.

NEUMANN, ERICH (1954). *The Origins and History of Consciousness*. Routledge and Kegan Paul, London.

NIANE, D. T. (1965). *Sundiata: An Epic of Old Mali* (translation G. D. Pickett). Longmans, London.

O'FLAHERTY, WENDY D. (1975). *Hindu Myths*. Penguin Books, Harmondsworth.

ONIANS, R. B. (1973). *The Origins of European Thought.* Arno Press, New York.

PAGEARD, R. (1961). Soundiata Keita and the oral tradition. *Présence Africaine*, **8,** 53–72.

PERSON, Y. (1973). Oral tradition and chronology. In *French Perspectives in African Studies* (Ed. P. Alexandre), pp. 204–220. Oxford University Press, London.

POLANYI, M. (1969). *Knowing and Being.* Routledge and Kegan Paul, London.

POPPER, KARL (1969). *Conjectures and Refutations.* Routledge and Kegan Paul, London.

RANK, OTTO (1959). *The Myth of the Birth of the Hero.* Vintage Books, New York.

SKINNER, E. P. (1964). *The Mossi of the Upper Volta.* Stanford University Press, Stanford.

SOUTHWOLD, M. (1966). Succession to the throne in Buganda. In *Succession to High Office* (Ed. J. Goody), pp. 82–126. Cambridge University Press, Cambridge.

WINNICOTT, D. W. (1974). *Playing and Reality.* Penguin Books, Harmondsworth.

Reflections on a Cut Finger: Taboo in the Umeda Conception of the Self

Alfred Gell

MY THEME IN this paper is the nature of taboo and its role in the definition of the self, and in the articulation of the self into a social world. Partly, I have attempted here a revision of the too-featureless "ego" whose presence in symbolic anthropology has hitherto mainly been that of a detached bystander "classifying out" an already constituted world.

Instead of a "transcendental" ego, occupant of a zero point at the centre of a cognized world while always remaining somehow external to it, I have sought to delineate the ego as immanent in a network of relations, defending an at best vicarious transcendence, not always successfully.

I am concerned with grasping the oscillatory movement whereby the ego both recoils from the world in constituting itself and is simultaneously drawn back into the world in accomplishing its projects. I argue that the notion of "taboo" stands for the negative, denying aspect of ego-hood, while the corresponding notion of "lapse" stands for the reabsorption of the ego into the world.[1]

[1] The absence of references in the text is the result not, I hope, of vanity but of a desire to keep the argument as simple as possible and to avoid being sidetracked into debates with the literature along the way. I have a precedent in the literature in the form of Berger and Luckmann's *The Social Construction of Reality* (1971) which is a whole book, not just a short article, constructed on the same principle of confining references to the *apparatus*, and which benefits as a result, in my view.

The "phenomenological" stance I adopt in this essay is derived from Merleau-Ponty, whose *Phenomenology of Perception* (1962) I was constantly reading in the field. A great deal also derives from Alfred Schutz (1962) and Berger (1973). Robert Murphy's *The Dialectics of Social Life* (1972) was another immediate stimulus. The basic idea of the "cycle" of hunting, sexuality and asceticism was worked out some time before, however, as a result of being asked to lecture on Umeda at the University of Sussex, an exercise from which I greatly profited.

The investigation is set among the people of Umeda village in the West Sepik District of Papua New Guinea, where I carried out field research.[1] The topic with which I am concerned is sufficiently narrowly defined as to render any detailed discussion of the Umeda setting unnecessary, except perhaps to forestall a possible misconception that the ensuing text will be devoted to accounts of pig-festivals, big-men or ceremonial exchange. Suffice to say that all three are remarkably absent in the vicinity of Umeda, isolated as it is either from the sea or river trade-routes and situated in a most unproductive terrain from which the inhabitants derive a slender subsistence based on sago. The village and its neighbours form a collection of exogamous hamlets, permanently occupied by one or more patrilineal clans, whose relations with one another take the form of matrimonial exchange and matrilateral alliance. Viewed from afar, the individual hamlets resemble becalmed ships amid an ocean of trees, each one perched on a ridge too low to make it more than barely discernible above the forest plain. The huts are clustered in little groups beneath the shade-giving coconut palms, and may be abandoned, for much of the time, by occupants who prefer to live among their hidden and somewhat desultory gardens, or in hunting lodges deep in the bush.

Such, very briefly, is the social and physical context of the present investigation: an equable, low-keyed existence, dominated by the monotony of sago production and the hardly less monotonous quest for game, and punctuated by too-infrequent hunting successes and annual performances of ritual of surprising splendour.

But with these I am not concerned here.

It is apposite that an investigation which focuses on the twin notions of "taboo" and "lapse" should commence with the analysis of an incident, involving myself, which well exemplifies both.

I happened once, during my fieldwork, to be peeling a stick of sugar-cane together with some companions from Umeda village. Clumsily, I allowed my knife to slip and it embedded itself in my finger. Unhurriedly, but still unthinkingly, I deposited the offending kitchen knife and the still unpeeled stick of sugar-cane and raised my bleeding finger to my lips. The external world ceased momentarily to exist for me, conscious only of the familiar saltwater taste on my tongue and a just perceptible pulsation where the sting would be. My world contracted to a simple circuit, a chain of actions and sensations

[1] I have described the Umedas in a monograph (Gell, 1975).

completed by finger, lips, and tongue tentatively exploring the extent of the wound, which was only slight, in fact. Slight enough to be in itself entirely unremarkable, and the momentary lapse into unreflectiveness prompted by it equally so, were it not that, reflected in the distorting mirror of an alien, or at least partially alien, set of cultural categories, my lapse of consciousness was a lapse indeed, as the shocked countenances and expressions of disgust evinced by my Umeda companions told me soon enough, just as soon as I recovered my wits and looked about me.

Naturally my curiosity was aroused and my observation somewhat sharpened by this incident. It was evident that I had, in Umeda eyes, *broken a food taboo*, though one so fundamental as not to figure in the recitations of such taboos which my highly taboo-bound informants would readily provide – and of which the prime one, as had been impressed on me from the very first days of my stay in Umeda, was the *taboo on consuming self-killed game*. It did not need much to perceive the kinship of my own unwitting "breach of taboo" with what was, for them, the taboo *par excellence*. It occurred to me, as it had not done previously, that Umeda ideas of taboo had little or nothing to do with real or supposed anomalies within their system of animal or plant classification, and everything to do with avoiding eating one's own self.

Nothing, I subsequently learnt, prevented Umedas from ingesting blood, *per se*, but ingestion of one's own blood was in the highest degree revolting. Pig's blood – derived from a pig killed by somebody else, of course – was a most acceptable delicacy. It was the auto-cannibalistic aspect of my behaviour which they so remarked, the more so in that Umedas disdain to practise cannibalism in any guise, while continually harping on its terrors in their myths and stories. With opened eyes, I was enabled to see the significance of the entire absence of auto-cannibalistic habits among the adult population, the absence of such things as nail-biting, moustache-chewing, the swallowing of dried nasal mucus, etc. – practices which among ourselves vary in degree of niceness without ever attaining the status of major sins.

It was, then, but a short step from the realization that to lick blood from a cut finger was to breach a taboo which protects the body in all its aspects from auto-cannibalistic violence and confusion, to the further realization that the whole spectrum of Umeda food taboos might repay examination from precisely this point of view. For it is not only the debris of the body which is protected in this way, but everything in the environment which stands as an emblem or appurtenance of the self. And it is tabooedness, specifically, which singles out these entities, emblems, for this particular role. In Umeda, taboo clarifies the phenomenology of the self, in placing under its interdictions those parts of it whose separateness, far from disqualifying them for this function, permits them to express its individuation and separateness from its congeners.

It may be helpful to cite an example at this point.

An important food tȧboo prevents children and ritual novices from eating the river fish *pannatamwa*, whose red markings are said to recall the red body-paint sometimes worn by this category of persons. The "category of persons who taboo the *pannatamwa*" are distinct from the rest of society precisely, and perhaps only, in that they *do* observe the taboo: of broadly comparable social status, their shared category membership is by no means founded on overwhelming resemblance between observers of the taboo as individuals. They differ in age, in clan and hamlet affiliation, in physiognomy, in accomplishments and in the esteem in which they are held. In everything, in fact, but the tabooed status that *pannatamwa* has for them, they are situated differently *vis-à-vis* the total society, yet, in the light of the taboo in which they all share, they do form a category, and do have a common status. Because the taboo, in this instance, applies to the whole species, all of whom appear to resemble one another in every minutest particular, it serves to codify the less palpable resemblances which unite the category of those who must observe the taboo. Should we say, then, that the *pannatamwa* is tabooed "because it stands for the self"– because it situates the self in an intelligible order? But just as the class of "persons who taboo the *pannatamwa* fish" has no basis outside the actual observance of the taboo, so, it seems to me, outside the specific acts, observances – and taboos – which specify a self as *my* self, there is nothing for an emblem of the self to be an emblem of.

To observe a taboo is to establish an identifiable self by establishing a relationship (negative in this case – *not* eating) with an external reality such that the "self" only comes into existence in and through this relationship. In phenomenological language, the self only comes about in "intentional acts" and the observance of a taboo is such an "intentional act". It is nowhere except in what it accomplishes.

Umeda food taboos establish and specify the individual at a number of levels: (i) through taboos incumbent on humankind in general such as the incest taboos, the taboo on eating self-killed game, on cannibalism or the eating of dogs; (ii) through other taboos which are incumbent on certain social categories such as the *pannatamwa* taboo, or a taboo which prevents little girls from eating pandanus sauce; (iii) through taboos which apply only to individuals whose careers have been marked by certain specific incidents, such as a taboo which prevents men who have undergone a certain curing ritual at which white cockatoo feathers are worn from eating these birds; and finally, (iv) through taboos which are entirely personal and idiosyncratic, though always socially recognized, as when a man taboos a variety of sago in memory of a deceased wife, or a fruit tree from whose branches he once suffered an unlucky fall. The Umeda individual, at any given point, is always observing a specific constellation of taboos, some collective, some personal, and many perhaps unacknowledged. In this constellation of taboos one may discover the outlines of a *soul* or *personality*, no longer a shadowy even if believed-in counterpart of the physical body, though the body is included, but immanently present in a privileged segment of intersubjective reality. The "I" does not stand apart from the world in placing a portion of it under a variety of interdictions: it is present only in the network of intentionalities which bind it to the world, its contours outlined in the very substance of that world. Taboos on eating, on killing, on sexual intercourse, on looking at, touching etc., together circumscribe a "hole" in the texture of shareable intersubjective reality which, privileged with respect to a specific individual, constitutes his soul, or ego, or personality. Taboo does more than express the self: it constitutes the self.

Such a philosophical account of taboo, whatever advantages it might possess in terms of generality, does not, at first glance, seem to offer very much by way of cultural insight. Culturally, it implies no more than that a system of food taboos, or taboos of any other kind, functions as a set of diacritics situating the observers of taboos within an intelligible social order. I want, in what follows, to focus attention more narrowly on "eating" and "not eating" in Umeda, not so much as indices of status as aspects of a culturally specific personality system. Let us suppose that I have established my view of the anthropological "ego" as a network of relations, having its origin in intentional acts: it is now desirable that I should reconstruct, in more detail, the actual form that this network of relations takes in Umeda. In order to do this I have narrowed the field down to just one aspect of this general system, namely the relations subsumed under the Umeda verb *tadv* meaning "eat".[1]

Or, to be more precise, I am concerned with "*tadv* relations" as constitutive of the ego both positively, eating (and also drinking, biting, striking, shooting, killing, and copulating with, since *tadv* means all these things), and negatively (not eating, not striking or killing, not copulating with, etc.). In Umeda such *tadv* relationships, fanning out from each individual, punctuate intersubjective reality and set up a series of fields of identity at various levels. *Tadv* has no "basic" meaning, since the context determined which of a wide variety of *tadv* or *tadv-maivem* (not eating) relations is the operative one. But in all contexts in which *tadv* relationships are found identical principles apply. We may approach the elucidation of the *tadv* relation system by bearing in mind the following criteria:

i. I distinguish three basic **modalities** of *tadv* relations. These correspond to the separate "meanings" of *tadv* in various contexts in which it is used, that is "biting", "striking", "shooting with an arrow", "copulating with", "eating" and so forth (or any of these preceded by "not"). These may conveniently be reduced to just

[1] I am not saying that no food taboos reflect taxonomic anomalies, "interstitial" categories, etc. (Leach, 1964; Douglas, 1966). I am saying that Umeda food taboos are not of this kind. I am well aware that paradoxical consequences can be drawn from my assertion here that Umeda food taboos reflect an "identification" between the thing tabooed and the observer of the taboo. For instance many male-dominated societies in New Guinea impose taboos on young men forbidding them to consume foods which can be plausibly said to be identified with women, feminine sexuality, menstruation, etc. (Meigs, 1976). Such taboos would appear to be definitive of the ego by negation, rather than by association, as here. We are by no means required to make a choice between these alternatives.

Umeda men or women would not eat menstrual blood, or faeces or earthworms or any of a large class of entities thought to be "disgusting" (*ehe*). These are at one level certainly in a different class from entities which are "emblems of the self" such as *pannatamwa*, trees bearing the same name as ego, self-killed game, etc., that is, things known to be desirable to eat apart from their tabooedness. My point is not that tabooed entities have to fall into one or other category, but that whichever category they do fall into the effect of taboo is to create a relationship in the *public* sphere between "ego" and an external reality communicated by *acts*. Taboo creates and specifies an ego. Umedas, in fact, predominantly taboo things which are independently known to be good to eat. But the total structure of the food system is too complex to analyse completely here. We have to distinguish among: things which are good to eat and are eaten, things which are good to eat and are not eaten, things which are not good to eat and are not eaten and an apparently paradoxical class of entities which are known not to be good to eat but which are nonetheless eaten – such as the dogs' penises that Baktaman novices are forced to consume, or, less spectacularly, the ultra-hot sago Umeda bachelors have to swallow (Barth, 1975, p. 65). No matter how taboo and "prescriptive eating" are distributed among these categories, which would vary from culture to culture, I think my essential point would stand.

My emphasis on the public character of the self descends at some removes from Wittgenstein (1953) and Ryle (1949). Barth's monograph on the Baktaman (1975) contains a chapter on "Taboo", whose argument is in some respects parallel to the one advanced here.

three modes, viz., the **sexual, gustatory** and **aggressive** modalities of *tadv* relations.

ii. Next, we may distinguish two possible **senses** or "directions" of *tadv* relations: the **active** sense (*tadv* is transitive) or the **passive** sense, in which ego is defined as undergoing the *tadv* activities of others.

iii. Finally, we may distinguish a number of **planes** of *tadv* relations, that is, the plane of the individual's own sexual–gustatory–aggressive experience, the planes of his vicarious experience, his dreams, myths, sociological constructs, etc.

Utilizing these three criteria as the dimensions of a coordinate system it is possible to define *tadv* relations and *tadv-maivem* relations in terms of a "semantic space" having three dimensions: modality, agency-passivity and immediacy-transcendence. And if, as I would suggest, the *tadv* relation system in Umeda subsumes the fundamental ego–world relationships (the structures of relevances which define the Umeda ego) a model of the *tadv* relation system is also a model of the ego itself.

More interesting, though, than the mere static outlines of such a system, are the consequences of the interactions of events in different senses, modalities and planes of *tadv* relations within the ongoing life process. A *tadv* relation, that is to say, is not simply a "point" in the coordinate system, but is generally found to correspond to a spectrum of other *tadv* relations on other planes, in different modalities, etc., which are "activated" simultaneously. A *tadv* relation is not single-stranded by nature, but comes as part of a bundle of such relations. These co-activated relations are discussed below as the "paradigmatic equivalents" of a particular *tadv* relation. An example is needed for clarification here: let us take the sexual mode of *tadv* relations as a case in point.

Anthropologists are familiar with languages, such as Umeda, which use the same word for both "eat" and "copulate". The sense of this transaction, as expressed in speech, is overtly man/eater/active *versus* woman/eaten/passive. But even a purely physiological interpretation of the situation, as it would be conceived by the Umedas, would not make the transaction appear entirely one-way. If their language is understood by Umedas as making the man the eater, the situation is reversed when one takes into account the masculine role in reproduction, also as understood by the Umedas. In the one act the man both "eats" the woman and also contributes semen which is the food of the embryo, that is, he is himself "eaten". Hence the practice, widely encountered in New Guinea and elsewhere, of continuing sexual intercourse during the earlier months of pregnancy, supposedly to further the development of the unborn infant: the Umeda father is simultaneously a consumer (active sense of *tadv* relations, sexual mode) and a nourisher (passive sense of *tadv* relations, gustatory mode). This reciprocity of senses in the eating/sexuality nexus is nicely brought out by the Umeda words for the female sexual organs: a trio of closely related words mean, respectively:

i. daughter, young girl, vagina *(mol)*
ii. fruit, daughter (metaphorically) *(movwi)*
iii. gullet, vagina (euphemistically) *(mov)*

The vagina has a double significance both as what is "eaten" (that is, fruit and girls) and as the organ which consummates eating, the gullet down which the eatables disappear.[1]

The same point can be made in a more general way. The reciprocal of the verb *tadv* is the verb *yahaitav*. This verb expresses the notions of (i) "dying, being killed" (the reciprocal of the aggressive modes of *tadv*); (ii) "fainting" including experiencing orgasm (reciprocal of the sexual mode of *tadv*); and (iii) "being satiated", "falling asleep" (reciprocal of the gustatory mode of *tadv*). It is derived from the adjective *yahoi* which means basically "soft" and in addition "ready to eat" of cooked food, sago, fruit, etc., and "ready to faint, sleep, die, etc." Umeda men discuss their sexual experience explicitly in terms of "fainting" and "dying" thereby revealing the reciprocal character of sexual–aggressive "eating" of the other (women also "die" in the sexual act). The same is true even if one is merely talking of food; eating food – which is seen incidentally as an incitement to love, as well as sleep – warms and excites the body, as a prelude to softening and relaxation followed by fainting and death. Food is an active as well as a passive substance; while it submits to being eaten, the eater must also submit himself to the power inherent in it, as is seen in the usage which demands that a young man must eat his sago as hot as possible, and is forbidden to blow on it so as to cool it. He has to submit to the "heat" of the sago in order to conserve and augment his own "heat".

[1] Cf. Gell (1975, chapter 3), on Umeda lexical symbolism.

The situation becomes still more complex and nuanced when we bring into consideration parallel sequences of events, not only in different modes or senses but also on different "planes" of *tadv* relations. A *tadv* relation, let us say the sexual one we have been considering, has correspondences with other *tadv* relations on other planes. The plane of the dream is a case in point. In terms of the standard repertoire of Umeda dream interpretations a sexual *tadv* relation corresponds to the following dream: "your sister comes to you bringing a gift of food" – this being the dream which is supposed to foretell imminent sexual gratification. It will be apparent, and this is not fortuitous, that the dream which prefigures a *tadv* relation (sexual) is itself a dreamed-out *tadv* relation, but not a sexual one. The "crossing over" from the physiological to the symbolic–prefigurative plane of events (whose mechanics I will consider in more detail below) is accompanied by a shift, not in the sense of the relation, for ego is active in the dream (as eater), but in the modality of the *tadv* relation. The dream representation of having sexual access to a woman is receiving food from the hands of a sexually inaccessible one. Sexuality becomes eating. But there is also, in the patterning of the dream, a reference, which is less obvious, to yet a third plane of *tadv* relations, the sociological plane. For why should ego be in receipt of a gift of food brought by his sister? Such a gift is not simply a token of affection, but represents a structural feature of Umeda society. It is not biological individuals alone who become bound together in the nexus of *tadv* relations: social groups, sibling sets, patrilines, hamlets and whole villages are definable in terms of such relationships. In Umeda, ego is by definition a member of a group whose relationship to other groups is mediated in the form of the transfer of women, the passage of gifts of food, and on occasion by mutual violence. Relations between social groups are *tadv* relations; the structure of ego's *tadv* relation system is integral with the structures of *tadv* relationships which define his group membership. Returning to the dream, then, the "sister's gift of food" is an aspect of *tadv* relations on the sociological plane. Ego's married sister returns periodically with gifts of food whereby affines reciprocate the sexual rights they have in ego's sister – with whom ego himself identifies and whom he definitely does not eat. It need hardly be said that the incest taboo can be most readily incorporated into the approach to taboo I have adopted here.

Accordingly, a twofold shift from the original plane of physiological events can here be seen: (i) a shift from the "real" meaning of the dream to the dream events themselves wherein "sexuality" is replaced by "eating", and (ii) a further shift from these dream events (posited as "real") to their sociological interpretation. Here a second transformation occurs in the mode of *tadv* relations, which results in their assuming the sexual mode once more, in that ego is being reciprocated with food for being sexually "eaten" (in the person of his sister) by his affinal group. But the sense of the transaction is inverted, passivity replacing the active sense of the transactions figuring on the planes of physiological and dream events: *qua* wife's brother, ego submits to the sexuality of the other.

A *tadv* transaction, in whatever mode or plane, can therefore be seen as forming part of a set of **paradigmatically equivalent** transactions in other senses, on other planes, or in other modes. The example just given of the correspondences between bodily experience and dream events, and between dream events and a certain sociological reality comprises such a set of paradigmatic equivalents, though an incomplete one no doubt. But rather than explore the merely paradigmatic aspects of the system of *tadv* relations further – since of such substitutions there is perhaps no foreseeable end – I should like to look in more detail at the enchainment of events within the reality of everyday life. How is it that certain among the constellation of *tadv* relations encompassing ego become salient from moment to moment, how are they articulated to his vital interests, and how are they translated into specific patterns of action?

In other words, having sketched in the *tadv* relation system as it is paradigmatically, I turn now to the problem of **syntagmatic** ordering in the enchainment of *tadv* relations in the flow of social life. And by contrast with the paradigmatic axis, along which *tadv* relations are seen as equivalent to one another, when viewed syntagmatically *tadv* relations are characterized by being mutually exclusive, even mutually inimical within one plane of events. This discussion will also lead me back to the themes of taboo and lapse with which I began.

A *tadv* transaction is by no means an isolated event; it is integral with the texture of interconnected events which make up the social process. A *tadv* transaction has its origins in events which are themselves *tadv* transactions, and it has consequences, and these consequences are further *tadv* transactions, and so on. For detailed examination I have chosen the hunting/sexuality nexus. Not only are these the pivotal elements in Umeda masculinity, but an analysis of the relationship between hunting and sexuality enables one to see, in a particularly striking fashion, the orderly – that is to say, repetitive or oscillatory – character of the enchainment of *tadv* transactions within the social process.

Our initial situation is as follows: a young Umeda man, having waited patiently and sleeplessly in his deserted garden by the light of the moon, succeeds, at length, in shooting and killing a marauding wild pig. What are the *tadv* relations involved here? Up to the moment of the pig's demise the man was in a *tadv* relation with the pig, and it with him, indirectly, in that it was from his garden that the pig came to steal. Subsequently, though, the situation is transformed: having consummated his relation with the wild pig in the modality of hunting, the killer is precluded, by the very strict taboo on eating self-killed game, from consummating the relation subsequently in the modality of eating.

Or, where we find paradigmatically:

killing = eating

syntagmatically, we find:

killing → *not* eating

Identifiable here is a basic principle having implications for the whole spectrum of Umeda behaviour, which asserts that if, on the plane of real life events, say, a relationship, A *tadv* B, is paradigmatically, equivalent to A′ *tadv* B′ on another plane (for example, dream) then the latter relation, A′ *tadv* B′, is inimical to or contraindicative of the original relation A *tadv* B, should it occur on the same plane. This has profound consequences, for if the relation A *tadv* B corresponds to ego's vital interests, then it must be that the relation A′ *tadv* B′ will be shunned, or, in other words, A′ *tadv-maivem* B′. Hence, if "ego shoots pig" is paradigmatically equivalent to "ego eats pig", as indeed it is on the basis of the general schema, *tadv* = hunt = eat = make love, etc., it follows that ego cannot eat the pig he has killed. The "principle of syntagmatic exclusion" motivates both the taboo and its sanction, for the consequence of eating self-killed game is not being able to hunt successfully subsequently.

To return to the situation of the hunter: the death of the pig has the consequence of creating a *tadv-maivem* relation which prevents him from eating its carcass. At the same time this constitutes a redefintion of his "field of identity", since, as I argued above, the observance of taboo creates a privileged segment of intersubjective reality, so far as ego is concerned, not so much *his* as *him*. Having witnessed the demeanour of Umeda men at the butchering of wild pigs they have killed, the diffident, sidelong, almost embarrassed glances they direct towards the dismembered animal, I am convinced that I am not being fantastic in suggesting that they are personally strongly identified with their hunting prey.

In the working out of the logic of *tadv* transactions, it is the hunter himself who now becomes the passive object.[1] The pig, edible, but inedible by him, now enters the sphere of matrilateral–affinal food exchanges briefly alluded to above. His closest relatives, his father, his mother if he is an eldest son, his elder brothers and certain individuals with whom he is ritually associated, may no more eat the pig than may he, since they are too closely identified with him and his kill. It is another matter with the members of his opposite hamlet moiety, his mother's brothers and their families, or, if he is married, his wife, brothers-in-law and wife's parents. These "others" now eat ego's pig. In this guise ego is now, in a sense, dismembered and eaten, most significantly by those with whom he has, or may have, *tadv* relations of a sexual kind. These are: wives, marriageable girls, and female cross-cousins who, though actually too close for marriage, are the likeliest partners in unsanctioned liaisons.

Ego is not passive in all respects even during this phase of "dismemberment". Ego, as food, is active inasmuch as food is a potent substance in its own right. Even in being the object of *tadv* relations in the gustatory mode, entering the bodies of ego's potential sexual partners, food becomes the instrument of ego's active *tadv* relations in the sexual mode. Food softens the hearts of wives and girlfriends in a remarkable way, and it is the accepted consequence of hunting

[1] What motivates this "principal of exclusion" cognitively? Why should a sequence of events on a "higher" plane, such as dream, mean something *else* when transferred back to mundane reality? Essentially, I think, this arises from a separation, which has to be maintained, between "metaphors of experience" and what is *meant*. The principle of exclusion keeps the metaphors which generalize experience "meta-". The switch-over in modality which accompanies a crossing over from one plane to a higher one is a frame-marking device: metaphorical reality, dream reality, give access to vicarious transcendence, but only while they can be kept separate logically from the "paramount reality of everyday life" (Schutz, 1962, p. 341) from which they all start. On psychological "framing" cf. Bateson (1973, p. 157). The metaphor of *tadv* relations, which generalizes the ego–world interaction (eating, aggression and sexuality) at the same time motivates an Umeda preoccupation with keeping separate in reality what metaphor unites in terms of a cognitive paradigm.

success that ego will now become the target of amorous advances, to which he will succumb.

A paradoxical situation ensues, for love-making is a paradigmatically equivalent *tadv* transaction to hunting success and is, both according to our hypothesis and in Umeda eyes, highly inimical to it. The dream betokening a sexual conquest was, it will be remembered, a gift of food: the dream betokening a hunting success is dreaming of making love. The hunter's integrity, the virtue he derives from the strict rein he places upon his appetites in order to succeed in the chase, is dissipated at the very moment of coming to fruition. Triumphant, he falls into the arms of his amorous cross-cousins, who play the role of so many Delilahs to his Samson.

We may now begin to grasp the pattern in its totality. Ego is embroiled in a sequence of active and passive movements: first active (pig-killer) then passive (food provider) then active again (sexual conqueror) then passive again, since ego is "softened" by his sexual partners, just as he softened them originally with his gifts of meat. At this point, these active and passive oscillations of *tadv* relations are interrupted, since ego, physically and morally threatened by his love-making, must now eschew *tadv* relations altogether and resume the ascetic mode of life of the hunter awaiting his kill, patiently watching by night in the lonely forest.

Two types of rhythmic alternation can be sensed here. First "short cycles" of active/passive *(tadv/yahaitav)* alternations: "eating" followed by "softening" and dissipation. *Tadv* relations, modalities of ego–world interactions which constitute the ego as an open, energy absorbing system, contain also, because of their intrinsically reciprocal character, the promise of the ego's dissolution and incorporation into the other as a thing "softened", eaten, and destroyed. But these short cycles of *tadv/yahaitav* alternations, tending towards dissolution and death, are only episodes within a longer cycle of indulgence, activity, followed by asceticism and withdrawal from activity. The hunter has consummated his vital interests in the realms of venery – in both senses of that convenient homophone – but only at the cost of placing himself in jeopardy from which the only escape is via asceticism, that is to say, via taboo. If the short cycle is definable as a *tadv/yahaitav* alternation, then this, the longer cycle, is definable as *tadv* (consummation) followed by *tadv-maivem* (taboo). *Tadv-maivem* (taboo) is the condition of rejecting both "eating" and "softening", since the latter only follows on the former. Taboo restores the ego by reconstituting it as a closed system, protected by the *tadv-maivem* relations which demarcate an inviolable region. Having first of all described taboo as the means whereby the ego comes into existence as a privileged segment of intersubjective reality, we are now able, by tracing the vicissitudes of the ego in the flow of social process, to grasp taboo as a "moment" in the dialectics of the ego–world interaction.

But there is more to it than this. The phase of ascetic withdrawal at which the hunter has arrived is not a *terminus* but is only a stage on the way to the renewal of the overall cycle of events. We need to understand the mechanism whereby this alternation (eating/tabooing) becomes prolonged. The mechanism involved is the dream.

Umedas explicitly associate dreaming with the ascetic mode of existence. The fully fed man, the sexually satisfied man, will sleep a sound and untroubled sleep, while the man who is neither tosses and turns beside his fire and dreams. The impoverishment of his waking hours is compensated for by the enrichment of his vicarious experience, the nobler for not being real. Our ascetic hunter, benighted, hungry, and solitary, also dreams. He dreams of the women from whom he has voluntarily absented himself in order to restore his integrity, and of gifts of food brought to him by his sister. In either case, the dream is a negation of actuality, while being also, according to the logic of the system of dream omens, a prognostication of what is to come. Detached from the entanglements of worldly *tadv* relationships, the ascetic has access to the sublime, to symbolic truths unavailable except in dreams or in the world-ordering magical formulae of his hunter's incantations over his dog.[1] A spirit will guide his steps to the pig's lair in the forest, and a wonderful dream about women, of which he must say nothing subsequently on pain of its losing its efficacy, will set the seal of ultimate success on his endeavours. Awakening from his ascetic trance, he encounters a world subtly transformed by the action of the dream into one demarcated as the scene of his future projects, its inner constitution now laid bare, inviting him, drawing him in. He picks up his bow, whistles for his dog, and sets off in search of his predestined pig. And not in vain: crouching by a gap in the perimeter fence of a garden he first hears a rustling, a snuffling in the underbrush, which can mean but one thing. A dark form looms and in the same instant his arrow flies from his bow. . .

[1] In a paper related to the present one but concerned with Umeda magical perfumes (Gell, 1977), I have discussed Umeda hunting magic and its mechanisms in more detail.

The cycle is complete: we have arrived at our point of departure.

Vita activa, vita contemplativa – between these contraries we are forever vacillating, and in Umeda as elsewhere. Gorging, love-making, as well as the noble pursuit of killing pigs, constitute vital interests in the eyes of the Umeda male, but their consummation comes in the moment of **lapse**, which in turn carries with it the suffering, dissipation and extinction. Contemplation, transcendence, asceticism, re-establish the integrity which is threatened by lapse, but also, by giving access to apodictic symbolic knowledge, re-open the mundane sphere for renewed activity. In this way an oscillation is established which corresponds to the life-process, between immanence, involvement, entropy (*tadv/yahaitav*, agency/passivity, tending towards death and absorption) alternating with transcendence, asceticism, negentropy which only succeeds in directing the ego back towards its immanent role in the world (Fig. 1).

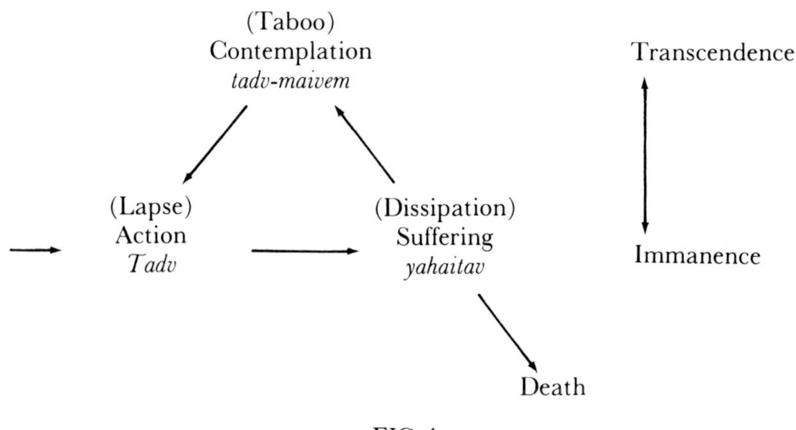

FIG. 1.

References

BARTH, FREDRIK (1975). *Ritual and Knowledge among the Baktaman of New Guinea*. Universitetsforlaget, Oslo. Yale University Press, New Haven, Connecticut.

BATESON, GREGORY (1973). *Steps to an Ecology of Mind*. Paladin, London.

BERGER, PETER (1973). *The Social Reality of Religion*. Penguin Books, London.

BERGER, PETER and LUCKMANN, THOMAS (1971). *The Social Construction of Reality: A Treatise on the Sociology of Knowledge*. Penguin Books, London.

DOUGLAS, MARY (1966). *Purity and Danger: An Analysis of Concepts of Pollution and Taboo*. Routledge and Kegan Paul, London.

GELL, ALFRED (1975). *Metamorphosis of the Cassowaries: Umeda Society, Language and Ritual* (LSE Monographs in Social Anthropology, no. 51). Athlone Press, London.

GELL, ALFRED (1977). Magic, perfume, dream . . . In *Symbols and Sentiments: Cross-Cultural Studies in Symbolism* (Ed. Ioan Lewis), pp. 25–38. Academic Press, London and New York.

LEACH, EDMUND (1964). Anthropological aspects of language: animal categories and verbal abuse. In *New Directions in the Study of Language* (Ed. Eric H. Lenneberg), pp. 23–63. MIT Press, Cambridge, Massachusetts.

MEIGS, ANNA S. (1976). Male pregnancy and the reduction of sexual opposition in a New Guinea Highlands society. *Ethnology*, **15**, no. 4, 393–407.

MERLEAU-PONTY, MAURICE (1962). *The Phenomenology of Perception* (translation Colin Smith). Routledge and Kegan Paul, London.

MURPHY, ROBERT (1972). *The Dialectics of Social Life*. George Allen and Unwin, London.

RYLE, GILBERT (1949). *The Concept of Mind*. Hutchinson, London.

SCHUTZ, ALFRED (1962). *Collected Papers I. The Problem of Social Reality*. Martinus Nijhof, The Hague.

WITTGENSTEIN, LUDWIG (1953). *Philosophical Investigations* (translation G. E. M. Anscombe). Blackwell, Oxford.

Tambu: the Shell-money of the Tolai

A. L. Epstein

WHEN, IN 1875, the Wesleyan missionary George Brown landed on New Britain he encountered a people whose ways contrasted sharply with those of the Samoans with whom he had previously lived for many years. In their political organization, their modes of government, as well as so many of the arts of life, the Samoans evidently enjoyed a much more advanced culture than the Melanesians; but what impressed Brown no less forcibly was the difference between the two groups in regard to their commercial attitudes and activities. "A Samoan gives, a New Britain native sells or lends at interest. . . . There were no markets in Samoa, but every district in New Britain had one. There was no money or any recognized standard of value in Samoa like the *diwara* or *tambu* in New Britain, for the fine mats, or other property given at marriage or funeral feasts, had no fixed negotiable value." (Brown, 1910, p. 434.) Other early visitors to this part of New Guinea were no less intrigued by the local monetary system and the way in which *tambu* was intricately woven into the very texture of social life. One such traveller commented that New Britain was the only savage country he had visited where the natives had a true money currency of a standard value. "With this money you can buy anything you like, a wife if desired. It is as much a standard coin of the realm as the sovereign is of the British Empire." (Pitcairn, 1891, pp. 178–179; cf. Romilly, 1886, p. 24.)

Within a short time, fuller and more scholarly accounts of New

Britain shell-money began to appear in the ethnographic literature (e.g. Danks, 1887; Kleintitschen, 1906; Parkinson, 1907) from which the major features of the system emerged quite clearly, even if certain of the claims made for *tambu* were to be received sceptically by later anthropologists (see Malinowski, 1921). More recently a number of professional anthropologists have carried out extensive field research in different parts of the Gazelle Peninsula, and they have reported not only on the continuing use of *tambu* in the contemporary setting but they have also attempted to elucidate and clarify the traditional working of a very complex institution (see Epstein, A. L., 1963, 1969; Epstein, T. S., 1968; Salisbury, 1966, 1970). As between these various accounts and analyses there are certain differences of emphasis and perspective and, indeed, on occasion, of interpretation, but what is common to all is the treatment of *tambu* as a cultural artifact, a "social fact" to be handled and understood in relation to other "social facts". Thus Danks, another early Wesleyan missionary, in a paper that might fairly be regarded as anticipating the brand of functionalism that Malinowski was later to develop, pointed out that there was not a custom connected with life or death in which shell-money did not play a great and leading part, and suggested that if *tambu* were removed from the people their whole way of life would collapse. By contrast, Scarlett Epstein, in the context of her discussion of Tolai economic development, has been primarily concerned with *tambu* as a monetary institution, while Salisbury, with rather similar interests, has emphasized the importance of *tambu* in the emergence of local entrepreneurs and the part they play in the political system. I have no quarrel with these various approaches as such. Together, and in their several ways, they have helped to make *tambu* perhaps the best known and best understood among primitive currencies. My claim is, however, that in paying inadequate attention to the dimension of affect, such analyses leave many questions about *tambu* unanswered and, indeed, unasked. To take but one example for the moment: the term by which the Tolai refer to their shell-money is also the one by which they denote that class of phenomena usually categorized in the anthropological literature as taboo. Is this a matter of coincidence to be explained, or rather dismissed, after the fashion of Malinowski, as another example of homonymy (see Leach, 1958)? If not, what is there about their shell-money that leads to its association with the category *tambu*? As I hope to show, many of the attitudes, ideas and practices that pertain to shell-money are permeated by a profound emotional charge. In Freudian terms, *tambu* is highly cathected, suggesting that behind its pragmatic uses powerful unconscious impulses are also at work. The aim of this essay is to explore this possibility and to trace out some of the implications that stem from it. Before embarking on this task, however, it is necessary to retrace some of the ground, to describe by way of background something of the social setting and circumstances of the Tolai, and to outline the main features of the *tambu* complex.

Tolai society

The Gazelle Peninsula of New Britain offers an environment at once harsh and fertile; isolated from the rest of the island to the south and west by a rugged range of mountains, the landscape and topography of the area also testify to continuing tectonic activity over long periods of time. Volcanoes or their extinct craters dominate the skyline around Blanche Bay, picturesque but threatening – the last major eruption in 1937 transformed a small island in the bay, which had itself been thrown up in another eruption some sixty years earlier, into a substantial hill connected to the mainland, wrought havoc in the town of Rabaul, and claimed the lives of more than a thousand Tolai. On the other hand, soils enriched by volcanic deposits made possible one of the densest populations throughout the whole of Melanesia.[1] The marked degree of ecological diversity, particularly striking in so tiny an area, may also perhaps be associated with this history of vulcanism. Such diversity, expressed in a great variety of highly localized products, provided a matrix within which an indigenous trade could develop.

To its earliest European observers the Gazelle Peninsula presented something of a puzzle. It was not simply that men and women went completely naked or that head-hunting and cannibalism were regularly practised. It was rather that the people appeared to possess few of the familiar indices of cohesion and social solidarity. They acknowledged no common name for themselves as a group, and designations of the land, the people, and the language as Gunantuna or Kuanua were merely usages adopted by the incoming Roman Catholic and

[1] According to Salisbury (1970, p. 19), the population density at the time of first contact was more than 100 per square mile. At present it is probably around 300 to 400.

Methodist missionaries respectively.[1] There was a common language, referred to simply as *tinata tuna* – the true or proper tongue – but dialectal variation was often considerable, even among neighbouring communities, and the contemporary homogeneity of the language owes a great deal to the influence and efforts of the missions. Again, there was no substantial body of historical lore common to the group as a whole; legends of origin tended to vest in particular clans *(vunatarai)*, telling of more or less recent immigration into the area from New Ireland or of movements within the Gazelle Peninsula itself.

But what probably served most to convey the impression of almost total anarchy was the lack of any centralized political institutions. People lived in small and sometimes scattered hamlets, each surrounded by its own fence, within territorial units known as *gunan*. The *gunan* or village had a population that rarely exceeded 300 or 400 individuals who, while they did not always actively cooperate among themselves, nevertheless saw themselves as a unit in opposition to other like units. With the inhabitants of these other villages they arranged alliances or marriages and carried on trade, but they guarded their autonomy jealously and, as Salisbury (1966, p. 113) put it, wars were continually fought to avenge slights to village self-esteem, which usually involved the theft of pigs or the seduction of women. The absence of judicial mechanisms for securing law and order was also evident. While the earlier ethnographers perceived dimly that Tolai society was not given over entirely to utter lawlessness, their puzzlement is seen clearly in the way each sought the key to its fragile integration in a different direction: Kleintitschen in the power commanded by the wealthy; Parkinson and Brown in the role of the *dukduk*, a masked dancer and the central figure in the secret male cult, while Meier sought for the means of law enforcement in the work of the sorcerer (see Sack, 1974).

The traditional Tolai polity was thus highly fragmented and marked by a pervasive parochialism. Yet countervailing processes were also at work within the social system, binding people into wider and more complex networks of relationship. Apart from the presence of trade and markets previously mentioned, there was an elaborate kinship system built up around the principle of matriliny. One aspect of this was the dual organization in the form of two exogamous units

[1] The use of the term Tolai as a group designation has no sanction in tradition, and is in fact of quite recent origin (cf. Epstein, A. L., 1969, p. 13).

or moieties, which operated throughout the Gazelle Peninsula, the neighbouring Duke of York Islands, and part of New Ireland, to regulate marriage. Marriage links might therefore be fairly widespread, creating intricate webs of obligation between otherwise hostile communities. There was too a rich and varied ceremonial life. Certain prominent individuals, known as *ngala* (literally big-man) or *luluai*[1] were in a position to sponsor the performance of large-scale mortuary rites or to initiate the activities associated with the secret male cult of *dukduk* and *tubuan*. Such festivities, usually marked by a ban on fighting, involved the participation of, and competition between, individuals and groups from many different villages and so served to create new ties as well as to cement established ones. All of these various activities, as I shall discuss presently, turned on the capacity to command considerable resources of shell-money.

In the hundred years that have elapsed since first sustained contact with the outside world, the Gazelle Peninsula has seen many changes. In this period the Tolai have moved from a condition that Danks once referred to as "commercial savagery" to becoming the most sophisticated and wealthy of all the indigenous people of contemporary Papua New Guinea. Yet the passage has not been an even one, nor free from stress. Times of rising prosperity and heightened expectation have alternated with periods of slump and frustration, reflecting not only the Gazelle's increasing involvement in the world's economy, but also in its political system. For the Tolai have experienced at close quarters a succession of imposed regimes, civil and military, each with its distinctive policies and programmes and style of approach.

In the Gazelle Peninsula the Germans found an ideal setting for the establishment of a colonial plantation economy, but they also stimulated indigenous economic development by the creation of a road system, by encouraging increased production of food and cash crops, and by introducing schooling which prepared students for a variety of relatively skilled occupations. Then, on the outbreak of the First World War, the Germans were supplanted by the Australians. Through the inter-war years New Guinea was administered by Australia under Mandate of the League of Nations and the town of Rabaul, established by the Germans, remained as the capital and

[1] In some parts of the Gazelle the term *luluai*, which was adopted by the Germans to describe a Government-appointed village headman, referred traditionally to a war-leader. In others, so I was assured by my oldest informants at Matupit, it meant simply a man of wealth, one who had ample stocks of *tambu* at his disposal.

main seaport of the Territory. The Mandate imposed certain obligations for the development of the country in the interests of its people, but for the most part they received little more than lip-service, for the Australians took few positive steps to carry further the developments initiated by the Germans. It was a period which few Tolai recall with notable enthusiasm, and even though they sometimes refer to it as "the good days" *(ta ra boina bung)* this must be understood less as an expression of nostalgia and more as a way of marking off the years that immediately preceded the coming of the Second World War.

The entry of the Japanese into that war marked the beginning of a period of great hardship for the Tolai. Within a short time the Gazelle Peninsula came under military occupation and later, when the Japanese found themselves cut off from their lines of supply, their regime became increasingly oppressive. Many Tolai died through punishment at the hands of their new masters, others through malnutrition and lack of adequate medical supplies, while yet others were killed in Allied bombing attacks. In addition, in some areas the coconut plantations, on which Tolai pre-war wealth had been built, were destroyed and many years would have to pass before they could be restored. In some parts too accumulated stocks of shell-money were seriously depleted, in some cases because *tambu* had been seized and destroyed by the Japanese, in some cases because it had been used up in the purchase of food from more fortunately placed communities.

The ramifying consequences of the war for the Tolai are difficult to assess, but what is at least clear is that once peace was restored, and the Australian administration re-established, few were in a mood to return meekly to the *status quo* of the pre-war period. At the same time Australian policy, previously quiescent, was suddenly seized with a new urgency. The stage was thus set for rapid changes in every sphere of social life; in the economic there was, for example, the setting up of the Tolai Cocoa Project; in the political, the introduction of Native Local Government Councils to the Gazelle, the first of their kind in the Territory. Serious attention was also being given to improving services in the fields of education and health. The result of these various developments is that today the Tolai area has come to occupy a position of prominence in the affairs of the country out of all proportion to its tiny size. For many years, its contribution to the Territory's revenue, based in large measure on the efforts of Tolai producers, has been quite disproportionate when simply measured against that of other Districts. Over the years too, increasing numbers of Tolai have held a variety of relatively skilled jobs in many parts of the country clearly less advanced than their own, so it is not surprising that they should have come to develop a view of themselves as an indigenous elite. Though the situation in this regard has begun to change gradually, Tolai predominance in certain "white-collar" occupations is still especially striking.[1]

There is, however, another side to the coin. For some time there has been ample evidence of mounting social tension on the Gazelle to impress even the most casual observer. Most dramatic perhaps was the emergence of the new political movement known as Mataungan (see Epstein, A. L., 1970), and the later killing of the District Officer at Rabaul. The Mataungan movement was founded avowedly to oppose the establishment of a Multi-racial Council that would have replaced the existing Gazelle Local Council, a Tolai body, but at its roots lay a variety of interconnected social ills and problems: population growth of quite startling proportions; a seemingly intractable land problem; a situation of rising unemployment exacerbated by the presence of a high proportion of sixth-form "drop-outs", and so on. All of this has been going on in an atmosphere of growing uncertainty among the Tolai about the political future of the Territory, and of the position of their own area within it.[2]

This review of the recent social history of the Gazelle has been necessarily cursory and selective, but it is essential to my analysis, not simply by way of providing background information but in order to make a number of important points. Together, and in their several ways, the various developments just outlined have generated a considerable strain on the traditional fabric of Tolai social life. Indeed, given all the surrounding circumstance, one might readily imagine that little of the pre-contact social organization or culture can have survived, save perhaps as folk-memories. It is true of course that the world of the modern Tolai is vastly different from that of his great-grandfather, but it is no less true that in certain fundamental respects Tolai society remains recognizably traditional. Making a basically

[1] The case of teaching affords a vivid illustration of the point. According to an index provided by Finney (1971), calculated for the purpose on the basis of teachers per 100,000 head of population, the figure for east New Britain (that is, the Tolai area) was 472; for the Madang District, with an equally long history of contact, 43; and for Chimbu and the Eastern Highlands populous areas, which were only effectively opened up after the Second World War, 8.

[2] For rather fuller discussion of these issues see Epstein, A. L. *et al.* (1971).

similar point, Salisbury (1966, p. 115) observes that in the village of Vunamami the religious ceremonies of the *tubuan* are carried out virtually unchanged from Parkinson's descriptions based on his observations in the 1880s, and that land tenure still operates in terms of the traditional, highly flexible matrilineal system. The island of Matupit, where my own research was conducted, and perhaps the Tolai community in which cultural erosion has proceeded furthest, presented no less striking evidence of continuity, leading me to take this as one of the central themes of my own monograph (Epstein, A. L., 1969).

This situation is not quite so paradoxical as it might seem at first sight. From the earliest days of contact, the Tolai have shown themselves receptive to new ideas and willing to adopt new practices – but selectively and only on their own terms. Salisbury (1970, p. 97) has commented that withdrawal rather than argument is a usual Tolai reaction to European experts who think they know best, and I have myself frequently observed Matupi respond in this way. Among administrative officers and other Europeans such behaviour has earned them a reputation for obtuseness. Thus one observer of the contemporary New Guinea scene, having paid tribute to Tolai responsiveness to schemes put forward by the government for their advancement, goes on: "But they are not a tractable group: they do not consider themselves particularly obliged to the administration for its special attention to their advancement. They do not respond with unquestioning loyalty and affection. On the contrary, some Tolai clans tend to be stubborn and at times violent." (Williams, 1964, p. 51.) From the standpoint of the anthropologist, however, such behaviour appears rather as a fairly typical expression of defiance, a response in an unequal power situation to demands made by the more powerful figure which the other regards as a threat to his autonomy. We shall see later that such displays are not confined to interactions between Tolai and *kiap*s;[1] they find expression no less frequently in a variety of purely indigenous contexts. They point to a fierce sense of personal independence, a prickliness and assertiveness in all forms of social intercourse, and a refusal to acknowledge any man as one's master. Along with such traits there goes a refusal to yield, a tenacious clinging to that with which he closely identifies himself, and through which he seeks to assert his autonomy. Nowhere is this more

[1] The term *kiap* commonly applies throughout New Guinea to a government officer who is concerned with native affairs.

clearly revealed than in the persistence of the Tolai's attachment to shell-money. But this is an issue we cannot explore further until we have learned a little more of the uses to which it is put, and the meanings, conscious and unconscious, with which it is invested.

The uses of shell-money

Tambu consists of the shells of a small mollusc, the main source of which for the Tolai for many years has been Nakanai on the north coast of New Britain. The journey today is not hazardous as it was in the past, but since the collection of a sizeable quantity is a slow business it may still involve for the party making the trip an absence from home of some months. Collection, however, is only the first part of the task, for the shells do not become *tambu* until they have been properly treated. This consists in the arduous process of cutting the whorl of the shell away from the lips and then stringing the lips on lengths of rattan (Salisbury, 1970, pp. 281–283). A further point mentioned by Brown (1910, p. 295), which I shall refer to again, is that when first acquired the shells have a dull brown colour; they only became valuable as in the course of time they were bleached.[1]

The ease with which the threaded shells can be divided into strips of different length makes *tambu* particularly serviceable for use as a currency. The standard unit of measurement is the fathom *(a pokono)*, calculated as the distance between one's two outstretched arms. There is in addition a whole series of smaller units, measured off in terms of the distance between different points of the body, for example, between outstretched fingers and the middle of the chest (half a fathom) or the inside of the elbow (quarter of a fathom), until one comes to the smallest units of all which are counted in pairs of shells. It is clear that the larger units cannot always be of uniform

[1] Brown was uncertain how the bleaching was accomplished and attributed it to light, time and constant handling. However, according to Powell (1883, p. 56), it was achieved by burying the shells in the earth. Of interest in this connection is a reference by Pfeil (1899, p. 119) to counterfeit shell-money. Apparently early European traders had found it necessary to make use of *tambu* in their transactions with Tolai. Noting that the amounts in circulation were inadequate to meet the demand for it, some of them conceived the idea of having *tambu* manufactured in Europe. The venture was unsuccessful. The Tolai recognized the introduced shells as counterfeit and refused to accept them. Unfortunately, Pfeil does not tell us to what features of the manufactured shells the Tolai objected.

length, but minor variations do not appear to worry the Tolai. Presumably these balance out over a series of transactions (cf. Salisbury, 1970, p. 288). More pertinently, the units are not immediately convertible among themselves; units of different length cannot be totted up in one's head to yield a total in fathoms. This can only be done by placing all the pieces together and measuring them off against a strip of vine.

At first glance then it would appear that, despite certain deficiencies, *tambu* has a close generic resemblance to money as understood among ourselves. But my concern here is not to measure the attributes of *tambu* against a model of a monetary system derived from quite different socio-economic conditions, an approach against which Dalton (1965) has rightly cautioned. Nowadays, as it happens, Tolai operate with both cash[1] and *tambu*, and there will be an opportunity to discuss the relationship between the two in a later section. The present task must be to describe the varying uses to which shell-money is put, the different spheres of relationship and social context into which it enters, and the attitudes that are held in respect of it.

The situation in which a visiting European is first likely to encounter the use of shell-money is at one of the main market-places: Rabaul or Kokopo. While he will pay in coin for his choice among the wide variety of fruits, vegetables and other local produce on display, he will discover that Tolai may hand over *tambu* in exchange for the same items. Closer familiarity with the area would reveal that any transaction between Tolai in respect of goods or services can be mediated through shell-money: today, as in the past, everything has its price, be it food, goods manufactured by another, such as a drum or a canoe, or the services of a man who has cured one's sickness or designed one's dance costume. The major difference in this regard as between past and present is that whereas formerly the Tolai only had *tambu*, nowadays they have a choice of currencies.

Such a picture suggests a highly "monetized" economy, an impression which is heightened by the presence of concepts concerned with regular ways of dealing in *tambu*: borrowing, lending, pawning, and so on.[2] An acute commercial sense is also revealed in the concept

[1] Papua New Guinea now has its own currency, the basic unit of which is the kina.

[2] According to Danks (1887, p. 308), the people of the Duke of York Islands had a clear concept of interest *(wawaturu)*, but he noted that among the Tolai the idea was less fully developed. Indeed, having described Tolai practice, he then adds, "But the idea in the native mind does not seem to be so much interest, as an expression of thanks for a favour." Here again we have an excellent instance of the need for extreme care when we take a concept which is used in a technical sense in one system and seek to apply it in another.

of the *vuvuvung*, an "account" or "fund". Thus a man who purchased, say, a new canoe would hire it out to others, including his close kin, for a fee in *tambu*; all that he received in this way went into a separate canoe "account". The expression *pal na vuvuvung* refers to the house in which a man stores his own accumulated stock of shell-money together with that of others who may deposit with him.

Tambu was also used in a variety of ways that are non-commercial. Mention has been made of the lack in traditional Tolai society of any differentiated institution for the enforcement of law and order. Danks (1887), however, has described how exchanges of shell-money served to restore peace after fighting had broken out in which people had been killed or injured, as well as a general means of making atonement for wrongs. Even today in some Tolai communities, as I have myself observed, the handing over of *tambu* by way of atonement or compensation remains the appropriate way of settling certain kinds of dispute.

Such uses point to the role of shell-money in adjusting social relationships that have become disturbed. There is also a wide variety of contexts in which the passage of *tambu* operates to redefine or change the character of an existing relationship, as in the case of the adoption of a child or the removal of the avoidance taboo between a man and his wife's mother. There is also the institution of the *turguvai* (literally, a "standing together") whereby a person who regularly helped another in his enterprises by contributions of shell-money might come to be regarded as a member of that other's descent group despite the fact that such a claim could not be substantiated on genealogical grounds. But above all it is in marking the change of status as the individual passes through the various sequences of the life cycle that *tambu* figures most prominently: birth, initiation of boys into the cult of *dukduk* and *tubuan*, marriage and death. Around these events there revolves a rich ceremonial life, in which all the sense of pageantry and the artistry of the people in song, dance and the carving of painted figures can find full scope for expression. Most of these ceremonies require on the part of their sponsors a heavy expenditure of shell-money, and they are also accompanied by complex distributions of *tambu* among the participants.

For Tolai it is the part that *tambu* plays on these occasions that marks off the value of shell-money from that which attaches to cash. "*A mani ure ra nian, a tambu ure ra minat*", they say; money pertains to food, that is the secular or profane, *tambu* to death, to what is sacred.

So far as shell-money itself is concerned, the passage between these two realms is marked in the most tangible way. As we have seen, the natural shells are transformed into *tambu* by being specially treated and threaded. In this form the average Tolai is likely to carry a fathom or two around in his arm-purse for small everyday purchases. Larger amounts in the form of skeins are kept at home, or are deposited for safekeeping with a trusted kinsman or elder, against heavier outlays. What the Tolai most ardently desires, however, is that his stock of *tambu* should accumulate rapidly to the point where it can be bound into a large round coil called a *loloi*. Once in the form of a *loloi*, which may contain anything from fifty up to a thousand fathoms, *tambu* no longer circulates in the ordinary way. Instead, the coils are carefully stored away until, on the occasion of a major ceremony, they are brought out to adorn the specially erected scaffolding called a *leo*, or they are publicly "cut" and the shell-money within distributed.

In former days the desire to accumulate *tambu* was bound up with doctrines about the afterlife. When a person died the corpse was wrapped in the fronds of a coconut palm, the orifices were plugged with pieces of *tambu*, and shell-money was also strewn on the grave. The explanation offered for these practices was that the spirit was now equipped to make the appropriate responses when it arrived finally at the Abode of the Dead. In the traditional view, without the accumulation of shell-money during one's lifetime and its cutting up and distribution on one's death, there could be no entry to the *matana kaia* or *tingena tabaran*, the Abode of the Spirits; instead the spirit of the deceased was doomed to an existence of everlasting wretchedness in the land called IaKupia.

Describing Tolai funerary customs, a Roman Catholic missionary, Winthuis (1926, p. 58), records the lamentations of a mother bewailing the death of her son:[1] "Oh my son, now you have died leaving me. Oh, where have you gone? . . . You wonderful dancer, the plumage in my head-dress, now I will never see you dance again, leaping as though on glowing coconut embers. My body is torn with sorrow and pain. Who will now bury me when I come to die? Who will scatter *tambu* over my grave? All will revile me, for I shall have no shell-money left. Oh, woe is me, woe is me." It is as though the woman's grief is divided: mourning the loss of a beloved son, she laments too the prospect of her own death without a son to "cut" *tambu* at her burial.

[1] All translations of German texts offered here are the responsibility of the author.

Winthuis adds an explanatory gloss. The last sorrow, he points out, was a particularly heavy one because it was the desire of every Tolai to accumulate as much shell-money as possible so that his death would be followed by the finest mortuary rites imaginable, and the giving away of large quantities of *tambu*. "This is the greatest longing of every native, the central thought which occupies him every day of his life. All his life is nothing less than an attempt to amass shell-money: in this way he prepares himself for his own death." Nowadays, profoundly influenced by the teaching of Christian missionaries for close on a century, there are many Tolai to whom the older doctrines are no longer known. Nevertheless, the desire to accumulate *tambu* towards one's own death, or that of a close kinsman, remains a powerful incentive, even in those communities such as Matupit where social and cultural change have proceeded furthest.

Danks associated the propensity to hoard shell-money with habits of frugality and industry. These values survive, though the activities which generate wealth are much more varied now than in the past. On Matupit, where a high proportion of the population has long been accustomed to work away from the village for wages, local leaders try to impress upon young people the importance of maintaining those activities that yield *tambu*. In these circumstances one might easily imagine that accumulated wealth in shell-money is due directly to unremitting labour at traditional tasks, and the sale of the produce through market-trade. In fact, as Salisbury (1966) has demonstrated, the amounts yielded by such trade are paltry compared to the sums required to stage the major ceremonies known as *balaguan*. How then are these latter ends achieved? The answer is that *tambu* is not merely to be saved, it is to be worked with.

We touch here on the role of the entrepreneur who, as recent analyses make clear (for example, Epstein, T. S., 1964; Salisbury, 1966, 1970), is at once a financial and a political figure. The entrepreneur here makes his mark by his capacity to persuade others that because of his organizing skills and trustworthiness they should co-operate with him in some enterprise. Once successfully launched in this way, he may eventually graduate to the point where he can contemplate more ambitious ventures, such as acquiring a *tubuan* of his own and sponsoring the ceremonies associated with "raising" it. These ceremonies have a profound religious significance, yet Salisbury (1970, pp. 301–304) has shown in detail how it is possible to discuss *tubuan*-ownership as a business. And, indeed, it was in precisely these terms that my own informants at Matupit referred to it: "raising" the *tubuan*, they would say, was an activity that involved a heavy outlay of shell-money, but one from which in due course the sponsor could hope for a profitable return. At the same time it was in organizing these and other major ceremonies that one also staked out a claim to be recognized as a leader. The ceremonial ground was pre-eminently the domain of the big-man, the arena in which he sought to assert his dominance. A successful *balaguan* is an immense source of prestige; but more, it is the means of converting prestige into power through the deployment and distribution of *tambu*. The giving away of wealth is a most notable feature of these occasions, and is accompanied by tremendous excitement. Salisbury describes how, for each dance, a roll or coil of *tambu* is taken from storage and publicly cut before lengths *(pidik)* are thrust into the hands of each dancer. Giving, indeed, is the order of the day and it "reaches frenzied proportions in the evening as the dances finish" (1966, p. 121).

Power lies in the gift *(a tinabar* or *di tabar)* because it imposes an obligation on the recipient to make return in due course and because, by the same token, it represents a challenge. Hence at a *matamatam*, to cite Salisbury's account again, "normal Tolai penny-pinching is in complete abeyance" (1966, p. 121). "Any important man seizes the opportunity to *tabar* all and sundry, but especially other important men. He throws a fathom or so at the feet of a friend/rival, and his followers hurl *pidik*s onto the pile for the recipient to gather up. The latter then seeks out another friend/rival to *tabar*, and waits for the next *matamatam*, when he will reciprocate *(bali)* the gift he has received." (ibid.) Nowhere does the close association between command of wealth in *tambu* and political authority emerge so clearly as in these ceremonies, and nowhere is the point more clearly demonstrated than in a comparison of the two communities of Vunamami and Matupit. For the former area, Salisbury records twenty-six *matamatam* in the period 1937–62. Nine of these were initiated by three individuals who held the highest political office in the area during this time. The remainder were given by a number of Village Councillors and others who were, or who became, clan heads *(lualua)*. At Vunamami the big-man has remained a familiar figure. By contrast, many years have now elapsed at Matupit since the last major ceremony was staged there. Partly because of their involvement in wage-labour partly for other reasons, the Matupi have become paupers so far as *tambu* is concerned. This is not to say that they have abandoned the pursuit of shell-money. On the contrary, as I shall discuss in a later section, many continue to skimp and save in order to raise the bride-wealth, to obtain certain foodstuffs such as taro from inland communities who insist on payment in *tambu*, or to purchase the canoes without which they cannot easily reach their gardens. But they lack the resources to pursue the ceremonial life in any but a skeletal form. In these circumstances, matrilineage elders may continue to play a role, while at the same time new kinds of leaders emerge, but there can be no more big-men cast in the traditional mould (see Epstein, A. L., 1969, pp. 241–245).

At this point, having set out with minimal comment a certain amount of ethnographic data relating to shell-money, it may be useful to try and draw the threads of discussion together in a preliminary way. I began by asking what there was about shell-money that led to its verbal association with the category *tambu* (taboo). We are now in a position to move part of the way towards an answer. We have seen that traditionally *tambu* was intimately bound up with views about the afterlife. In this connection Winthuis (1926, p. 8) comments that for the Tolai *tambu* is not just ordinary money, but rather "divine" (*Gottesgeld*). Some of my oldest Matupi informants sometimes spoke in a similar vein. *Tambu*, they would say, was our God; it gave us life (*tambu a kalou kamavet; i ga valaun avet*).[1] Yet, as we have seen, while the conscious rationale has almost entirely disappeared, since almost every Tolai today belongs to one or other Christian congregation, the pursuit of *tambu* continues unabated. So let us approach the matter first from a sociological perspective.

Traditional Tolai society was what we now term a "stateless" society; it lacked any centralized organs of authority. The various local communities who now speak of themselves as Tolai shared a common tongue, as well as many customs and institutions, but they guarded their independence jealously and none regarded itself as subordinate to another. However, they were also linked in overlapping and intricately criss-crossing networks forged by ties of marriage and reinforced by participation in joint ceremonies organized and spon-

[1] *Kalou* is a Fijian word introduced by the first evangelists and subsequently adopted by the European missionaries as the word for God. *Valaun* means literally to cause life, hence also to save. The expression *a tena valaun* is heard most frequently with reference to Christ the Saviour.

sored by ambitious big-men. In all of these activities, as indeed in the defining of any new social relationship, *tambu* was a *sine qua non*. At the same time, no society exists in the present only; it has to have the means to define relationships between the generations. Among the Tolai land provides an important link of continuity. Land is held to vest in the *vunatarai*, a descent group whose living members enjoy it during their lifetime, holding it on trust from their matrilineal ancestors for future members still unborn. It is in celebration of the dead of the *vunatarai* that the ceremonies of the *tubuan* and *matamatam* are held. From one point of view then *tambu* emerges as the lynch-pin of the social system, the crucial mechanism defining and maintaining the bonds between various social groups as well as providing the nexus between the realm of the living and the realm of the dead. From another point of view, it is possible to speak of *tambu* as lying at the heart of the traditional Tolai system of values, the central component in their conception of the moral order. In either case, if we adopt the Durkheimian view that the origins of religion lie in the apotheosis of society itself, then, in the Tolai context, what could be a more appropriate symbol of the sacred than *tambu*?

Unfortunately, the matter is not quite so easily disposed of, for too many questions are still left unanswered. Radcliffe-Brown (1952, p. 134) has noted the ambiguity of the Polynesian term *tabu* (or *tapu*) from which the anthropological usage taboo derives. On the one hand it can be applied to any sort of prohibition; on the other, it refers specifically to what Radcliffe-Brown calls ritual avoidances, violations of which are likely to be attended by mystical dangers. In precisely the same way, the Tolai word *tambu* covers not only simple interdictions, but also more complex situations. Thus the casual visitor around Rabaul will frequently come across signs bearing the words *"I tambu"*, meaning simply "Keep off this property"– and this is fully in accord with Tolai usage. Again, many Tolai-owned village stores prominently display a notice *"I tambu ra dinau"* advising customers that credit is not allowed. However, the same term *tambu* is also used to refer, for example, to the prohibition on the husband of a pregnant woman approaching the beach where his fellows are engaged in seine-fishing. In this last case, it is said, violation of the taboo would affect the behaviour of the fish, and the catch would be lost. It is difficult at first sight to see what these three situations have in common beyond the fact that in each instance there is something that is forbidden. Closer analysis, however, shows that they rest upon a more complex underlying idea: all exemplify the concept that taboo serves as a pointer to boundaries that should not be crossed. In its most elementary form, as in the first case, *tambu* means simply "Don't trespass". In the second it is a reminder to customers not to introduce considerations of kinship, neighbourliness or friendship into what should be strictly a commercial transaction; quite different sets of social relationships are involved here and they should be kept quite distinct if trouble is to be avoided and good relations preserved. The same point emerges no less clearly in the third example. Here the taboo expresses on the symbolic plane a relationship between categories which have been brought into association through some common property – in this instance pregnant women and bonito fish *(a tun)* are said to be heavy with blood – but which properly belong to different compartments within the conceptual system; if they are brought into conjunction there is a confusion of categories from which certain harmful consequences can be expected to follow. In all of these situations the use of the term *tambu*/taboo at once expresses or points to some latent source of conflict and provides the means for avoiding or resolving it.

Adopting this perspective, what is of immediate interest is that if one scrutinizes carefully the data relating to shell-money one becomes increasingly conscious of a number of seeming discrepancies and contradictions within the *tambu*-complex as a whole, that shell-money itself is a focal point of conflict. For example, in their everyday life Tolai give the impression of being quite pragmatic in regard to their use of shell-money; if one's observations were confined to the market-place one might conclude that they used it simply as a form of currency. In fact the most casual inquiry would quickly reveal a more compulsive interest in it, that it is invested with a degree of affect that would be quite out of keeping with its function simply as a medium of exchange – *tambu*, one soon discovers, is not to be parted with lightly, even if it is only a matter of making a purchase; as far as possible it should be saved.[1] Then again, we are told by Danks (1887, p. 308)

[1]My wife learned this lesson very early in her fieldwork. Discovering that certain items could be acquired for either cash or *tambu*, and that there was no parity of purchasing power between the two currencies (see further, p. 193ff.), she once sought to purchase a chicken with shell-money she had already managed to acquire, which seemed to her the better bargain. She was at once severely admonished by her Tolai companion, who proceeded to give her a lengthy lecture on the proper use of *tambu*; she should have made her purchase with cash, and saved her shell-money.

that children were taught, almost as soon as they could understand anything, that the acquisition and retention of wealth was an important, if not the most important, duty of life, yet its central purpose was directed towards the celebration of death. It is indeed in contexts relating to death that the emotional intensity that surrounds *tambu* is most closely to be observed. Most of the major *balaguan* are mortuary rites of one kind or another, and in their performance we discover the curious pattern of alternation so characteristic of behaviour in regard to shell-money, a sharp oscillation between clinging on the one hand, and lavish, even abandoned, giving on the other. Yet even on these occasions the giving is not done without evidence of conflict: those who "cut" the coils of shell-money prior to its distribution arm themselves with a magical device *(a vaimkor)* to ensure that the entire coil is not given away, and some of the wealth of its owner is saved. Finally, we may notice that if *tambu* serves as an appropriate symbol of solidarity, it is no less a symbol of individual and group pride and assertiveness, as evidenced in our earlier reference to behaviour in the context of a *matamatam*.

All of these seeming contradictions are contained within the symbolism of *tambu*; in a sense, indeed, they are cloaked by it. Viewed as a symbol, shell-money serves as a pointer to various conflicts within the Tolai system of values, some of which I hope the ongoing discussion can help to illuminate. Behind these, and congruent with them, are other kinds of conflict of an intrapsychic character. My point of departure here is the view of the symbol offered by psychoanalytic theory, according to which the power of the symbol derives from the fact that it is rooted in the unconscious. Like the symptom, the symbol represents a compromise-formation, the outcome of a struggle between impulse and repressing forces. I want to suggest that, in its symbolic aspects, *tambu* represents a formation of this kind in the sense defined by Ferenczi (1913), that is, it owes its affective overemphasis to unconscious identification with some other thing (or idea) which has been repressed and to which the surplus of affect really belongs. In adopting this approach I hope in the remainder of this essay to be able to clarify certain features of the *tambu*-complex as well as to reveal threads of connection with other aspects of Tolai ideology and behaviour not hitherto remarked.

Tambu and anal erotism

As it happens, mine is not the first attempt to examine Tolai shell-money making use of psychoanalytic insights, for Géza Róheim, so far as I am aware the first to combine the practice of psychoanalysis and anthropology, considered it many years ago in his paper *Heiliges Geld in Melanesien* (1923).[1] Róheim raised there, and sought to answer, a number of the questions with which I too am concerned, and to some of these I will return in due course. In general, however, the paper appears to me to illustrate well a dictum of Freud (1918, p. 97) that it is a methodological error to seize on a phylogenetic explanation before the ontogenetic possibilities have been exhausted. In this instance Róheim's concern with *tambu* was to trace the phylogeny of money, that is, to seek its psychic origins as a universal institution. A number of questionable assumptions underlie this particular approach, some of which have been noted by other psychoanalysts and will be considered again later; for immediate purposes its major defect is that it leads Róheim to ignore many of the particularistic features of shell-money, how these are interconnected to form a coherent system or complex, and how this complex in turn contributes to the Tolai ethos. To this end I find it more profitable to begin with the classical exposition of the concept of anal erotism.

This concept has to be understood in the context of Freud's theory of infantile sexual development. Sexuality, he holds, is not an eruption which suddenly makes its presence felt with the onset of puberty; it is seen rather as developing in a sequence of epigenetic stages, in the infantile phase each stage being associated with a particular zone of gratification: the mouth, the anus, and then the genitals. Each stage affects the way in which succeeding ones are experienced, and in turn contributes in varying ways to the pattern of adult sexuality eventually achieved. Psychoanalytic attention was early drawn to the importance of the anal region, not simply because of the interest that infants display in their faeces but because the excitation of the anal canal was seen to be a source of pleasurable sensation; in a word, the zone was libidinized. The infantile interest itself takes a number of different, though closely interconnected, forms: the endeavour to derive as much pleasure from the act of defecation as possible; the effort to exercise one's individual control over the act; and fascination with the product itself. These experiences of pleasure, however, are repressed very early in life, and the original impulse is deflected into

[1] The paper does not appear to have come to the attention of anthropologists. At any rate, it is not listed in the two standard bibliographies of the area, Taylor (1965) and *An Ethnographic Bibliography of New Guinea* (1968).

other directions through the mechanisms of reaction-formation and sublimation. In the case of adult individuals psychoanalysis has frequently been able to show how distinctive character traits can be traced back to their origins in unresolved conflicts centred on the anal zone (for example, Jones, 1918; Abraham, 1921).

What has all this got to do with *tambu*? For answer we may refer briefly to Erikson's concept of the organ mode. The child's earliest encounters with his environment are mediated through the organs of the body; depending on the stage of psychic and motor development, each of the erogenous zones becomes in turn the focus of a mode of approach that gradually becomes generalized. Thus, from this point of view, for example, the anal-urethral sphincters are the anatomic models for the retentive and eliminative modes, prototypes of a great variety of behavioural forms (Erikson, 1963, p. 52). For the child the act of defecation is a yielding of part of himself, and the infantile experience of that act, and the wishes and fantasies which accompany or are woven around it, may come to colour his reactions to subsequent situations that appear to involve giving or retaining. It is in this way that, as Freud (1918, p. 72) has observed, "one of the most important manifestations of the transformed erotism derived from this source [that is, the anal stage] is to be found in the treatment of money, for in the course of life this precious material attracts on to itself the psychical interest which was originally proper to faeces, the product of the anal zone."

In a paper of particular interest in the present context Ferenczi (1914) has traced the steps by which the child passes from the original idea of excrement to the seemingly remote one of money, and shows how that which is so often regarded with distaste comes to be symbolically associated with what is most treasured. At first the infant finds great satisfaction in playing with his faeces. This soon becomes disagreeable because of the smell, but the original interest is still revealed in the pleasure found in making mud-pies. A further development occurs when substances which, because of their stickiness, moistness and colour are apt to leave traces on the body and clothing, become despised and avoided as "dirty things". The symbol is dehydrated, and the child's interest turns to sand, a substance which while the colour of earth, is cleaner and dry. Sand in turn is replaced by more acceptable substances which lack odour but are dry and hard: pebbles, stones and then marbles or buttons, which are not only collected but are used in childish exchanges. The transformation is complete when the original interest comes to focus on money: "an odourless, dehydrated filth that has been made to shine" (Ferenczi, 1914, p. 276).

Ferenczi's paper offers a number of suggestive leads into a discussion of the symbolism of *tambu*. The shells themselves used to be gathered in Blanche Bay but, it will be recalled, the main source for many years has been Nakanai on north New Britain. There the shells are collected by wading in the shallow waters at various points along the coast. There is then an immediate association of *tambu* with mud.[1] This at once serves to remind us of Brown's observation that when originally fished the shells have a dull brown colour and only acquire value as *tambu* when they have become bleached. It is also of interest to note that the childish practices and games referred to by Ferenzci are also a source of pleasure among Tolai children. In a game played by very small boys, called *a varpo*, one of the boys makes a number of little heaps of sand in which he hides something, as a seed, which the others then have to find. There is another game, called *a pip*,[2] of which Powell (1883, p. 184) has given an early account. Here the participants mould in their hands small oval cakes of sand which they throw into the air so as to land in the water. The point of the game is to see who can throw most cakes into the water without breaking apart; if they drop whole into the water they do so with a hollow sound and gain the thrower a score. Powell also mentions that he often saw grown men and women playing the game for hours on end. Children have also been observed making "toy" *tambu* from shells which they use in play among themselves, according to Romilly (1886, p. 25) driving as hard bargains with each other as their fathers would do with the genuine article. At the same time it should perhaps be mentioned that children are introduced to the uses of *tambu* at a very early age and in my own experience if children were present on the occasion of a distribution of shell-money they would be included among the recipients.

It is in dreams, fantasies and myths that symbolic equations or identifications are most readily detected. Unfortunately, not suffi-

[1] Although I did not hear the word used in this particular context, it may be worth noting that the adjective *pipia* which means sandy, as of the sea bottom, also means dirty. The same term is also used as a noun meaning rubbish or refuse.

[2] *A pip* also means a heap or mound. I am unable to say if there is an etymological link with the word *pipia* mentioned in footnote 1, above, or with another word *pipi* discussed in footnote 2, p. 173.

ciently alive to the issues at the time, I did not collect a great deal of material of this kind. However, the Tolai traditionally enjoyed a rich oral literature, a good deal of which has been collected by Meier (1909) and Kleintitschen (1924). One myth recorded by Meier, and cited by Róheim (1923, p. 399), is of particular interest because it relates to the origins of *tambu*. It tells of a small boy who once asked his parents for food. They replied: "Go and eat your own excrement and that of the other children with whom you play." Deeply offended, the child left. He took off on a journey carried on the back of a talking tree-trunk. At length they came to a foreign land where a hen was hopping on the beach. The hen asked the tree-trunk where the boy came from, to which the trunk replied that he hankered for the ejecta (*auswurf*) of the sea in Nakanai. Then, with thirty baskets filled with shell-money, they returned to the boy's home. The death platform and sacrifice had already been prepared. The huge expenditure of shell-money had impoverished the parents, but the lad was able to repay them and became rich. Since then, it is said, "We all yearn for the ejecta of the sea at Nakanai".

Our task, however, is not simply to establish a particular symbolic identification, but to understand it. Following psychoanalytic theory, where behaviour in regard to money shows strong emotional overtones it usually suggests that money has come to serve as a private copro-symbol, pointing in turn to the likelihood of contradictory attitudes in regard to the act of defecation. The theory indeed indicates a number of sources of conflict surrounding the act. There is, in the first place, the problem of balancing the pleasure of retention as against the pleasure of elimination. Linked with this is the effort to retain control over the act as against requirements to yield demanded endogenously or from the outside. Control here is associated with the development of the sphincters, as well as the general muscle system, giving the child, as Erikson (1963, p. 82) puts it, greater power over the environment in the ability to reach out and hold on, to throw away and to push away, to appropriate things and to keep them at a distance. There is, then, in the act of defecation a sense of achievement, a form of gratification that reinforces the child's narcissism, his pride in his own powers. By the same token, it is this very sense of achievement that is likely to bring the child into conflict with his environment – interference is apt to be met by fierce resentment, if not violent rage. Thus the act of defecation becomes the focus of a struggle for autonomy, ushering in the stage of anal sadism. Faeces, the product of the act, now become an expression of power, which may be used productively or destructively; displaced on to copro-symbols, these may be manipulated creatively or serve as instruments of hostile aggression.

A number of the best-known discussions of anal erotism in the psychoanalytic literature (for example, Freud, 1908; Jones, 1918; Abraham, 1921; Menninger, 1943) have taken as their central theme the importance of the anal zone for character formation. Although my own concern here is not with delineating the dimensions of Tolai personality – a task in any case it would be absurd to undertake by focusing simply on one stage of libidinal development – it may nevertheless be instructive to follow up a few of these leads. It was Freud who first drew attention to the regular combination of a number of character traits displayed by many of his patients, all of which appeared to belong together and to be linked to anal erotism: the analysands were especially orderly, parsimonious and obstinate. In considering this now classical triad of traits in the Tolai context, it is convenient to begin with parsimony, a caution in the use of one's products or possessions that readily shades over into miserliness. Among the Tolai, as we have seen, the retentive impulse is especially marked. "No man is held in greater contempt than a spendthrift . . ." "To let money go for nothing in return or to pay a shell more than is necessary for an article is considered the height of folly." (Danks, 1887, pp. 315, 308.) Even today there are still many individuals who maintain special houses or rooms where their accumulated wealth in shell-money is stored; to be invited to inspect the wealth, usually a matter to be kept secret, counts as a great privilege; to enter the *pal na vuvuvung* is to be reminded of the treasure-house of Midas.

A tendency towards miserliness is said to be essentially characteristic of the aged. I was present at the hearing on Matupit of one very bitter and protracted dispute between an old crone and her grown-up grandchildren. The dispute erupted because, the latter claimed, they had been "driven away" by their grandmother who had spoken harsh things of their deceased parents, and was clearly unwilling to contribute shell-money for the "purchase" of brides for her grandsons. After the hearing, which was brought to an inconclusive halt by an outburst of hysterical sobbing throughout the audience, one man explained to me that everyone knew the grandmother as an angry old woman who was always scolding those who went near her coconut trees. Another added that she was a *tamuk* or a *lagodo*, a grasping greedy woman who, as she approached death, was anxious to keep all her *tambu* to herself.

This is an extreme case, but it helps to illustrate how fine can be the line that separates parsimony, which is socially approved, from stinginess, which is socially condemned. The Tolai resolve this potential source of conflict by allowing the retentive impulse full play, but insisting at the same time that at some point it should be matched by an act of giving. As Salisbury (1970, p. 279) remarks of the process of making shell-money up into a coil – an act which removes it from circulation – it implies a promise that the coiler will eventually freely donate his *tambu* to all and sundry. In psychological terms what this means is that the primary injury to narcissism suffered by having to yield one's faeces is compensated for by expressions of approval accorded to the act of giving: one gives as an act of love and in return for love. In sociological terms, too, social approbation is given in fullest measure to him that gives most lavishly; giving, indeed, is the act around which the whole social system revolves. That both psychological and sociological processes are equally involved, that they reinforce one another, and that they have to be taken equally into account is, I believe, shown very clearly in the culturally defined attitude towards niggardliness. Tolai values in this regard have been well stated by Brown (1910, p. 252):

> Niggardliness, especially with regard to food, is always wrong. A man of good conduct must make plenty of feasts; he must buy dances both for his own benefit and for the pleasure of the people; he must be loving to his friends; he must look well after his children, and he must be a good fighter. A bad man is a stingy man, one who takes no interest in his children, is quarrelsome, one who speaks evil of others, and one who kills another without cause.

Now what is of particular interest here is the fate of the niggardly in the afterlife. In general, ideas about conditions in the Abode of the Dead are extremely hazy, save in one notable regard – the treatment of the niggardly. Brown (1910, p. 195) comments: "So far as I could gather, the punishment for this was the only kind of which they seemed definitely assured." Niggardly people had their ears filled with filth, and their buttocks were dashed against the buttress roots of a chestnut tree. In another context Brown (1910, p. 399) expresses puzzlement why the buttocks are selected as the most suitable part for punishment. I do not know what symbolic significance attaches to the chestnut tree;[1] nor can one be certain that the symbolism of afflicting the buttocks has not been overdetermined. Nevertheless, in terms of the preceding analysis, one meaning that can be reasonably inferred seems fairly patent: in his mortal life the victim had refused to part with his faeces (his possessions); now, to adopt the common vulgarism, they were beating the shit out of him.[2]

A second set of traits which derive by way of a reaction-formation from anal erotism relates to orderliness and cleanliness. Early observers on the Gazelle Peninsula were struck by these characteristics, all the more so perhaps because in so many other respects the Tolai appeared so irredeemably savage. Villages were made up of clusters of tiny fenced-off hamlets, each occupied by a small domestic group. Brown (1910, pp. 23–24) remarks that the interior of these compounds was kept scrupulously clean, while outside evidence of taste and appreciation of the beautiful was revealed in the planting of dracaenas, crotons, and coleus plants of the brightest colours.

Similarly, according to Powell (1883, p. 252), the strictest sanitary laws prevailed, all offal being removed by the women and either thrown into the sea or, if in the bush, buried some distance away. Yet it is clear that behind this behaviour there also lay considerations that have little in common with modern notions of hygiene. I refer here to the concept of *puta*, ejecta; excreta, nail clippings, the shell of an areca nut which one has thrown away and so on, should they fall into the hands of another, immediately leave one open to attack by sorcery. Sorcery, however, is not simply an expression of individual malevo-

[1] Danks (1909, p. 454) has recorded similar ideas, but he specifies the tree as a banyan (*a giau*). This tree, unlike the chestnut, is very rich in symbolic associations. In particular, it is regarded with great fear as a source of illness and death. The afflicting of the buttocks is also referred to by Parkinson (1907, p. 79).

[2] In daily life the observer is likely to gain the impression that Tolai are rather indulgent of their children and that they do not impose strict discipline. This impression was confirmed at a number of village meetings on Matupit when the question of upbringing of children was discussed; on these occasions various speakers referred to the need for firmer control. Nevertheless, it would be wrong to assume that children are never chastised. On one occasion I observed a young father switching his five-year-old daughter across the buttocks when she threw a temper tantrum, while nearby an old man expressed his approval. I have also seen the mother of a very small babe instructing it in what it might and might not touch by lightly switching the buttocks with the leaves of a plant lying to hand. The act of switching is referred to as *pipi* (*di pipia*). Although I cannot be sure whether it has any significance, it may be worth mentioning that *pipi* is also the word for lightning. In the traditional belief, a flash of lightning was said to mark the entry of a recently deceased person into the *matana kaia*, the Abode of the Dead.

lence; the capacity to control anti-human magic was also seen as an important attribute of traditional Tolai big-men. Before taking up, then, the broader theme of aggressive behaviour, of which sorcery is but one aspect, and the relevance of anality to it, it is necessary to take a closer look at the nature of power in Tolai society, its connection with wealth, and the ambivalence that attaches to its use both at the sociological and psychological levels.

I have mentioned earlier the impression made on Danks by Tolai frugality and industry, the way they devoted their energies to productive activities that would yield wealth in *tambu*. In this regard Tolai ideology has remained unchanged, and encouragement to work hard and produce new wealth by planting coconuts or cocoa trees is still a constant theme of elders' speeches at village assemblies. What Danks did not fully grasp, however, was the nature of the connection between wealth and power. That there is a close link is immediately suggested by the expressions that Tolai elders use when they are exhorting the young men to greater efforts: *ongor* or *dekdek*. These terms can be translated as "work hard", but more usually they refer to power or strength. Sometimes the connection emerges even more explicitly. Once, for example, an elder at Matupit was delivering one of these harangues, urging the people to labour more intensively in order to raise their living standards. At this point he referred to the position of the small, immigrant Chinese community. "In our day", he said, "we have seen the Chinese grow wealthy. They live well with their wealth. We too should be strong (should work hard) so that it is we who rule them, not they who rule us." Here, as in more purely indigenous contexts, the underlying idea is clear: hard work improves one's standard of living, but even more important, to produce wealth is the guarantee of one's autonomy, enabling one to proclaim that he is beholden to no man. Associated with this attitude are a number of behavioural characteristics commonly noted of the Tolai: self-willedness, obduracy, assertiveness, ambition and pride, all adding up to an aggressive individualism.

All of these qualities are socially esteemed and they are most frequently exemplified in the person of the big-man. Traditionally, as we saw earlier, the big-man was essentially an entrepreneur who converted command of wealth in shell-money into political power. His contemporary counterpart engages in more varied business enterprises of a modern kind, but in terms of temperament, modes of operation and goals there is remarkable continuity. Scarlett Epstein (1964) has provided an account of ToDugan, a prominent figure in the inland community of Rapitok, who is also fairly representative of the Tolai big-man of today. ToDugan conveys the impression of a restless man of seemingly unbounded energy whose every moment appears to be dedicated to the sole task of building up his various businesses and making money. The owner of a large truck and a copra-drier, as well as many cocoa trees, he puts the profits of each enterprise to work to finance the latest scheme he has conceived that will further increase his wealth. Yet all of this has been accomplished without any sacrifice of his "traditional" interests. On the contrary, ToDugan has remained as avid in the pursuit of *tambu* as he is of cash and, as a man who aspires to be regarded as a local leader, he has been an ardent sponsor of a number of major ceremonies. That he enjoys indeed a powerful position within the village is immediately evident. For, despite the fact that his multifarious interests and activities keep him constantly on the move and involve his frequent absence from home, few major decisions affecting the local community are likely to be reached without being referred to him. Routine matters of village government could be left to others; there was little doubt who the real big-man was.

Yet there is another side to all this. For there is an inherent contradiction within a social system that, on the one hand, encourages the emergence of big-men and, on the other, endorses an egalitarian ideology. Salisbury (1970, p. 287) has argued that a Tolai variant of the Horatio Alger myth serves to cloak the conflict; the way of advancement is open to every Tolai provided that he works hard and accumulates *tambu.* This is fine so far as it goes, but it does not get to grips with the problem of aggression. For if social value attaches to personal assertiveness and aggrandizement, we must also expect a high level of competitiveness and belligerency. Two examples here may serve to illustrate the conflict of values. The first relates to the handling of anger, *a kankan*, the second to envy or covetousness, *a varngu*.

In their interpersonal relations Tolai can be warm and friendly, but they also tend to be prickly and quick to take offence. Older people in particular can be highly sensitive to slight, real or imaginary, and are given to outbursts of anger. The term *a tena kankan* is used disapprovingly of those individuals who are known for their irascibility and hot temper. On the other hand, it is said, if one is annoyed with another one should speak out, purge one's anger, for in wrath stored up *(a kankan ivai)* are the seeds of sorcery and death. Frequently in speaking of their forefathers, the *ngalangala* or great ones of the past, Matupi would refer to them as *aumana tena kankan*, men of fierce disposition who were quick to anger. But the ambivalence conveyed on these occasions was unmistakable. On the one hand, the expression put a distance between themselves and their ancestors by contrasting their own mildness and reasonableness with the latter's ferocity. What was no less clear was the admiration that tinged their remarks, for that anger was also a mark as well as a source of their power. The big-men of the past are recalled not only for their lavish generosity and the great ceremonies they sponsored, but also as men who inspired fear, in particular the fear of sorcery.

We find a similar picture in regard to envy. Tolai themselves do not always appear to distinguish carefully between the concepts of jealousy and envy. Thus the expression *a varngu* may sometimes be used in a situation of sexual jealousy, but the contexts in which I most commonly heard it rarely involved reference to women. Rather they were situations in which envy was generated by another's enterprise and prospective success.[1] Thus, one case that I recorded at Matupit was overtly a dispute over land, but it was soon transparent to many of those present at the hearing that it was an attempt, inspired by covetousness, by two older men to prevent a younger one from putting up a new store on a site that promised the development of a lucrative business. Afterwards one of my Matupi friends commented: "Such are our ways [*kaveve mangamangana damana*] . . . It's just the same with cocoa. A man plants cocoa and when you see that his plants are beginning to bear fruit you step in and claim that he has planted on your land. It is the spitefulness of the people [*a varngu kai ra tatrai*]." Suspicion *(a vartakun)* is the handmaiden of envy and jealousy, and while it is generally rife in everyday life it is on the occasion of death that it becomes most evident. Despite their long exposure to Western ideas, the Tolai still find difficulty in assimilating the concept of death through natural causes. Today on Matupit the immediate explanation of a death is likely to be a naturalistic one, but

[1] For some discussion of the distinction between the concepts of jealousy and envy see Klein (1957). She defines envy as the angry feeling that another person possesses and enjoys something desirable – the envious impulse being to take it away or to spoil it.

rarely is there a lengthy passage of time before the first murmurings of sorcery are heard, and the "real" causes of death are sought in the machinations of some envious rival. Yet what is so striking in these cases is that it is precisely those qualities which inspire envy and jealousy that are also the most admired, and which successful big-men are said to embody.

Tolai do not appear to be consciously aware of these various conflicts in their system of values. On the other hand, their culture does provide them, I believe, with an unconscious model by reference to which the contradictions are resolved on the plane of symbolism. In Tolai mythology there is a whole series of tales relating to two brothers, the culture heroes ToKabinana and ToKarvuvu. ToKabinana is recalled as having introduced everything good and useful, the founder of every art and craft; he is the personification of wisdom and cleverness. ToKarvuvu, by contrast, is credited with all the barren and stony land and everything evil, hurtful, ugly or ill-formed. ToKabinana, that is to say, uses his energies creatively, he is the prototype of the man who works productively, so that if one has performed a task particularly well it will be said of him: "ToKabinana did [or made] it." ToKarvuvu, on the other hand, cannot undertake a job without bungling it, or worse, bringing utter disaster in his wake. Thus the two brothers may be seen as representing the two faces of aggression, the one associated with life-enhancing qualities, the other with destruction and death. In reality of course the creative and destructive aspects of aggression are so intricately interwoven as to be inseparable. From this point of view ToKarvuvu appears simply as the *alter ego* of his brother. The myth faces the problem, and resolves it, by making use of a simple "splitting-mechanism".

The use of myth as an unconscious folk model is illuminating, but I do not believe that the task of the anthropologist finishes at this point. It is also important to ask why the indigenous model takes the form that it does. In the present instance I believe that we can make some progress in this direction with the help of certain psychoanalytic insights. Thus one might say, in psychoanalytic terms, that ToKabinana represents a man who has sublimated his anal erotism and become a mature artist, whereas ToKarvuvu still "smears"; in the latter's efforts, that is to say, the original impulse is still direct and undisguised (see Fenichel, 1946, p. 153). This view receives some support from other comments I recorded about the two brothers.

ToKabinana, I have remarked, was the wise one. Before he spoke and acted he considered the matter. By contrast, ToKarvuvu was a man of quick temper, easily roused, who ranted and stormed first and only asked questions afterwards. For the Tolai, as I have said, ToKarvuvu represents man's capacity for destruction, and it is to him that responsibility for introducing death is attributed, but what is especially interesting is the way in which this capacity is consistently perceived in anal terms.[1]

A view of faeces as an instrument of hostile aggression emerges in a variety of contexts. It receives its most open and direct expression in verbal abuse. In disputes, or when tempers are roused, people will curse one another shouting *u a taka* (you shit), *una peke* (you will excrete), *i ang ra bitim* (your anus stinks) and many other expressions of a similar kind. One of the most abusive insults of all is to call a person a *lup taka*[2] which is equivalent to accusing him of indulging in homosexual practices. Verbal abuse is frowned upon, and sometimes the guilty party will be brought before the village assembly or *varkurai* (see Epstein, A. L., 1974) and ordered to pay a sum of shell-money by way of atonement; but it is not intrinsically dangerous. Sorcery is quite another matter. Tolai doctrine and practice in regard to sorcery are much too complex for extended discussion here. The point of immediate relevance is the importance of the concept of *puta* mentioned earlier. *Puta* refers to anything which has been closely associated with one's person, which one has cast away, and which can be worked upon by the sorcerer to achieve his nefarious purposes. Excrement is the prototype of *puta*, but any kind of ejecta may serve – as I discovered when I was once cautioned against the casual throwing

[1] Or occasionally urethral, as in the following myth I recorded. One day ToKabinana said to ToKarvuvu that he should lead the people to weed the gardens. (The word for weed used here was *mimie*, to clear the ground, which in earlier days was done with a digging-stick.) So ToKarvuvu went off with the people, but when he gave them instructions on what they should do he used instead the word *mim*, which means to urinate. So, from the top of the garden to the bottom, they urinated. At last ToKabinana arrived to see how the work was progressing, but he saw no evidence of *mimie*, only of *minim*, and he upbraided ToKarvuvu for his stupidity.

[2] *Lup* refers to a particularly strong liking or propensity for something. Thus a *lup nian* is literally a lover of food, that is, a glutton. By the same token a *lup taka* is a lover of excrement. Matupi sometimes spoke as though homosexuality was wholly unknown to them in the past, and only learned of through the introduction of prisons. There is some suggestion of homosexual practices in the earlier literature discussing the *iniet*. This was a society of sorcerers which the Germans quickly extirpated, and on whose activities it is now difficult to establish anything with much certainty. The extreme distaste with which Tolai respond to any expression of homosexuality might suggest an early and severe repression; the practices mentioned below (see p. 179) may offer further evidence in support of this view.

away of a cigarette. In this context then faeces are seen as a weapon of potentially destructive power.[1]

There are other connections of a direct kind between sorcery and anal sadism. Winthuis (1926) reports that when, after a number of attempts, a sorcerer has failed to achieve his ends by the use of magic, he may resort to more plainly physical means. The victim would be assailed in some isolated spot by the sorcerer and his assistants. They would then thrust a knife into his thighs or a spear into his rectum; the spear was then broken off, leaving the head lodged in the anus. Then the man was beaten and had his throat twisted until he no longer had the use of his voice. Thus he would die shortly afterwards without being able to disclose the manner of his death, which would be attributed to someone's powerful sorcery.

Sometimes the cloacal theme appears only thinly disguised, as when a man seeks to ensorcel another by casting a *lika*, a small stone or pebble formed of volcanic waste, over his victim's house. In other cases it is concealed behind a more complex web of symbolic associations. Thus Brown (1910, p. 195) reports, for example, the alarm that was felt if one had been sitting under a tree from which a flying-fox (*a ganau*) had been disturbed. "If anything should drop from the bat or from the tree on which it was hanging, it would be regarded as an omen either of good or bad fortune, according to the nature of the article which fell upon or near him. If it were useless or dirty, he would certainly apprehend some very serious results." These curious ideas become more explicable when related to others that are held about the flying-fox. Because the *ganau* inhabits caves and becomes active only at night, it is held to have close connections with the spirits of the dead. In particular, those who died without wealth in *tambu*, instead of being admitted to the *matana kaia*, might be left to take up their abode in a flying-fox. According to Danks (1909, p. 454), should this creature be disturbed during the day and fly across country, the people are full of fear until it settles somewhere; should it happen to do so on a tree overhanging a village, that village is greatly perturbed,

[1] It follows from this that the act of defecation is attended by a good deal of secrecy. The privacy of the act ensures that one is undisturbed, but even more that no evildoer will discover and thus be able to make use of one's faeces. One of the village sections on the island of Matupit is called Kilingalingen. This means literally to sit casting one's eyes back over one's shoulder. The section acquired its name because, before people started to build their houses there, it had been an area of bush which was sometimes used for purposes of defecation. But because it was also a somewhat exposed spot, they had to squat casting their eyes around against the presence of intruders.

especially if the villagers had recently taken part in killing and eating a person. In this instance the droppings of the *ganau* clearly represent the means by which the dead exact their vengeance.

Beliefs about sorcery or ideas held about such creatures as the flying-fox afford us a fleeting glimpse of the Tolai world of projective fantasy. To trace the structure of that world would be a major undertaking in itself, and one which may no longer be possible. For present purposes, however, it is enough to remark that for the most part it is the habitat of a bewildering variety of creatures or spirits, usually referred to collectively as *tambaran* or *kaia*. Sometimes these are perceived in human form, though with certain clearly distinguishable features, like the *tutana vurakit* which has four sharp instruments like nails in its mouth instead of teeth and so lacks the power of speech; sometimes they are envisaged as creatures of the most grotesque and bizarre kinds. Invariably they are malevolent and always to be feared as a source of danger and death. There is evidently a deep and pervasive fear of death which is associated (unconsciously) with both oral and anal aggression. There is at the same time, on the conscious or cultural level, a similar preoccupation with death, but phrased, as it were, in positive rather than negative terms: death remains a fearful thing, yet much of one's life is devoted to preparation for it by working towards the accumulation of *tambu*. What then is the relationship between these contrasting attitudes and behavioural patterns? More particularly, why is shell-money so intimately associated with death? It is to these questions that we must now turn.

Tambu and death

The question of the close relationship of shell-money to the cult of the dead was one of those to which Róheim (1923) chiefly addressed himself. Briefly, he found the answer in the drama of the primordial parricide; funerary rites, he argued, have their origins in the identification of the sons with the dead father to whom they offer by way of atonement their anal products (originally excrement, later money) in return for oral gratification (the body of the mother, that is, food). Róheim's fuller analysis offers a number of interesting suggestions, but his phylogenetic and pseudo-historic approach leads him to take little account of the riches of the ethnographic data, and away from any attempt to trace out their ramifications, psychological and sociological, for any particular social group. Just as the first responsibility of the psychoanalyst is to the primary, and in a sense unique, data produced by his patient, so the first responsibility of the anthropologist is towards the ethnographic material.

What is so striking about the Tolai in this regard is the special importance they attach to death and the central position it occupies in their culture. From one point of view of course death is a simple datum of existence; in the words of the Talmud, "for all creatures, death has been prepared from the beginning". Mortality therefore is something with which individuals and groups alike are all compelled to come to grips, to which they must seek to define a relationship. Hence, despite the universality of death, the responses and solutions arrived at by different peoples are often highly variable. The Matupi, for example, used sometimes to contrast their own attitudes towards death with those of the Japanese with which they had acquired some familiarity in the days of the Second World War. A Japanese, it was said, preferred death to the experience of pain. For themselves it was otherwise; death was what they feared above all. Aware of this geneal attitude, I was particularly interested to observe Tolai reactions one day when they were preparing a grave. The soil at Matupit is of volcanic origin and, having little to bind it, collapses readily. On this occasion one side of the grave suddenly fell in, exposing part of a skull. Somewhat to my surprise, this produced no marked reaction save to draw my attention to it in the most pragmatic way. I was made to realize that it was not so much the physical fact of death which is the source of fear as the ideas and fantasies that are woven around it.[1] In the absence of more direct evidence, these are best approached through those social contexts in which they chiefly find expression – funerary and mortuary rites.

As in other societies, the scale of the funerary ceremonies was a function of the social status of the deceased, and the most elaborate rites were for those who had achieved wealth and prominence in the community. A death was announced by the beating of the *garamut*, the slitgong drum whose origins are attributed to ToKarvuvu, and a wild

[1] A somewhat similar observation is made by Parkinson (1907, p. 81). Seemingly, in the past, the skull of a dead man might be produced at certain ceremonies, but it was no more than a visible sign of the presence of the deceased at the celebration in his honour. As evidence that no particular emotion or value attached to the skull, Parkinson records that after the celebrations he was able to buy the skulls for practically nothing without any difficulty.

outburst of lamentation among the women and children. Winthuis (1926) describes how women would throw themselves to the ground, tear their hair out, fill their mouths with earth and dirt and behave altogether as if they had been overpowered by sorrow. Winthuis adds that all this is usually show only. But if there is much behaviour on these occasions that is culturally enjoined, there is also much that is spontaneous, an expression of genuine grief and loss. At one funeral I attended the young widow was quite hysterical with grief, and it was only with the greatest difficulty that she could be restrained from throwing herself into the grave of her husband. I also knew one couple who went into a prolonged period of mourning on the death of a favourite child; during this time they appeared dressed only in black, the traditional colour of mourning, and observed a number of self-imposed taboos. Moreover, the concept of *niligur*, grief or sorrow, runs very deep in the culture, and its expression is not confined to formal occasions.[1]

In earlier days, when death was seen to be approaching, two structures were erected, one in which the corpse would rest and where he would finally be buried *(a pal na minat)*, the other a small cook-house nearby. After interment, a task formerly allotted to the brothers or uterine nephews, that is, members of the *vunatarai* of the deceased, a group of "watchers" were "locked" in the *pal na minat*, where they were attended in all their needs by a number of women who otherwise remain within the house of the deceased. Of this particular aspect of the rites it is said *A tarai dia gugu ma a varden dia va palai*: the men make merry and entertain the people while the women "sleep in hiding" and only emerge to serve the "watchers". Meanwhile, within the *pal na minat* two fires had been lit, one on either side of the grave. These were said to warm the dead person *(vamadir ra minat)* as well as to remove the foul odour that filled the hut. On the fire were also cast the maggots that emerged from the grave; when they ceased to appear this part of the rite came to an end. Then there was a feast for all those who had taken part, and a distribution of shell-money.

[1] Here, as in other regards, my own observations amply confirm those of Parkinson (1907, p. 80). The men, he notes, are by nature uncommunicative and deem it improper to display their grief openly but, he goes on, "I have seen tears rolling down the cheeks of old men when I showed them photographs of sons or wives who were dead for some time. Women were much freer in the expression of their feelings, and one often came upon them in the gardens or in the bush shedding tears for the dead." Similarly, when I paid a return visit to Matupit after a lapse of eight years, many of the women who saw me immediately started weeping. It was then explained that this was because of my association with their husbands who had died in the meantime.

However, this was by no means the end of the matter; in the case of someone of particular prominence it was merely the prelude to a series of ceremonies that might go on over a period of years. These might include a *balaguan*, held from three months to a year after death, when the house of the deceased was ceremonially destroyed to the accompaniment of dancing, feasting and yet further distributions of *tambu*. Some time later there might be a performance of the *tatabar*, an offering of food to the spirit of the deceased. This was placed high on a tree near the spot where the dead man reposed. Then all the people departed the place and went to stay in the bush, leaving the spirit of the dead man to regale himself on the repast prepared for him. The rite, known as *a vinamut*, was brought to an end by the appearance of a masked figure known as *a tubuan na kurakuradui*, to whom offerings of shell-money were made. Finally, perhaps some years later, there might be a great festival of remembrance, *a balaguan na warwanuknuk*, to honour not only the dead man but all the members of his *vunatarai*. It should also be noted here that the *tubuan*, referred to frequently in passing, has particularly strong associations with death, and may appear at a number of the rites; in this connection it will be recalled that the *matamatam*, the climactic rite in the cult of *dukduk* and *tubuan*, is always in commemoration of the dead.

Even in the past there was considerable variation between different Tolai communities in regard to mortuary customs, but the underlying themes and concerns were universal. Today in many of the villages a number of customs and practices have fallen into desuetude, but even in places like Matupit, where the entire ceremonial life has been seriously eroded, strenuous efforts are still made to ensure that the dead are properly honoured in the traditional fashion.[1]

All of these ceremonies contribute to what Goodenough (1955), describing a somewhat similar situation in Nakanai on north New Britain, has aptly called the pageant of death. For the Tolai death is feared above all, but within the framework of their culture they have made it a major focus of celebration. I have noted the theme of grief, *a niligur*, and this is given expression on every ceremonial occasion. Whenever the *tubuan*, which always carries the name of an ancestress

[1] For an account of the rites which followed the death of one prominent Matupi while I was on the island see Epstein, A. L. (1969, pp. 232–236).

of the *vunatarai*, or even a representation of the figure,[1] appeared publicly I always observed that while it was greeted with loud exclamations of triumph *(dia kabinge)*, numbers of women would at once burst into weeping. The appearance of the *tubuan*, I was told, recalled to memory a close kinsman who had died.

In the major ceremonies, however, grief is subordinated to the expression of emotions of quite a different kind. The *balaguan* is preeminently an occasion of triumph and pride, in which personal assertiveness and competitiveness are allowed the fullest expression. Brown (1910, p. 86) describes the boastful behaviour that is a mark of these performances. At one point the big-man, the sponsor of the ceremony, will stand up and *ababut*, that is "show off in fighting attitude, will speak and brag, tell of his wealth, of the men he has killed, of the dances, charms, songs, etc., which he has brought, etc., and will also tell of what he intends to do". When he has finished, he presents some small portions of *tambu* to the other big-men present who proceed to boast in similar fashion. This may be followed by a challenge from the sponsor to all present to try and remove his *butur*. The *butur* is a small tree on which in the past the big-man would have placed his offerings to the dead. Now, prancing around and brandishing a spear, he would invite his audience to challenge his supremacy. Only those who were wealthy in *tambu* could rise to the bait, for if they were successful in removing the *butur* they would be presented with *tambu* and other gifts which would have to be returned at some future date; it was in effect a challenge to stage a *balaguan* of equal splendour.

I myself never heard the term *ababut*, which appears to be peculiar to the Duke of York Islands. At Matupit the word associated with this kind of boastful behaviour was *a varpin*. If a man felt he had been slighted or insulted he would exclaim angrily in terms of self-aggrandizement: "*U toia upi u tata ure iau? Iau a iap. Pata tikai i taun iau*" ("Who are you to talk about me? I am the fire that burns. There is none who surpasses me"), and much else in similar vein. In everyday life such boasting is strongly condemned. A braggart, *a lup tinata na varpin*, it is said, does not live long. In the context of the *balaguan*, how-

[1] At Matupit they perform a ceremony known as *a namata* for a young man about to be married. He is required to spend some time living secluded in the bush, attended only by a number of his companions. Then, on the appointed day, he is led back to the village under a kind of tabernacle, *a pal na mamarikai*. A great deal of artistry goes into the construction of the tabernacle, which is often topped by a carved representation of the *tubuan* figure. The design immediately identifies the name and the *vunatarai* it represents.

ever, such behaviour is not merely permitted, it is an integral part of the ceremony and *a varpin* attached to every aspect of the day's events: the number of dances put on, the skill of the dancers, the beauty of their decorations, and the amounts of food and *tambu* distributed. It is as though what is forbidden in secular life becomes legitimate in the context of rite and ceremony. Ceremony "tames" the impulse, transforms it by specifying the conditions under which what is ordinarily illicit becomes socially acceptable and even enjoined.

The symbolism of the *butur* must remain obscure, for many years have elapsed since the custom was practised at Matupit, and I was unable to explore the matter very far. Consideration of the role that *tambu* plays in these ceremonies as a whole suggests, however, that among the impulses that find their expression on these occasions are those particularly associated with anal erotism. I have mentioned that the anal phase of infantile development, in psychoanalytic theory, is the focus of a variety of intrapsychic conflicts: as between the demands of retention and elimination, and in regard to the struggle for autonomy and the handling of aggression. We may see Tolai ceremonies, I suggest, as a projection and resolution of these conflicts through their expression in disguised form. I have argued that *tambu* is a copro-symbol, a displacement of the original infantile interest in excrement. By means of this cultural device, which emphasizes the importance of accumulating *tambu*, Tolai are able to gratify the retentive impulse to the maximum extent possible: until death, when it is yielded up and distributed to the accompaniment of praise and acclamation in the rites that mark one's passing. Through *tambu*, too, they are provided with a means of giving expression to the aggressive impulses that have their sources in anal erotism, as well as resolving the conflicts associated with that phase. Freud (1918, p. 81) points out that "faeces are the child's first *gift* [italics in original], the first sacrifice on behalf of his affection, a portion of his own body which he is ready to part with, but only for the sake of someone he loves. To use faeces as an expression of defiance . . . is merely to turn this earlier 'gift' meaning into the negative." We are confronted here with the two faces of aggression. Both find their full representation in the context of the mortuary rites.

Faced with a case of conflict over the modes of retention and elimination, the psychoanalyst will expect his patient to entertain, as Erikson (1963, p. 59) puts it, peculiarly messy fantasies and violently hostile wishes of total elimination against selected individuals, especially those close to him who by necessity are forced to make demands on his inner treasures. Erikson goes on to comment that while the patient's deeds of passive and retentive hostility often remain unrecognizable to him and to his intended victims, he would be constantly compelled to undo, or to make amends, to atone for something done in fact or fantasy. We have seen something of these "messy fantasies" in Tolai preoccupations with sorcery. Such notions, however, are essentially the projection of one's own hostile impulses and a measure of one's own guilt. It is wholly appropriate therefore that death should also be the occasion of sacrifice, the final act of atonement, the yielding up of one's *tambu* which alone ensures acceptance into the Abode of the Dead.

That *tambu* is also a symbol of hostile aggression, a transformation of the anal impulse, is evident in a number of ways. The cutting of the coils of shell-money is held to be mystically dangerous, and those who are to undertake the task protect themselves by daubing the body with *a matatar.*[1] In cutting up a coil the man hacks at it furiously (Fig. 1). Then he moves round the assembly, breaking off small lengths of shell-money which he casts contemptuously at the feet of the recipients. They, for their part, studiously ignore the "gift". In these acts there is a plain hostility, but its sharpness is blurred as it becomes fused with a more positive expression of competitiveness.[2] We may also recall here the custom relating to the removal of the *butur* or Salisbury's account of the *matamatam* where the big-men and their followers move around casting *pidik* at the feet of their friends/rivals by way of challenge. However, the *balaguan* is more properly to be regarded as a whole, and in this regard, like the *moka* exchanges of the Western Highlands described by Strathern (1971, 1974), it is an elaborate form of "ritualized conflict". Recalling such an occasion, a man will speak

[1] The basic substance is *a tar*. This is described as *a pia na pikai*, mud which is deposited as a result of volcanic activity, or as the Tolai would prefer to express it, a product of the *kaia*, the demon associated with a volcano. Gathered by the women, *tar* is burned until it acquires a reddish colour. In this form it is used as a kind of paint on a variety of ceremonial occasions. It is also said to be used to medicate shell-money when it is being made up in the form of a *loloi* or coil. *Tar* itself appears to serve as a copro-symbol. If this is so, the idea underlying its use in the last instance would seem to be analogous to the immunity conferred by the use of a vaccine to activate antibodies or, more colloquially, setting a thief to catch a thief.

[2] Since at Matupit my opportunities to observe the major ceremonies were necessarily restricted, I cannot say whether one would be able to detect in the course of a ceremony that transformation of the symbol from one pole of meaning to another that Turner (1967) has postulated.

proudly of his own moiety: "We, the Pitalaba, stood together so that the Marmar should see our strength." In its thematic structure the *balaguan* is, from our point of view, merely a variation of the prototypical game called *a pip* which I described earlier; the *balaguan*, how-

FIG. 1. Cutting up a coil prior to distribution.

ever, is a "game" for men, a great competitive event fought out with *tambu*. The greater the amount of shell-money expended and distributed, the greater the success of the ceremony, and the more widespread and lasting the fame of its sponsor. In this context, then, *tambu* expresses the creative aspects of aggression and pride, the sense of power and achievement that legitimately belong to the man who, through his own efforts and enterprise, is able to stage a successful ceremony.

All of these contending motives and impulses are given their most concentrated expression, and find their reconciliation, in the symbol of the *leo*. An essential prop in the staging of any ceremony designed to leave a mark on the memory, the *leo* is a huge scaffolding made of bamboo supports, surmounted by carved representations of *dukduk* and *tubuan*, and hung, for all to admire, with numerous coils of *tambu* (Fig. 2). In the light of the whole of the preceding discussion, it appears to me not too fantastic to suggest that the *loloi*, in appearance like a great wheel, is a transfigured representation of the anus. In this way, holding the centre of the stage, the *leo* stands as a supreme symbol, affirming and reconciling the conflicting values of triumph and contrition, dominance and submission.

In his account of the case of Wolf-Man, Freud (1918, p. 72) remarks: "We are accustomed to trace back interest in money, in so far as it is of a libidinal and not of a rational character, to excretory pleasure, and we expect normal people to keep their relations to money entirely free from libidinal influences and regulate them according to the demands of reality." Crucial here is the final reference to reality. For if the Tolai display in their behaviour traits that might strike the outside observer as characteristic of certain obsessionals, it is important to stress that their reality is not that of the neurotic individual of Western society who requires psychiatric help. If much of their behaviour in regard to *tambu* appears compulsive, it is at the same time socially prescribed, necessary to the maintenance of their social arrangements, and in full accord with their social values. We may state the issues in rather different terms by saying that their social system appears to demand the development of certain anal characteristics. But if this is so, then at the same time ways have to be devised for handling the conflicts, both intrapsychic and social, that must accompany such a development. In the main this is achieved, I believe, through the ceremonies that surround death. On the sociological plane these have obvious functions in maintaining the economic and political system. On the psychological plane they provide the occasion for an expression of the intrapsychic conflicts, and their transcending, in symbolic terms. On both levels they

FIG. 2. Coils of *tambu* garlanding the *leo* at a *balaguan*.

provide simultaneously, to adapt the language of psychoanalysis, an elaborate mechanism of defence.[1]

My account has necessarily failed to answer many questions of detail. It also raises other questions of a more general nature. To draw attention to some regular pattern or set of relationships in the data is not to explain them. If it is the case that certain Tolai social arrangements are closely linked to the development of anal characteristics, how is such a development achieved? What has been the mechanism by which it is generated? To such questions I cannot give any certain answers, but it is important that at least some attempt should be made to discuss them. Before doing so, however, it is necessary to consider the status of shell-money under contemporary conditions.

The persistence of *tambu*

Gluckman (1964) has pointed to the traps that await the anthropologist who is tempted to stray across disciplinary boundaries and is thus led beyond "the limits of naivety". The dangers lie not simply in moving out of the field of one's own professional competence, but in the likelihood that one will be led into confusing different frames of reference, for example, by offering psychological explanations of "social facts" or vice versa. The psychoanalyst, for his part, is no more immune to such temptations, and the psychoanalytic literature is unfortunately replete with examples that testify to the weight of Gluckman's argument. Róheim's article on "holy money" is a case in point, for it will be recalled how he sought the origins of the social use of money in terms of intrapsychic processes that were phylogenetically given. However, the objections to which this particular kind of approach leaves itself open have not escaped other psychoanalysts, most notably perhaps Fenichel, who also points the way out of the seeming dilemma of employing psychological concepts in sociological contexts. Fenichel (1938) castigates those who would derive the origins of complex social institutions, such as money or capitalism, from instinctual impulses associated with anal erotism. Anal erotism produces the desire to collect, he points out, but an irrational desire

[1] Dr Don Tuzin has pointed out to me in a personal communication that my argument here comes fairly close to certain ideas proposed by Spiro (1965). I was not familiar with Spiro's paper at the time I drafted the passage. Professor Spiro, who was kind enough to read an earlier version of my essay, was presumably too courteous to make the point himself.

for possession merely occupies itself with money, it does not itself create money. To deduce, as Róheim does, the function of money from anal sources, Fenichel remarks, would be like drawing from the secret sexual meaning of walking in the hysteric, shown by psychoanalysis, the deduction that we walk for the sake of sexual pleasure and not in order to get from one place to another. Nowhere then among the "instinctual" goals does money appear as such; "only the presence and the function of money in the social system furnish these unspecific instinctual drives with this specific object." Thus for Fenichel impulse and social reality are seen as mutually interacting; his view, indeed, envisages a relationship that we would now describe in terms of a mechanism of negative feedback. Thus, for a child brought up in a modern capitalist system, "not only does an interest in money arise from the primitive conflicts of anal eroticism, but the interest in money which is and must be instilled in the child also increases his anal eroticism and in turn arouses the conflicts which formerly raged about the latter" (1938, p. 103).[1] This interplay of sociological and psychological factors is well illustrated in, as well as being essential for the understanding of, the continuing use of shell-money under contemporary conditions.

Almost from the earliest days of contact, Tolai became accustomed to Western money, at first in the form of German marks, then the pounds, shillings, and pence of Australian currency, more recently Australian dollars, and now the kina of Papua New Guinea. Over the years the experience intensified as they became increasingly involved in wage-labour and cash-cropping, and developed new wants that could only be met by the possession of money. Today the Tolai count as an affluent people, certainly by New Guinea standards; their command of cash is immediately visible in the large numbers of cars and trucks they own, in the way in which they throng the stores, offices and banks of Rabaul, or in the modern style homes that they now build in their villages. Money is as indispensable to their modern way of life as it is to the Europeans or Chinese resident among them. Alongside of money, however, they also continue to make use of *tambu* in traditional ways.

[1] Although Freud himself recognized from time to time the importance of social or cultural factors, in general he was content to take over the concept of instincts then current in intellectual circles. Fenichel's approach represents a departure from the classical view in that the "instincts" are no longer seen as being simply biologically determined, but also as depending to a large extent on social factors. For a more recent discussion of "instinctive behaviour" along these lines see, for example, Bowlby (1969).

If I am correct that attitudes towards *tambu* express a transformed anal erotism, then we might expect that these attitudes would be readily transferred to money. And it is evident that in some regards this has indeed occurred. The opening of savings accounts with banks is of interest in this connection. I have no information about banking facilities in German times, but it appears that Tolai had commenced to hold such accounts quite early on in the days of the Australian Mandate (Ainsworth, 1924). In 1969, according to information collected by my wife, there were more than 35,000 Tolai accounts held with the Commonwealth Savings Bank at Rabaul, and total deposits at all banks were estimated at around $A4 million (Epstein, T. S., 1970b, p. 21).[1] The very high proportion of accounts (in a total population at that time of around 60,000) is explained by the fact that many Tolai hold multiple accounts with separate books for each member of the family, including the children. This is in full accord with the traditional practice of setting a special basket aside for a child some time after its birth. The parents might then plant, as many frequently still do, a crop of groundnuts which would be sold for shell-money. This would go into the basket, an opening of his "savings account" in *tambu*, to which further contributions would be made from time to time as the child grew up, and to which he too was expected to add whatever shell-money he happened to earn or acquire.

There are other regards in which contemporary Tolai economic behaviour appears to me to reflect continuity with the past and reveals the same underlying motivation. Thus it has been noted that while production has both diversified and expanded and income regularly increased, the pattern of wants has not always expanded in line with growing wealth. In this connection, for example, Scarlett Epstein (1968, p. 92) has recorded of Rapitok, an affluent inland community, that the prosperity of the village in 1960, founded on the marketing of copra and cocoa beans, was still unmatched by any significant improvement in living standards. Indeed, as the same authority comments elsewhere (1970a), a decreasing marginal propensity to consume, so clearly exemplified among the Tolai and other New Guinea groups, is a feature that serves to distinguish the economy of contemporary New Guinea groups from that of so many other under-

[1] In addition to such savings, a certain amount of money was simply hoarded (Epstein, T. S., 1968, p. 102). Bank managers in Rabaul frequently complained of the shortage of coin, which they attributed to Tolai hoarding.

developed countries. Sometimes, if one asked one's informants what they proposed to do with their money savings, they would speak of providing appropriate funerals for all the members of the *vunatarai*. Such responses again reflect traditional ideas, but they also have to be read in the context of opportunities available for investment. Just as *tambu* was not simply to be hoarded, but should be worked with, so too now in their use of money Tolai are not only "conspicuous savers", they are also "conspicuous investors". However, as the local demand for retail stores and transport has become almost saturated, a major problem has been posed for the Tolai by the dearth of alternative avenues for investment (Epstein, T. S., 1970b, p. 22).

Yet if the evidence points to some transfer of attitudes, it is equally plain that money and *tambu* are not psychological equivalents. If they were, cash, with its more varied uses and stronger purchasing power, would by this time have displaced shell-money. The two currencies cannot be equated psychologically because they cannot be equated sociologically; they have their roots in quite different sets of economic and social arrangements, the one in an integrated market economy, the other in a particular cultural and social system. Hence, in the one case, one cannot hope to purchase a car or a transistor radio with *tambu*, while in the other, up to the time of my fieldwork, the Tolai still adamantly refused to acknowledge that money could be used for the *varkukul*, the "purchase" of the bride,[1] or the garlanding of the *leo* at a *balaguan*.

The fact that the Tolai operate simultaneously with two currencies raises immediately the question how the two coexist. Moreover, as shell currencies elsewhere have often shown little resistance once Western money has entered the economy, there is the further problem of accounting for the remarkable persistence of *tambu*. The two issues are closely connected and I shall discuss each in turn.

Tolai today operate in a number of different, and to some extent distinct, fields of relationship, in which money and *tambu* have separate roles. Those, for example, who are in wage employment outside the villages receive the rewards of labour in Papua New Guinea

[1] I did come across a couple of instances on Matupit where money was used in this way, suggesting yet another area where the traditional system was coming under strain. One of these concerned a man around thirty who, having been married and divorced a number of times, was now unable to win the support of his kinsmen in acquiring another bride. Accordingly, he undertook the marriage arrangements himself and, having no *tambu* of his own, offered the *varkukul* in cash. This confirmed the popular view that he was a thorough scapegrace, but no less angry expostulations were directed at the parents of the girl who accepted the money.

currency, and no store in town of course accepts shell-money. On the other hand, there are certain transactions involving only Tolai where, as we have seen, cash is regarded as inappropriate and only *tambu* is acceptable. Between these poles is an area of overlap in which cash and shell-money serve as alternative media of exchange or may be used in combination. One curious feature of this situation is that different "conversion" rates may operate for different items. Thus for taro or fish the equivalent rate for a fathom of shell-money might be 20 cents, for slaked lime 30 cents, and for a chicken 50 cents. However, there is no attempt to manipulate these different exchange rates. This is partly due to the small size of the *tambu* market, and the ensuing risk of loss involved (Epstein, T. S., 1964, pp. 57–58). Beyond this is the fact that direct competition between the currencies is avoided by the lack of convertibility between them. Relating to different spheres of social value, the balance between them is maintained by individual acts of choice. So a woman concerned with finding a bride for her son will insist on receiving *tambu* for her produce, while the owner of a lorry who is preparing for a ceremony may stipulate that for a particular journey his passengers pay the fare in shell-money only.

On the other hand, even though money and *tambu* are not usually brought into direct competition, there are very real sources of conflict between them, well illustrated in developments on the island of Matupit. Older people there constantly deplored their poverty in shell-money and, contrasting their position with that of more prosperous communities, would discuss endlessly possible schemes to remedy the situation. All of this was so much whistling in the dark, for in reality there was little they could do to halt the decline, still less to restore *tambu* to the importance it formerly held in their lives. Most of the younger people worked away from the village for wages – many of them in remote parts of New Guinea – and had few opportunities for engaging in those activities which traditionally yielded shell-money. In any case, as they would frequently point out, few of the things they now wished to acquire could be purchased with *tambu*. As for the older men themselves, for all of their exhortation of their sons and nephews to be "strong for *tambu*", they too were compromised by their own dependence upon cash. To give but one example: fishing at Matupit is one of the main traditional sources of *tambu* revenue there, but during my stay on the island there was a pressing need for cash to buy the materials for the completion of a new church. The people were urged to form small fishing cooperatives to help raise the funds: the catches were therefore sold for money, not for *tambu*. The Tolai live in a real world which often confronts them with difficult choices, and where a choice made in one area sets up constraints on behaviour in others. In this way, as seen in a community like Matupit, the balance appears to be swinging rapidly against *tambu*.

Yet prediction of its early demise could well prove foolhardy, for *tambu* has shown remarkable resilience. From the earliest days of contact it has been subjected to pressure from various sources. The Roman Catholic missionaries have consistently preached against it, seeing in the passing of shell-money possibilities for the improvement of family life (Salisbury, 1970, p. 278). Again, the Germans were at one point compelled to introduce a decree prohibiting the use of shell-money in trade by Europeans, and would have liked to eliminate it altogether, though in this they signally failed. Later, the Kenyan official, Ainsworth (1924, p. 20), called in by the Australians to advise on "native policy", also argued for its abolition on the grounds that it was harmful to the general progress of the people. Today the pressures against *tambu* are of a rather different kind, but even where its decline is most evident, as at Matupit, what is no less striking is the way people continue to make strenuous efforts in order to acquire it. Clearly, *tambu* refuses to die easily.

Discussing the tenacity of primitive currencies in the face of Western money, Mary Douglas (1967, p. 142) suggests that those types of primitive money which display vitality are those which have what she calls a coupon function in controlling status in the social system.[1] Her point appears to be that while their medium-of-exchange function may be easily replaced, they survive as long as they retain their importance for determining social status. What is interesting about *tambu* is that it has retained its medium-of-exchange function and, for my part, I find it difficult to imagine how it could survive if that function were lost completely. One of the reasons why Matupi are compelled to continue the pursuit of shell-money is that other Tolai groups upon whom they are dependent for brides or for the satisfaction of other requirements still insist on payment in *tambu*. But behind such rational calculation it is not difficult to detect the pre-

[1] In fact Douglas offers only two examples in support of her view, one the *tambu* of the Tolai, the other the use of manillas in the Cross River area of Nigeria. My impression is, certainly within Melanesia, that shell currencies have shown less tenacity than she supposes.

sence of other, more emotional, considerations which touch the sensitive issue of Tolai identity.

In the past, as we have seen, the local groups which today make up the Tolai community were independent and often mutually hostile. Yet in their language, and in the social ties forged through participation in shared institutions – marriage, trade, and the cult of *dukduk* and *tubuan* – as well as in their relations with other groups indigenous to the Gazelle Peninsula, the seeds of an ethnic identity already existed. Thereafter contact with the outside world fostered the awareness of their common bonds, generating an increasing sense of their own distinctiveness as a people in relation to other indigenous groups within the wider society of Papua New Guinea created by colonialism. I have discussed this process of identity formation elsewhere at some length (Epstein, A. L., 1970, 1978). What needs to be emphasized here, as both Salisbury (1970, p. 278) and I (Epstein, A. L., 1969, pp. 311–317) have noted quite independently, is the way *tambu* has come to serve as a symbol of the new Tolai identity. This is not merely an inference on the part of an observer, but something of which Tolai are consciously aware and of which they frequently speak. I have cited elsewhere (Epstein, A. L., 1969, p. 317) the comment of an English-speaking Tolai who in the course of a conversation once spontaneously remarked: "You have read the book Treasure Island? Well, *tambu* is our treasure. If we didn't have *tambu*, we would not be Tolai; we would be a different people." Sometimes indeed they formulated the idea in quite explicit sociological terms, referring to shell-money as the skeleton or bones around which their whole social system was built, and without which the entire structure would collapse (cf. Epstein, T. S., 1968, p. 95; Salisbury, 1970, p. 278).

When therefore young wage-earners at Matupit go out of their way to purchase rice out of their wages so that it can be sold in exchange for shell-money, or when they spend part of their weekends fishing or collecting megapode eggs which will yield *tambu*, they are expressing quite deliberately their profound desire to be and to remain Tolai. *Tambu* serves here as a peculiarly appropriate symbol expressing the retentive impulse in a new guise: the desire to cling to their ethnic identity. Yet, as we might by now expect, this is only one side of the picture. For, particularly among younger Tolai in the various communities around Rabaul, talk of shell-money can arouse quite hostile responses reflecting what Erikson would call a crisis of identity.

The complex and contradictory attitudes held by these younger people towards shell-money are revealed in a variety of contexts. Many of the more thoughtful will argue that the pursuit of *tambu* should be maintained so that one can fulfil one's obligations on the death of a near kinsman or for the proper payment of bridewealth. But what happens if, for example, the bride is not Tolai? During the course of my fieldwork the announcement of a forthcoming marriage between a Matupi lad, who had been to school in Australia, and an Australian girl aroused a great deal of discussion within the village. Among the more conservative, both young and old, there was strong opposition to the union on various grounds. Among a number of the younger people, however, including those who spoke in favour of retaining shell-money for the *varkukul*, there was a feeling that intermarriage between black and white should be encouraged. In this way, it was said, the cultural standards of the Tolai would be uplifted and their transition into a modern society eased.

Sometimes these conflicts are expressed in more forceful terms. Once, for example, I was having a long, meandering conversation with a man called ToPirit, with whom I was very friendly. ToPirit at the time was a man in his middle thirties, employed as a clerk in one of the government offices in Rabaul and beginning to make his mark within the village, where he frequently served on the "committee" when disputes were brought for hearing before the village assembly. Previously, I had always known him as a quiet man of equable temperament with a pleasant and easy-going manner. Now, as we chanced on the topic of shell-money, something within him seemed to snap, and he burst out: "*Iau* hate *go ra tambu*" ("I hate this *tambu*"). The conversation was in Tolai, but he interposed the English word presumably because he could not find a vernacular term sufficiently strong or apt to express his feelings. Shell-money, he went on to explain, was one of the things which stood in the way of achieving their political independence. Its continued pursuit divided their attentions, preventing them from raising their living standards. As long as young men stayed at home and worked for *tambu* the old customs would continue, and as long as they continued the old men would retain their power. For ToPirit then *tambu* was an obstacle to their development as full citizens in a modern society, which ought to be removed. Yet these convictions were not always consistently reflected in his behaviour. In other contexts he often appeared as a spokesman for traditional values. He was also one of those who would seek to convert part of his wages into shell-money, and he himself already possessed a *loloi*, a coil of about 100 fathoms, which he stored with a maternal uncle in another community lest, he once explained, it was stolen at Matupit.

ToPirit represents the dilemma of an increasing number of younger Tolai. They are at present attempting to face in two directions at the same time. The processes of social change have generated on the one hand a strong sense of Tolai consciousness, but those same processes have resulted at the same time in increasing Tolai involvement in the wider society of contemporary Papua New Guinea. Imbued with a deep love of their own part of the country, and a pride in themselves as Tolai, they yet look to horizons beyond those of the village. Clinging to their Tolai identity, they seek at the same time identity as citizens of a new nation. These conflicts in their scheme of social values are immediately reflected in their contradictory attitudes towards shell-money: on the one hand, to make great efforts to retain it; on the other, as one Tolai once put it, to collect it all together and deliver it into the hands of the tourists who call at Rabaul or, more simply, to dump it in the sea. This tug-of-war at the level of behaviour and overt attitudes is sharpened, however, because it also represents processes at work within the psyche, reviving in a new form earlier infantile sources of conflict. I have sought to show how in the past sociological and psychological processes worked in tandem, mutually supporting one another. *Tambu*, on this view, provided a cultural device whereby the energy generated by the conflict between the retentive and eliminative impulses or the struggle for autonomy was harnessed to socially approved ends, reconciling the oppositions on both the social and the intrapsychic planes. For the present, however, as the traditional social system crumbles, *tambu* becomes rather the focus of a fierce ambivalence for which existing institutions and social arrangements provide no resolution.

Conclusion

The focus of this essay has been on Tolai shell-money in its affective dimension. This has led us into many highways and byways of Tolai behaviour, both spontaneous and enjoined, in secular and ceremonial contexts, as well as aspects of their ideology and symbolism. At a variety of points, and on different planes, I have drawn attention to the conflicts within their system of values. Yet these conflicts reveal a striking consistency; they express in disguised forms, I have argued, the contradictions that surround the infantile experience of defecation. Anal erotism runs like a thread through so much of the data I have presented.

The psychoanalyst, confronted with a patient who displays evidence of a fixation at the anal phase of psycho-sexual development, is accustomed to trace its roots to some early injury to infant narcissism brought about by toilet training that was too early or too rigid. Applying these ideas cross-culturally, some anthropologists, using Rorschach and other tests of personality, have observed that the postulated relationship between infant training and adult structure is not supported by their data (see, for example, Straus, 1957). Some of these studies seem to me, however, to be misconceived in that they assume simple causal relations where psychoanalytic theory stresses complexity. As Menninger (1943, p. 162) has observed, merely to relate a particular symptom to, say, the anal phase is too general, because it is never possible to differentiate in an adult clear-cut examples derived exclusively from a particular phase of infantile development. No character is purely oral, anal, or genital. Moreover, insofar as such studies rely simply on projective techniques they ignore the importance of social context; they do not examine the actual behaviour of those who instil toilet-training, how such behaviour is experienced by the child, nor in particular the ideas and fantasies woven around the experience, in a word, its phenomenology.

Unfortunately, having become alive to the problems with which this paper deals only after I had completed my fieldwork and began to ponder the data, my knowledge of Tolai infant-training is woefully inadequate. So far as the act of defecation is concerned, for reasons mentioned earlier, Tolai parents are careful to remove the child's excreta, but until the child has passed its first year it is not reprimanded if it is found playing with its faeces or smearing them on its body, because it has not yet learned that faeces are "bad" *(i kaina)*. However, according to one of my informants, from the age of about eighteen months the child is expected to be clean. Should he wish to defecate in the night he should call his parents to take him outside. If, having been instructed in this way, he misbehaves he will be punished by being lightly switched across the buttocks. But what is important in all this, as I have previously stressed, is less a matter of a particular act (or acts) performed by the parent so much as the way in which the child is handled, how he interprets the experience as well as the social context in which it occurs. In the absence of any hard data on these matters, I can only venture a few very tentative suppositions.

I have repeatedly stressed Tolai concern with death. If I may be permitted to twist a line of Keats, they appear at times as a people half in love with fearful death. The concern is evident in their secular life, but it is above all in the ceremonial context that it finds pre-eminent expression. It appears to me that the *balaguan* reveals a conjunction of a number of major themes: mourning and loss, atonement, and triumph. Out of what experiences are these various emotions born and brought together in this way? It is not enough to point, with Róheim, to the primordial parricide, for the oedipal situation, and the castration fears associated with it, are experienced within a specific natural and cultural environment. Recent work on mourning and loss offers some clues. Thus for Bowlby (1961, 1969, 1973) the prototype of grief is to be found in detachment from the mother: once the child has formed a tie to a mother figure, which ordinarily occurs by the middle of the first year, its rupture leads to separation anxiety, grief and anger and sets in train processes of mourning. The relevance of this in the Tolai context is that there is an increasing detachment of the mother from the child as she becomes pregnant again, and finally gives birth, a sequence of events that will ordinarily coincide with the period in which anal erotism achieves maximum intensity, between the eighteenth and twenty-fourth months.

A Tolai child at this time is familiar with the fact of his mother's pregnancy. One young father once referred to his first-born son, then about twenty months, and still unable to talk. The mother was now expecting another child and sometimes, playing with their son, they would ask: "Where is your brother? Where is your sister?" The child would then toddle over to his mother and pat her on the belly.

It would be extremely interesting to know how the child responds to these events, in particular how it fantasies the facts of conception and birth. What does seem clear is that the mother's pregnancy introduces a new regime that demands a variety of adjustments on his part. Tolai themselves recognize that this is so for they say that when the mother conceives again, *a bul i malakak*, the child begins to pine or languish.[1] It may also develop a variety of complaints, for example, *a pal a kovakovo*, a kind of rash which is said to be very painful and irritating. Such symptoms the Tolai explicitly relate to the child's awareness that his parents are no longer lavishing the same attention on him as before. The outside observer may see in them the expression of more complex forms of conflict arising from the coincidence of pregnancy, the emergence of a sibling rival, and the onset of toilet-training, all of which are carried forward into the oedipal situation. Róheim has, I think, made out a case for the Tolai response to death in oedipal terms; what I believe emerges more clearly now is the reason that they respond to loss in an anal way. According to Bowlby the child responds to loss by grief and anger in an effort to recover the beloved object. But because, as I have suggested, detachment from the mother tends to coincide in time with the child's attempts to assert its autonomy in the matter of defecation, separation also fosters its sense of guilt towards her, which can only be assuaged by an act of atonement: through the proper yielding of his faeces the child recovers the mother's love. Such a view helps to shed further light on the symbolism of *tambu*. For the Tolai, the coil of *tambu*, which I earlier discussed as a transfigured representation of the anus, may now be seen too as a symbol of the vagina, through which one achieves rebirth. Earlier in this essay I drew attention to the way the concept of *tambu*/taboo serves as a boundary marker between different realms, social and symbolic; *tambu* not only indicates the areas where trespass is forbidden but it also serves to mediate the passage between these realms or to make reparation when the taboo is violated. This applies no less to the most fundamental prohibition of all: the incest taboo. Hence, just as the "cutting" of *tambu* in the mortuary rites affirms the taboo, so in a sense it abrogates it at the same time. In these rites the Tolai finds his triumph over death as, purged of guilt, he is able to enter a new life in the Abode of the Dead. This, I suggest, is the most profound significance of the *loloi*, the great wheel of *tambu*, that in death one is finally able to return to the mother and be born again.

[1] A couple of Tolai practices relating to birth may be worth mentioning here. It is forbidden to sever completely the umbilical cord (*bitono*); part of it remains attached to the child. This part, I was told, becomes hard and black like a stick of trade-tobacco until it finally falls off. The mother then takes it and stores it away carefully where none shall discover it. A couple of weeks after its birth they perform what is called *a nirarang na bul*. This consists of passing the child over a fire. In this way, it is said, the child is cleansed of sputum and black faeces (meconium), and thus freed from disorders of this kind. Such practices hint perhaps at the presence of a cloacal theory of birth (see, for example, Jones, 1918, pp. 694–695), but I lack direct evidence on the point.

Acknowledgments

The ideas which I have sought to explore in this paper were stimulated by a six months' stay as a visitor at Miss Anna Freud's Child-Therapy Clinic in Hampstead, London in 1971. The opportunity to work them out in their present form arose when I was invited to spend the academic year 1974–75 as a Fellow at the Center for Advanced Study in the Behavioral Sciences at Stanford, California. To both of these institutions, and their staff, I am extremely grateful. For helpful comment and criticism on earlier drafts of the paper I also wish to express my gratitude to Professor Derek Freeman, Australian National University, Canberra, to Professor Mel Spiro and Dr Don Tuzin, University of California at San Diego, and to Professor David Pocock, University of Sussex. None of these of course is responsible for any of the views which I have expressed here.

References

ABRAHAM, KARL (1921). Contributions to the theory of the anal character. *Selected Papers on Psycho-Analysis* (1949), pp. 370–392. Hogarth Press, London.

AINSWORTH, J. (1924). *Report on Administrative Arrangements . . . affecting the Interests of Natives in the Territory of New Guinea*. Government Printer, Melbourne.

BOWLBY, JOHN (1961). Processes of mourning. *International Journal of Psycho-Analysis*, **42,** 317–340.

BOWLBY, JOHN (1969). *Attachment and Loss*. vol. 1, *Attachment*. Hogarth Press, London.

BOWLBY, JOHN (1973). *Attachment and Loss*. vol. 2, *Separation: Anxiety and Anger*. Hogarth Press, London.

BROWN, G. (1910). *Melanesians and Polynesians*. Macmillan, London.

DALTON, G. (1965). Primitive money. *American Anthropologist*, **67,** 44–65.

DANKS, B. (1887). On the shell-money of New Britain. *Journal of the Royal Anthropological Institute*, **17,** 305–317.

DANKS, B. (1909). Some notes on savage life in New Britain. *Australasian Association for the Advancement of Science*. Report of Twelfth Meeting, Brisbane (1910), vol. 12, 451–457.

DOUGLAS, MARY (1967). Primitive rationing: a study in controlled exchange. In *Themes in Economic Anthropology* (Ed. R. Firth), pp. 119–147. Tavistock, London.

EPSTEIN, A. L. (1963). Tambu: a primitive shell money. *Discovery*, **24** (December), 28–32.

EPSTEIN, A. L. (1969). *Matupit: Land, Politics and Change among the Tolai of New Britain*. Australian National University Press, Canberra.

EPSTEIN, A. L. (1970). Autonomy and identity: aspects of political development on the Gazelle Peninsula. *Anthropological Forum*, **2**, 427–443.

EPSTEIN, A. L. (1974). Moots on Matupit. In *Contention and Dispute: Aspects of Law and Social Control in Melanesia* (Ed. A. L. Epstein), pp. 93–112. Australian National University Press, Canberra.

EPSTEIN, A. L. (1978). *Ethos and Identity: Three Studies in Ethnicity*. Tavistock Publications, London.

EPSTEIN, A. L. *et al.* (1971). Under the volcano. In *The Politics of Dependence: Papua New Guinea 1968* (Eds A. L. Epstein, R. S. Parker and Marie Reay), pp. 48–90. Australian National University Press, Canberra.

EPSTEIN, T. S. (1964). Personal capital formation among the Tolai of New Britain. In *Capital, Saving and Credit in Peasant Societies* (Eds R. Firth and B. Yamey). Aldine, Chicago, Illinois.

EPSTEIN, T. S. (1968). *Capitalism, Primitive and Modern: Some Aspects of Tolai Economic Growth*. Australian National University Press, Canberra.

EPSTEIN, T. S. (1970a). The setting for socio-economic planning. In *People and Planning in Papua and New Guinea*, New Guinea Research Bulletin no. 34, pp. 42–61. New Guinea Research Unit, Australian National University, Canberra and Boroko.

EPSTEIN, T. S. (1970b). Indigenous entrepreneurs and their narrow horizon. In *The Indigenous Role in Business Enterprise*, New Guinea Research Bulletin no. 35, pp. 16–46. New Guinea Research Unit, Australian National University, Canberra and Boroko.

ERIKSON, E. H. (1963). *Childhood and Society*. Norton, New York.

Ethnographic Bibliography of New Guinea (1968). 3 vols. Australian National University Press, Canberra.

FENICHEL, OTTO (1938). The drive to amass wealth. In *Collected Papers*, second series (1954), pp. 89–108. Norton, New York.

FENICHEL, OTTO (1946). *The Psychoanalytic Theory of Neurosis*. Routledge and Kegan Paul, London.

FERENCZI, SÁNDOR (1913). The ontogenesis of symbols. In *Contributions to Psycho-Analysis* (1916), pp. 233–237. R. Badger, Boston.

FERENCZI, SÁNDOR (1914). The ontogenesis of the interest in money. In *Contributions to Psycho-Analysis* (1916), pp. 269–279. R. Badger, Boston.

FINNEY, R. S. (1971). *Would-be Entrepreneurs? A Study of Motivation in New Guinea*. New Guinea Research Bulletin no. 41. New Guinea Research Unit, Australian National University, Canberra and Boroko.

FREUD, SIGMUND (1908). Character and anal erotism. Standard Edition, vol. 9 (1959), pp. 167–175. Hogarth Press, London.

FREUD, SIGMUND (1918). *From the History of an Infantile Neurosis.* Standard Edition, vol. 17 (1955), pp. 1–133. Hogarth Press, London.

GLUCKMAN, MAX (Ed.) (1964). *Closed Systems and Open Minds.* Oliver and Boyd, Edinburgh.

GOODENOUGH, WARD H. (1955). The pageant of death in Nakanai. *University of Pennsylvania Museum Bulletin* no. 19, 18–43.

JONES, ERNEST (1918). Anal-erotic character traits. In *Papers on Psycho-Analysis.* 3rd edition (1923). William Wood, New York.

KLEIN, MELANIE (1957). *Envy and Gratitude: A Study of Unconscious Sources.* Basic Books, New York.

KLEINTITSCHEN, A. (1906). *Die Küstenbewohner der Gazelle-Halbinsel.* Herz-Jesu-Missionhaus, Hiltrup bei Münster.

KLEINTITSCHEN, A. (1924). *Mythen und Erzählungen eines Melanesierstammes aus Paparatava.* (Anthropos Bibliotek vol. 2). Mödling bei Wien, Münster.

LEACH, E. R. (1958). Concerning Trobriand clans and the kinship category *tabu.* In *The Developmental Cycle in Domestic Groups* (Ed. J. R. Goody), pp. 120–145. Cambridge University Press, Cambridge.

MALINOWSKI, BRONISLAW (1921). The primitive economics of the Trobriand Islanders. *Economic Journal*, **31,** 1–16.

MEIER, J. (1909). *Mythen und Erzählungen der Küstenbewohner der Gazelle-Halbinsel (Neupommern).* Aschendorffsche Buchhandlung, Münster.

MENNINGER, W. (1943). Characterologic and symptomatic expressions related to the anal phase of psychosexual development. *Psychoanalytic Quarterly*, **12,** 161–193.

PARKINSON, R. (1907). *Dreissig Jahre in der Südsee.* Strecker und Schröder, Stuttgart.

PFEIL, J. G. (1899). *Studien und Beobacktungen aus der Südsee.* Friedrich Vieweg, Braunschweig.

PITCAIRN, W. D. (1891). *Two Years among the Savages of New Guinea.* Ward and Downey, London.

POWELL, W. (1883). *Wanderings in a Wild Country.* Sampson Low, London.

RADCLIFFE-BROWN, A. R. (1952). *Structure and Function in Primitive Society.* Cohen and West, London.

RÓHEIM, GÉZA (1923). Heiliges Geld in Melanesien. *International Zeitschrift für Psychoanalyse*, **9,** 384–401.

ROMILLY, H. (1886). *The Western Pacific and New Guinea.* John Murray, London.

SACK, PETER (1974). The range of traditional Tolai remedies. In *Contention and Dispute: Aspects of Law and Social Control in Melanesia* (Ed. A. L. Epstein), pp. 67–92. Australian National University Press, Canberra.

SALISBURY, R. F. (1966). Politics and shell-money finance in New Britain. In

Political Anthropology (Eds M. Swartz, V. W. Turner and A. Tuden), pp. 113–128. Aldine, Chicago.

SALISBURY, R. F. (1970). *Vunamami: Economic Transformation in a Traditional Society*. University of California Press, Berkeley.

SPIRO, MELFORD (1965). Religious systems as culturally constituted defense mechanisms. In *Context and Meaning in Cultural Anthropology* (Ed. M. Spiro), pp. 100–113. Free Press, New York.

STRATHERN, ANDREW J. (1971). *The Rope of Moka: Big-Men and Ceremonial Exchange in Mount Hagen*. Cambridge University Press, Cambridge.

STRATHERN, ANDREW J. (1974). When dispute procedures fail. In *Contention and Dispute: Aspects of Law and Social Control in Melanesia* (Ed. A. L. Epstein), pp. 240–270. Australian National University Press, Canberra.

STRAUS, M. (1957). Anal and oral frustration in relation to Sinhalese personality. *Sociometry*, **20,** 21–31.

TAYLOR, C. R. H. (1965). *A Pacific Bibliography*. Clarendon Press, Oxford.

TURNER, V. W. (1967). *The Forest of Symbols*. Cornell University Press, New York.

WILLIAMS, M. (1964). *Stone Age Island*. Collins, London.

WINTHUIS, P. J. (1926). Krankheit, Tod und Begräbnis bei den Gunantuna der Gazelle-Halbinsel, Neupommern. In *Jahrbuch des Missionärtzlichen Institute*, Würzburg.

Stone as a Symbol in Apache Folklore

L. Bryce Boyer

THIS PAPER SUGGESTS: (1) that aboriginal belief systems as inculcated and reinforced by Chiricahua and Mescalero Apache socialization practices produced people who have certain dominant intrapsychic conflicts; (2) that their folklore assists them in expressing such typical conflicts without excessive guilt and anxiety; and (3) that their use of stone as a symbol is largely the same as has been found to be common among psychoanalytic patients with other cultural backgrounds.[1]

As noted in Bascom's (1954) excellent survey article, anthropologists have focused generally on the group functions of folklore: its amusement factors, its role in validating culture, its educational utility and its part in maintaining conformity to the accepted patterns of culture. Psychoanalysts, who are in full accord with those group functions of folklore, have been more interested in its furnishing individuals with psychological supports and, particularly since the introduction of ego psychology (Freud, 1923; Boyer, L. B., 1977, and in press),

[1] This paper was presented at a symposium on anthropology and psychoanalysis which was held in honour of my good friend, George Devereux, at the Annual Meeting of the American Anthropological Association, Mexico City, November 1974. It constitutes a revision of a paper published originally as "Stone as a Symbol in Apache Mythology", *American Imago*, 1965, **22**, 14–39, which appeared also as "La piedra como un símbolo. Datos ulteriores. (Temas pre-edípicos y edípicos en la mitología Apache.)" *Cuadernos de Psicoanálisis*, 1963, **1**, 123–145. A shorter version of the present article has appeared as "La piedra como símbolo del regionalismo Apache". *Norte*, 1975, No. 264, pp. 53–60.

its role in the formation of a character structure (Arlow, 1961) that is adaptive (Hartmann, 1939) to the needs of the culture in which the folklore arose, or which obtained it through diffusion and embodied it into the idiosyncratic folklore of the group (Dundes, 1965, pp. 53–56). Psychoanalysts view folklore as offering group-supported means through which individuals can avoid total repression or total expression of intrapsychic conflicts and thus express them without experiencing undue anxiety or guilt.

Psychoanalysts have concluded that each theme or element in a folklore representation can be viewed as a symbol and that symbols, as used in dreams, daydreams, hallucinations, symptoms, prose narrative, rituals and religions, are products of repressed impulses and inhibiting influences.[1] With anthropologists, psychoanalysts assume that the nature of the dominant intrapsychic conflicts which will exist in the typical member of a group will be determined by the interaction between his innate human endowment and the socialization processes which were used to make him an acceptable member of his group.

The Mescalero and Chiricahua Apaches are closely related in both social structure and socialization processes. Their aboriginal subsistence areas overlapped and there has always been considerable intermarrying between them (Basehart, 1959, 1960; Hoijer, 1938a, 1938b; Opler, 1933). It has been suggested that their aboriginal personality organization was very similar, if not identical (Boyer, L. B., 1964).

The puericultural patterns of the nomadic, hunting, gathering and raiding Apaches at some time in the remote past evolved into those that produced individuals with personality traits adaptive to their highly mobile style of living. These techniques became, probably through trial and error (Lubart, 1970), means of producing people

[1] Reference is made to a recent monograph on trauma and symbolism (Waldhorn and Fine, 1974). The report on symbolism is an attempt to synthesize biological, developmental, and metaphysical approaches to the subject. Three main findings are presented: (1) every symbol involves both instincts and defence; (2) the number of things symbolized are few and involve the instinctual interests of childhood, while objects for symbolization are almost infinite in number and variety; and (3) symbol formation represents a particular type of mental functioning which, though discernible as a manifestation of conflict, yet may at the same time be present in many aspects of mental life outside of, and independent of, conflict. The prerequisites, precursors, and conditions necessary for symbol formation are delineated. Symbolism links multitudinous sensory phenomena from the external world to bodily functions, feeling, and body parts and relates these to objects and experiences of gratification and/or frustration, making them familiar and integrated through ordering and organizing them. It thus serves all three psychic institutions through all phases of development.

with a great reservoir of aggression, who were hardy, alert and suspicious. It was also adaptive that the Apaches have relatively shallow emotional ties, inasmuch as their lives were fraught with dangers that could result in the loss of loved ones at any time and, further, there was a high infant mortality rate. Were their emotional ties to be deep, in the face of these frequent encounters with death they would have been subject to debilitating depressive reactions which would have made them incapable of alertness and immediate decisions and actions.

The aboriginal child rearing patterns of the Apaches, techniques which persist today in so far as prelatency training is concerned, frustrated children at each stage of their psychosexual development and produced exceedingly aggressive people (Boyer, R. M., 1962; Boyer and Boyer, 1972). The hostile feelings of the young were initially directed toward their mothers, their first meaningful frustrators. But the socialization practices also provided group-supported objects on to which that hostility could be projected and against which it could be discharged, as must occur if a group is to survive.

The earliest and most influential bases of character formation are to be found in the interactions between mothers and infants. The interactions between Apache mothers and their young are grossly inconsistent and produce fundamentally suspicious people who lack what Erikson (1950) designated to be a sense of basic trust. The id–ego differentiation of the typical Apache has been stunted and the establishment of self- and object-representations has not become well established as a result of the traumata to which he has been subjected during his oral period of psychosexual development (Hartmann *et al.*, 1949; Jacobson, 1964). His thinking and behaviour remain influenced heavily by the primary process (Freud, 1915; Laffal, 1964).

Longitudinal studies by psychologists of growing infants and children indicate that they go through a developmental stage when they perceive themselves to be fused with their mothers, who are not seen as separate objects, the symbiotic phase described by Mahler (Mahler and Furer, 1968; Mahler *et al.*, 1975). Observations of today's Apache mothers clearly reveal that they periodically view themselves as psychologically fused with their infants. Their attitude no doubt reinforces the view of the child and makes his later individuation more difficult. Reversion to this period of life remains a constant unconscious primitive wish of the child whose early interactions with his mother are psychologically traumatizing, as is certainly true of those of the Apache child.

The infant who is subjected to inconsistent care becomes both orally dependent and sadistic. All children perceive their teeth to be the first weapon which can effectively express aggression. Before his id and ego have become well-differentiated, the youngster perceives his hostility to have limitless magical powers, but at the same time he projects his rage on to his mother whom he views as omniscient and omnipotent and he fears punishment for aggressive wishes according to the *lex talionis*, the tooth-for-a-tooth philosophy (Klein, 1957). He perceives his gratifying mother and frustrating mother as separate beings, the good- and bad-mothers. The typical Apache mother was, and is, intensely gratifying. When she was in a receptive mood, the child's slightest vocal signal of distress brought the breast, regardless of the source of his discomfort. She helped fixate in him the mental set that oral satisfaction and its derivatives were the solution to all problems, thus interfering with his structuralization of drives. She was also intensely frustrating. Apaches are wont to have precipitous mood shifts. When the narcissistic selfishness of the mother prevailed and she wanted to be elsewhere, either to "fool around", or relieve the monotony of everyday life in pursuit of more enjoyable duties than those of the household, she might leave him to the care of "just anyone" for hours or days at a time, or suddenly abandon him, often without informing anyone of her planned actions. Aboriginally, with the matrilocal residence patterns (Boyer, R. M., 1964), her mother or sister might then be available to take over the largely physical care of her baby. Today, when those female kin might not be immediately available, she might leave her infant to be cared for by tiny children. In a recent extreme example of this pattern, one mother left her infants frequently for days to be cared for by a sibling no older than five years of age. On three occasions, the house burned down and once a sick infant died. All of her children, whom at times she treated with the utmost consideration, were constantly ill and only sporadically treated, although the Public Health Hospital was less than a quarter of a mile away and there was a family shaman. Others of her children died, obviously from complications of malnutrition, although her family had sufficient income and female kin lived nearby.

Almost every Mescalero and Chiricahua family of today, regardless of generation, has without apparent guilt given at least one child away, rationalizing, sometimes correctly, that the youngster would be better cared for by someone else. The Apache words for this practice mean "thrown him away". At times, obtaining genealogical information produced grossly inaccurate results because Apache parents had forgotten the existence of children they'd "thrown away".

Underlying all forms of dangers conceptualized by these Apaches are to be found oral-oriented, primary process-dominated thinking. Threat of abandonment to a bogy is the most common form of discipline administered to the toddler. Discipline is customarily administered by the mother. The disobedient child will be told, for example, "*jajadeh* will get you" or "*awshee*". *Jajadeh* takes the form of the whippoorwill during the daytime but at night becomes a woman with a basket into which she will place a crying child and carry him away, perhaps to a mountain. She is reminiscent of the Navajo blunderbore "Spider Lady" (Reichard, 1934). The Apache child fears *jajadeh* will eat him; the Navajo child is told overtly he will be devoured by Spider Lady. The word *jajadeh* is a synonym of *gahe*, to be described below. *Awshee* means "the ghost is coming". The appearance of the ghost heralds death, as does the owl it is reputed to inhabit; some Apaches hold that witches are people who have been inhabited by ghosts. The ghost is thought to enter the body of a victim, either through his mouth or during inspiration. Children see that their sibs or young neighbours are "thrown away". Their observation reinforces their fear of abandonment.

Even after the child's ego maturation has allowed him to see his mother as a whole rather than as a split object, he retains an unconscious view of her and her later psychological surrogates as good- and bad-mothers. Apachean folklore supplies such representatives in their holy medicine men on the one hand and their real or imagined enemies (Erikson, 1939; Murphy, 1957), witches (Adair, 1948), ghosts (Spiro, 1952, 1953) and cultural *bêtes noires*, such as the snake, the cougar and the bear, on the other.

The youngest child is, within the narcissistic limits provided by the inconsistent parents, monarch of the household. When he is a toddler and his next sib is born, he is abruptly and sometimes brutally displaced. If his clamour for attention is too urgent, in extreme cases, he might be kicked in the face. The intense rage that he experiences is insecurely repressed. In the past, some of the child's aggression could be turned inward upon the self and the self-representations (Jacobson, 1964) in manners that made the child capable of undergoing privations while simultaneously developing self-esteem. Today, aggression is turned inward in self- and group-destructive manners (Boyer and Boyer, 1972).

The dreams and fantasies of analysands who have been severely traumatized by sibling rivalry often reveal that they picture the mother's womb to be constantly pregnant with other potential sibs whom they want to kill or displace, having the fantasy that intra-uterine existence is edenic. They symbolize such rivals usually as insects, spiders, birds and small animals. The Apache mother of today is in fact usually pregnant. Although aboriginally the policy existed that children should be spaced three years apart (Opler, 1941), today's aged informants state such spacing to have been very unusual. The fantasies of Apache children include the same sibling-rival symbols as those of analysands. In actual life, rejected by the parents when the new baby is born, they turn to their brothers and sisters for support, which they get very inconsistently, as a substitute for the affection and attention they would prefer to have from their parents.

The Caucasian child can learn to manipulate his parents, who are vitally interested in his cleanliness training, through his excretory behaviour. Apache parents seem to have always been indifferent to cleanliness training or inconsistent regarding it and their children have not had such means of controlling their parents. Although Apache parents refer to excrement and even clean underpants as "dirty" or "nasty", a child might wear faeces-laden and dripping diapers for many hours at a time and, if he drops his diaper on the floor, it might simply be kicked into a corner of the room, to remain there fly-covered until the house is cleaned the following morning. Aged informants relate that previously, when the child might spend long hours in his cradle board, the grass or weed which served as absorbent material might be changed infrequently. At the same time, children are taught that excreta can be used for witchcraft purposes. In Apache witchcraft (usually) invisible arrows are shot into the person who is being bewitched. The arrows carry on them pieces of cadavers, or discarded parts of living humans, such as hair, nail-clippings, faeces or menstrual effluvia.

The sexual activities of Apaches seem never to have been hidden from their very young children. At the same time, the little ones have been taught that they must ignore or forget what they have observed.

Their parents view them as somewhat less than human, "not even alive", until at least the age of two. Although the death of an adolescent might require, and of an adult surely necessitated, a ghost-chasing ceremony to avoid behaviour on the part of the ghost which would cause family members to become insane and either commit suicide or foolishly allow themselves to be killed (Opler, 1945, 1946; Boyer, L. B., 1964), no such ceremony was held when children died. The young observers of parental sexual intimacies, relations which were in fact typically accompanied by overtly hostile actions much of the time, were supposed to repress their excitement and the oedipal strivings which were awakened so early, and their rage that they were not included in the intimacies. Young children identify with the excitements of both partners in observed sexual intimacies and such observation no doubt contributed to insecure sexual identities, at least on the part of the Apache males (Boyer, L. B., 1964). Youngsters perceive genital activities in terms of their levels of psychosexual maturation and fuse them with their oral and anal sadistic interpretations. The ascription of hostility to the sexual act by Apache children was, and is, reinforced by their actual observations. The ideational fusion of mouth and vagina which is common to young children was reinforced by the overt Apache teaching that vaginas had teeth in them, a lesson which aged informants yet today claim to be necessary to reduce the boy's sexual wishes toward his mother and sisters. An occasional Apache jokes about teeth inside the male urethra; others reveal anxiety about the oral-destructiveness of the penis through stories about the fangs of snakes, whether they merely tear flesh or eject poison. It will be recalled that snakes are cultural bogies for these Indians.

Ophidophobia has been known from the earliest recorded times and constituted a theme in the folklore of many ancient and modern cultures. Sperling (1964) wrote of the special meanings of ophidophilia to an analysand who suffered from ulcerative colitis and problems of sexual identity. That man not only thought of his penis as endowed with teeth but, using the body–phallus equation, identified himself with a snake which could eat and fuse with snakes as surrogates for both of his parents.

Although these Apaches ignore or deny the open masturbation of their young children and do not interfere with their excited sexual play in the outhouses, they also refer to all sexual matters as dirty or nasty. This parental behaviour serves to enhance the youngsters' fusion of anal and sexual activities, supporting their earlier interpretation of sexual intimacy with anal sadism.

Apache child-rearing took place in a social structure which fostered dependency on group rather than internalized standards for behavioural control. As seems to be true among other Athabaskan groups, at least the Tanaina and Upper Tanana Indians of Alaska (Hippler *et al.*, 1978b, 1978a) and the Kiowa Apaches (Freeman, 1968), individuals were and are not expected to become largely dependent upon their own standards for behaviour until they become grandparents. Their functional adolescence seems to have persisted until they were in their forties (Boyer and Boyer, 1976).

Thus, at each stage of the psychosexual development of the prelatency child, aggression was socialization-induced, aggression which would have to be deflected from the family for the good of the group.

Less obviously adaptive by-products of such child-rearing are the retention of oral–genital confusion, magical thinking and the ease of shifting from one ego-state to another and the impulsivity which is found consistently among people whose behavioural controls are not stably internalized. In the absence of much pragmatic knowledge concerning physiology and having been taught that diseases and other misfortunes result from the actions of affronted supernatural spirits or powers, they could place great credence in shamanistic, that is, faith, healing.

A partial analysis of an Apache legend and a myth will serve to illustrate some ways in which their themes and elements permitted the expression of typical intrapsychic conflicts without causing individuals undue guilt or anxiety. Special attention will be paid to the use of stone as a symbol.

Like the typical dream (Freud, 1900, pp. 241–496), some symbols have proved to be refractory to understanding. As recently as 1957, Fleiss (pp. 19–30) found stone, as a manifest element of dreams and fantasies, to constitute a symbol which in general defied understanding. Yet Stekel in 1935 (Stekel, 1943) had learned that it could represent incest. Many analysts have stated that stone symbolizes the phallus, as is epitomized in the common expression "hard-on" for the erect penis. In 1956 Kestenberg found that stone could represent the ancestor, faeces and the baby. She wrote: ". . . the inner genital of the little girl, which is not ready to deliver a live baby, psychologically appears inanimate, empty, dead, stonelike." (Kestenberg, 1956, p. 287). Her findings were supported by Sperling (1961). In 1967 Wilson noted: "The vagina dentata is represented in dreams as a rock cave, a stone passage or room, a bay or river with stones or submerged reefs." (Wilson, 1967, p. 421.) He found that some women express their wish for the vagina dentata through such imagery and that men used like symbols to express their fear of the vagina dentata and/or their wish for a devouring, toothed phallus. He opined also that stone expresses the reliability of the mother, as well as of the self and others (pp. 423–424). Wilson concluded that in dreams stone, at the deepest psychological level, symbolizes the tooth or teeth of the second oral libidinal phase, the stage of psychosexual development Abraham (1924, p. 398) had designated as "the most primitive form of sadism".

The basic concept of Apache religion is that of diffuse power which pervades the universe and can be used by its possessor for beneficent or baneful purposes at his will. This conceptualization of power mirrors that of the child whose thinking is still predominantly under the influence of the primary process, the type of thinking Freud (1915, pp. 172–176) attributed to the "System Unconscious" (or *Ucs.*), when he had developed his theoretical concepts only to the stage which he called "the topographical point of view". Freud wrote (1915, p. 186):

> The nucleus of the *Ucs.* (from the structural point of view, we would now say, the id and the repressed ego and superego) consists of instinctual representatives which seek to discharge their cathexis . . . (which) are coordinate with one another, exist side by side without being influenced by one another, and are exempt from mutual contradiction . . . (Contradictory wishes) do not diminish each other . . . but combine to form an intermediate aim, a compromise. There are in this system no negation, no doubt, no degrees of certainty: . . . In the *Ucs.* there are only contents, cathected with greater or lesser strength. The cathetic intensities [in the *Ucs.*] are much more mobile. By the process of *displacement* one idea may surrender to another its whole quota of cathexis; by the process of *condensation* it may appropriate the whole cathexis of several other ideas. I have proposed to regard these two processes as distinguishing marks of the so-called *primary psychical* process. (Author's insertions in round brackets.)

To sum up, the characteristics of the system *Ucs.* are "exemption from mutual contradiction . . . timelessness, and replacement of external by psychical reality" (Freud, 1915, p. 187). It has been demonstrated that the individual's perception of his environment is distorted by his needs (Spiro, 1953; Fisher, 1954).

The acquisition of supernatural power by the Apaches requires a "power dream", which can occur during wakeful altered ego states (Gill and Brenman, 1959; Frankel, 1974) or sleep, and also the undergoing of an ordeal.

A special group of shamans are the *gahe* or *jajadeh*, human representatives of supernaturals who inhabit the interiors of certain mountains. These supernaturals became accepted into the corpus of Apachean folklore quite possibly by diffusion from the Pueblo Indians. They did not exist among the Athabaskans from whom the Apaches and Navajos stemmed.

When the Pueblo Indians rebelled against their Spanish conquerors between 1675 and 1680, they finally exterminated their oppressors. However, they were unable to unite under a single leader and to present a unified front against the Spaniards, who soon sought to repossess their former territory. The Navajos had not aided the Pueblos during the insurrection of 1675–80 nor did they help them against the second coming of the Spaniards. Hollister has written:

> As either the Pueblos or the Spaniards presented an unprotected point, they took advantage of it to rob and plunder, and in this way accumulated stores of food, secured many sheep, and grew stronger while the Pueblos grew weaker. Upon the return of the Spaniards many Pueblos had joined the Navajos, preferring to become even Navajos rather than live again under Spanish rule. The deserters from the Pueblos were in sufficient number to add materially to the strength of the Navajos, and from that date the latter began to rank as the most powerful of the southwestern Indian tribes. [1903, pp. 80–81.]

While the Apaches had less regular contact with the Pueblos than did the Navajos, they have intermarried frequently with both groups since time immemorial. Whether their *gahe* or *jajadeh* became incorporated directly from the Pueblos or more indirectly from the Navajos is not known.

After undergoing an ordeal, an Apache man could become a *gahe* when he dressed like one for ceremonials.

A very old Chiricahua man related the following legend concerning the acquisition of the position of *gahe*:

> My father was a great *gahe* leader. Long ago he was out raiding in a small group. They had been out a long time and were doing very badly. They were starving and surrounded by enemies. They didn't dare use their guns. One afternoon my father

went away from camp and sat facing the east, on a big rock. He was looking at *zithtai*.[1] He heard a man's voice from over his head saying, "Why do you sit there, poor and in sorrow?" My father said he was indeed poor and sad; there were enemies all about and his people were starving. He said he was out there trying to get (supernatural) help for his people. Then he begged the spirit for a glimpse of his hand or his face, so that he would know to whom he was talking. The spirit said: "No. You cannot see me. Just answer my questions." My father repeated what he had said and then said he had only one thing of value, his horse, which was his legs. He asked again to see that spirit. He said: "I pray to you. Bless us. We're starving." The power said: "It will cost you something."[2] My father responded: "I have nothing but my horse." The spirit answered: "Go kill that horse. Call your group and feed them from that horse. Return here tomorrow at the same time and place. If you do what I tell you, I will help you." He killed that horse with an arrow, because a gunshot would have attracted the soldiers.

The next day the spirit met him again and this time the spirit said my father could expect a big, fat buck to come to their camp that night.[3] He told my father to meet him again at the same time and place. My father took another man out with him at dusk and they hid behind some bushes. Soon a big buck walked right up to them and my father shot it dead with an arrow.[4] He killed that big, fat, iron-grey horse for his people, the women, the men. He said: "I give this for the power. I have to give something alive to keep you alive." The people thought he was out of his head to kill his horse and didn't believe power had anything to do with it. But when he got that deer in the evening, they were all amazed and *then* they believed he had power.[5] The next day he returned to that same rock and sat facing toward *zithtai*, that holy place. The spirit came. He said: "You're here. Good. You done well. Now if you want to help your people, you go to *zithtai*. Don't get scared. Someone will take you into that place." He went to *zithtai* where a clown, *thlibayeh*, approached him.[6] He demanded why my father was there. My father told him all his troubles and said he'd been told

[1] *Zithtai, Tres Hermanas*, a three-peaked mountain, a sparsely brush-covered outcropping of stone in southwestern New Mexico, was allegedly one of the major sites in which the *gahe* lived.

[2] Whenever an individual seeks to obtain the services of a shaman or a supernatural power, he expects to pay in advance.

[3] At this point, the informant laughed at the ludicrousness of the idea that a small band of men could eat a horse in one day.

[4] Here, the informant interjected: "I didn't listen to my father when I was a boy. When I had already come into my manhood, he wanted to teach me to be a *gahe* leader but I was too interested in baseball. I learned all the songs and all the prayers and how to paint the *gahe* on each of the four days (of the puberty ceremony for girls) and all of the dances, but I never got the power because I never had a spirit visit me."

[5] When a supernatural has been affronted by a mortal, he demands the life of that person. A shaman can use one of his powers to save the life of a person who has been condemned to death by a power. The insulted power, however, still demands a human life to assuage his anger, a concept which is consonant with the *lex talionis* philosophy of the young child. The shaman who saves a life must then substitute his own or that of a "loved one". That is, he must perform witchcraft to remain alive. This ambivalence toward the shaman reflects that of the Apache child toward his mother and his unconscious failure to fuse the good- and bad-mother objects of the period when he perceived her as a split object.

[6] The *thlibayeh* is the fifth member of a team of *gahe* impersonators and was formerly considered to be the most powerful (Opler, 1938). At times, a team will have two or more clowns.

to come, by the spirit. *Thlibayeh* told him to go into that cave with the narrow opening. He told him that inside there would be very frightening things, and gave him exact instructions how to proceed. He told him everything he'd see and what to do under each circumstance.

He crawled into the cave opening and there he saw big rocks before the front door. They were just going back and forth. (As the informant said these words, he moved his hands apart and together repeatedly, and simultaneously gnashed his teeth.) If a man went in there, he would be crushed. My father said, "*Sht*", and the rocks stopped open. He went through the first door. Then he met a huge snake. It was so big its mouth covered the whole tunnel. It had long teeth. He would have swallowed my father whole. He said, "*Sht*", and the snake's mouth stayed open so he could go right through the second door. There a huge lion growled and snapped his big teeth. "*Sht*". Next was a huge bear. "*Sht*".[1] When he got through the fourth door, he saw a beautiful country inside. There he was met by another *thlibayeh* who said mortals were not welcome there and asked what did he want. He told his troubles again and said he'd been instructed by the *thlibayeh* on the outside. The second clown told him to proceed to the Old Man and the Old Woman who sat far away inside. They just sat there, day in and day out, year in and year out. My father walked toward them. Every step of the way, insects, spiders, snakes, birds and animals of all kinds called to him. Each one said: "I'm God. Take me. I can give you what you want. Take my powers." But my father already knew they were evil and their powers were bad. They were *ch'idneh, entee*, witches. They had been entered by the ghosts of dead humans. So he paid no attention to them but just walked on to the old couple. Old Man challenged him as had each of the *thlibayeh*, and he repeated his story and his desire. He didn't talk much because the first *thlibayeh* had told him what to say. The old man told him it was good and if he wanted *diyee*, sacred supernatural power, he would have it. Then my father heard jingles, drums, singing and dancing and the hu-hu-hu-hu-hu sound those *jajadeh* make when they're dancing. The old man said that was good power from *yusn* (God) and asked if my father wanted it. He said he did want it. So he went in there where the *gahe* were dancing, using sabres, not the sticks the men who dress like *gahe* use, and there he was taught all the songs, dances, how to paint, prayers and everything, and there he finally got his power. And it took. He lived ninety-nine years and was always good. He didn't do what the men do now, he did all his good without pay. He had got the power for the good of his people and he used it that way.[2]

A second informant, the wife of a brother of the informant cited above, gave me a slightly different version of the same story of how her father-in-law had acquired his power. In her presentation, the various animals who threatened the man before the four doors of the tunnel

[1] The fauna met by the father of the informant were all cultural bogles of the Mescaleros and Chiricahuas. Only this informant and a handful of others presented this version of the origin of such *bêtes noires*. While it makes excellent sense when the manifest versions of the usual conceptualizations of the relationships among witches, ghosts and powers and blunderbores are analysed for their latent meanings, such a demonstration is outside the scope of the present paper. An aspect which is more important here will be presented below.

[2] The informant's ambivalence toward his father was very clear in other material he presented. It seems evident that he sought to deny the hostile side of his feelings toward his father with this denial that his father required payment for shamanistic services.

were replaced by huge, grinding stones which opened and shut until he said, "*Sht*". As she related this portion of the tale, she, as had the first informant, gnashed her teeth.

Another brother of the man whose version has been related in detail, presented a shortened rendition. In it, the only difference given was that there had been no snake, but instead, a panther. He also said that the animals in the tunnel were the monsters slain by Child-of-the-Water.

A story which is common among the Chiricahuas, Mescaleros and Western Apaches has been recorded also for the Lipans. The Lipans are more closely related historically to the Jicarilla and Kiowa Apaches than to the Mescaleros and Chiricahuas (Hoijer, 1938b, p. 1; Opler, 1940, p. 5). Nevertheless, the last known members of the Northern Lipans joined the Mescaleros in 1863, and the few remaining Southern Lipans at the turn of the century (Sjoberg, 1953). Here is offered a Lipan rendering of the myth of the acquisition of the *gahe* power:

> A blind boy and a boy who had no legs were alone. The clown of the *hactci* saw them crying. He went back to the mountain and told the other clowns of their plight. The head man instructed him to fetch the children. He found them and took them there. As he came up the side of the mountain he approached some rocks. He made a motion as though to open a door and they were able to enter. They went through two doors to where the clowns lived. Once they were in that cave, they were fed whatever they wanted. After four days, they were whole. [Opler, 1940, pp. 50–51.]

According to another version of the same tale (Opler, 1940, p. 50), after the children got inside the mountain they were cut to pieces every night for four nights. Each morning they were restored to their human shape and were stronger. On the last morning, they were whole.

One version of the legend was quite aberrant; it was the only one in which a female protagonist was involved. A blind and lame woman sought supernatural assistance. She entered a cave and emerged cured. She possessed supernatural power after her ordeal but could not be a *gahe*, a status reserved for men. The female who presented this version to me obviously envied the male status and her fantasies clearly depicted penis envy. Immediately after she told the legend, she began to talk of the witchcraft practices of the only Apache currently said uniformly to be a witch, a woman who had a "bad mouth". It was as though she were associating to a dream and her implication was clear: that the witch had obtained her power in that manner. The informant said that when the witch was performing her evil functions she danced naked with another woman and brandished a *gahe* stick as she did so, making thrusting motions with it toward her partner.

The myth of the origin of the Apaches reveals in its manifest content much preoccupation with oral-destructive activity. The condensed version which is related here was obtained from a modern, middle-aged informant of Mescalero and Chiricahua forebears, but it coincides, except for small details, with that obtained regularly from present-day informants.

> Long ago there was a race of people who, except for a virgin adolescent girl, were slain and eaten by *yeeyeh*, Giant, and four flesh-eating monsters. Giant wanted the maiden, White Painted Lady, *istsúneglezh*, Virgin Mary, for his bride and thus instructed the monsters to spare her. However, White Painted Lady heard the voice of *yusn*, God, and followed His instructions. She disrobed, lay on a mountain top and was impregnated by Him when rain entered her vagina.[1] She bore *tubajíshchineh*, Child-of-the-Water, Jesus, after four days.[2] *Yeeyeh* suspected that *istsúneglezh* had borne a son but she fooled him into believing otherwise and the baby grew quickly into young manhood. Child-of-the-Water, aided by other supernaturally-endowed Apache-speaking animals, tricked and defeated the monsters. He either relegated

[1] See also Hoijer (1938b, pp. 171–181, 183–188) and Opler (1942, pp. 1–20, 74–78). In other versions the early people were destroyed by a flood, an alleged event doubtless attributable to Christian influences, and, in one, White Painted Lady and Child-of-the-Water (*istsúneglezh* and *tubajíshchineh*) both survived the flood. That is, only the good mother and her infant son remained, as is consonant with the wishes of the youngster and Mahler's symbiotic stage of infantile development. According to some informants, before the old-time people were drowned or devoured, all of the animals talked Apache and were transformed into people. Here again we have the wishful removal of all rivals for the mother's attention.

In other myth narrations, different flesh-eating monsters existed, such as antelope, bull, eagle, snake, etc.

[2] In other renditions, a second culture hero, Killer-of-Enemies, and White Painted Lady remained. In further variations, *istsúneglezh* first bore Killer-of-Enemies and later *tubajíshchineh*, or had several children before Child-of-the-Water, all of whom were eaten. Killer-of-Enemies and Child-of-the-Water may also have been twins.

The position of Killer-of-Enemies in Chiricahua and Mescalero mythology is unclear. He is the principal culture hero of the Navajos, Western Apaches, Lipans and Jicarillas (Opler, 1942, p. 3).

In the versions in which the older children of White Painted Lady were killed, we have perhaps a reflection of the favouritism of Apaches for the youngest child. In the version in which Killer-of-Enemies and Child-of-the-Water were twins and only the latter survived, we have a reflection of the aboriginal killing of one twin, since twinning was assumed to have been the result of witchcraft, incest, infidelity or "too much sex". The twin to be killed was sometimes smeared with honey and placed on an ant hill, to be eaten – surely an obvious example of oral sadism. Regardless of the rationalizations given for the murder of a baby, we see here a reflection of Apachean parental ambivalence toward their young and perhaps support for the Rascovskys' (1970) conviction that parents harbour unconscious filicidal wishes. We see also the splitting mechanism, with a reversal of the good- and bad-mother introjects, now presented as good- and bad-babies.

them to the wilderness or permitted them to live nearby only after they had agreed not to molest his mother or himself or their progeny and to serve as food for the Apaches. Then he slew *yeeyeh*. In their battle, Giant hurled logs or long rocks at Child-of-the-Water, calling them his arrows, but the youth either deflected or destroyed them with his voice. Giant wore coats of stone but Child-of-the-Water penetrated them with his smaller arrows or with stones he called arrows, the fourth of which penetrated *yeeyeh*'s heart.

We turn now to a partial analysis of the legend of the acquisition of *gahe* power. Viewed one way, the first version of the story obviously recapitulates symbolically the child's quest for his infantile view of adulthood. By being a totally good, obedient child, he can eventually acquire the omniscience and omnipotence he ascribed to his parents while he was still under the dominant influence of the primary psychical process. Viewed another, it depicts the child's tremendously strong wish that he can regain his early fantasized fusion with the mother by returning to the womb.

The father of the legend is first presented as a hungry, helpless person, symbolically a small child. In the story, his rage is not apparent, that is, having been abandoned is repressed. His oral dependency is obvious. The first symbology of stone is that in it, *zithtai*, is to be found the magical gratification of the oral stage. The father, in an altered ego state, initially hears the voice of a spirit whom the informant later stated to have been the voice of *yusn*, God. In the renditions of Hoijer and Opler, the first supernatural being to approach the suffering supplicant was a *thlibayeh*. We can, then, assume that *thlibayeh* in this case is a representative of *yusn*. We recall that *thlibayeh*, the clown, was considered to be the ultimately powerful member of the *gahe* team, although today he is accorded less power (Boyer and Boyer, in press).

Soon it becomes obvious that stone represents the teeth of the oral sadistic phase, affirming Wilson's proposal. Gratification and abnegation of danger can be achieved through the vocalization, "*Sht*", reminiscent of the effects of the baby's distressed callings which, to him, magically resulted in the mother's solacing appearance. Once the projection of oral hostility on to the stones before the front door as the representative of the teeth has occurred, we then find the teeth of the snake, puma and bear without disguise. The obedient child gets past those dangers and then eschews the less than totally gratifying blandishments of the symbolic intra-uterine rivals, the insects, spiders and other animals.

Implicit in the legend is the child's entering into the digestive tracts of a series of parental symbols. The mountain itself represents a female: it has an opening which has the characteristics of both the mouth and the dentate vagina. Psychoanalysands often use the mountain as a female symbol and the anatomical name *mons veneris* reflects the symbolization of the pubic mound as a mountain and the trees or brush on the mound as pubic hair. The power seeking child-symbol gets past the stone-teeth of the cave entrance and enters the gullet of the mountain-mother. Then he gets through the teeth of the snake and enters into the oesophagus. The snake is a classical phallic symbol today and its having teeth reflects the Apachean notion of the penis with the dentate urethra. It is of interest that in some early Near-Eastern cultures, when their principal gods were conceptualized as female (Weigert-Vowinckel, 1938), the snake was sometimes used as an official symbol of the female. Then the father got past the teeth of the cougar and into its digestive tract. The puma is uniformly referred to by Apaches as "she". When they hear its scream at night, a sound which closely resembles that of a crying woman, they are fearful they are going to be devoured. To the Apaches, the bear is an androgynous symbol. Here we should recall Lewin's (1950) remarks about the wish to be eaten, thereby to regain fantasized fusion with the mother, and the version of the legend (Opler, 1942, p. 50) in which the children were cut into pieces inside the mountain on each of four successive nights, finally to emerge whole and possessing the supernatural power the young child ascribes to his mother. The portion of the legend which involves the helpless child's getting into the maternal digestive tract (reflecting childhood fantasies of oral impregnation) and emerging at its other end as a powerful figure, closely resembles childhood ideas of anal or cloacal birth. Viewed thus, the legend can be interpreted as a death and rebirth fantasy.

In the legend, the path to glory requires the re-entry into the womb. The narrow vaginal canal eventually opens up into the edenic intrauterine cavity. But there the protagonist is tempted by symbolic sibling rivals, the insects, the spiders and other small fauna. They offer him their powers but are rejected as witches. The small Apache child who has been spurned after the birth of the next sib turns to his older brothers and sisters for affection. But while they sympathize with his plight, with which they identify on the basis of their own past experiences, they are so hostile toward him that an Apache policy exists that the older child should not express any hostility toward the younger or even defeat him in athletic contests. Early in our more than twenty years of fieldwork among these Apaches, we often watched children of all ages playing football together; the little ones were allowed to score at will. On the other hand, when no adults were watching, older sibs often tormented their younger rivals. The blandishments offered by the symbolic older siblings of the legend would have been, if accepted, less gratifying than the attentions of the parent representates, the Old Man and the Old Woman.

Referring to the symbology of stone once again, we find confirmation of the proposal that stone can represent the genital of the female. The narrow cave, the vagina symbol, opens into the idyllic womb representation; both exist within the stone *zithtai*.

The interpretation of the legend as an enactment of the wish to obtain fusion with the mother and thereby regain the early fantasized symbiosis is implicit in the symbolized wish to be digested by her. To be sure, individuation is later accomplished when the child is reborn. But his reborn state represents retention of fusion, too, since, as the newborn *gahe*, he has become omniscient and omnipotent, sharing that fantasized state with the parent-symbols of his infantile imagination.

The legend can also be interpreted as a fantasy of incest and the reversal of the fear of castration. *Thlibayeh*, equated by the informant with *yusn*, God, He Who Created Us, Our Father in Heaven, does not forbid the weak adult son, otherwise represented by the blind or legless boy, to enter the symbolic vagina of the mother surrogate. Instead, the father uses his supernatural power to make the procedure possible and enable his son to undergo the dangerous procedure and emerge whole and in possession of supernatural power. Such power is often conceptualized by Apaches as being phallic in origin. The equation of omniscience and omnipotence with the possession of a huge phallus is clear in the following example. One time the woman who gave the sole version involving a female protagonist was allowed to continue her interview for some minutes after her session customarily ended. The next informant unceremoniously walked into my office. In mock apology, he said to her, "I didn't know you were here." She replied, "I thought you knew everything. Your third leg hangs to the ground." After further interchange, she also said she thought he could do everything.

The interpretation of the legend as a representation of incest involves use of the *pars pro toto* equation of the primary process. The body-phallus equation is common in the dreams and fantasies of analysands. The boy representative, the father of the legend, enters the symbolic vagina, that is, his body as a substitute phallus penetrates the mother representation. That Apaches, too, equate body and phallus is clear in the following joke. Two Apache men were enviously ridiculing a third, a man who was generally known as a "Don Juan". One said, "he has a big prick." The other replied, "He *is* a big prick."

The version in which the blind and lame woman underwent the ordeal and emerged whole is of interest. The informant who rendered it clearly envied men their penises; perhaps her version depicted a personal wish-fulfilment. She was a shaman whose status was diminishing and she feared she had lost some of her supernatural power. She was almost blind, arthritic and lame and one of the reasons for her attending interviews with the author was that she hoped he would cure those afflictions shamanistically (Boyer and Boyer, 1977). In her associations to the legend she had the witch, a shaman who chose to use her powers evilly, dancing naked with a woman toward whom she thrust the *gahe* stick, clearly a phallic symbol in this constellation. That is, in the view of the informant, the witch had emerged not only cured of blindness and lameness, but in possession of a phallus. The nude dancing scene apparently symbolizes intercourse.

We turn now to a partial analysis of the Apache origin myth. In the origin myth of the Apaches there existed a race of people who presumably were the children of He-Who-Created-Us, *yusn.* Except for White Painted Lady, all of them, including her parents, were devoured by Giant and the monsters. In dreams, crowds frequently represent a single person; in this case and context it seems reasonable to assume that the crowd represents the mother of the maiden. In the identification of *yeeyeh* there seems to exist another example of the splitting of the object. Many Apaches translate the myth in Christian terms and equate Giant with the devil, that is, they represent the moral and immoral aspects of one individual.

In clinical work we learn frequently that children are encouraged to behave in such manners that they gratify the unconscious wishes of the parents. Many communications report that parents of both sexes covertly or overtly seduce their children into latent or patent incestuous activity (Rangell, 1955). Devereux (1955) reported a counter-oedipal episode in the *Iliad*, emphasizing maternal sexual seductiveness. He had previously (1953) analysed the cause of Laius's death at the hands of Oedipus and concluded that Oedipus's cohabitation with Jocasta represented primarily an active homosexual triumph over the dead father. He suggested that, generally speaking, the attainment of full genitality presupposes also an at least imaginary homosexual victory over the father.

In the Apache myth of creation, the interpretation can be made that the father of White Painted Lady, represented by *yusn*, wanted his daughter as a sexual partner. In the overt content of the story, *yeeyeh*, a representative of He-Who-Created-Us, clearly did so. *Yusn* permitted or directed Giant to kill the mother of White Painted Lady. In Apache socialization, while parents officially disapprove of profligacy of adults and the incestuous relations of children, they directly encourage such behaviour. Also, sons sometimes marry their stepmothers or girls their stepfathers after a death or divorce, and sexual relations between teenagers of both sexes and adults easily old enough to be their parents are not infrequent. Aboriginally, maidens became marriageable with their puberty ceremonies and often married older men.

In the relations between Child-of-the-Water and *yeeyeh*, we see a distorted representation of the son killing his father and then cohabiting with his mother. Perhaps we have here, additionally, a validation of Devereux's interpretation that the fantasied fulfilment of the son's sexual relations with the mother involves a homosexual triumph over the father.

The battle of Giant and Child-of-the-Water, in most versions of the myth, was with arrows. Those of the father were huge, in fact logs, whereas those of the chronologically young boy were comparatively very small. People all over the world equate arrow and phallus; the Apaches clearly do in their everyday conversation. It seems tenable to interpret this portion of the myth to constitute a battle in which the father and the son seek to penetrate each other with their phallus-representations and the boy wins.

Thus far we have omitted the identification of the monsters, in our attempt to understand the genital aspects of this story. We have no direct information to assist us. However, since Child-of-the-Water slew them, in some cases with arrows, and since they performed similar functions in the myth to those of Giant, it seems reasonable to ascribe to them the identity of split-representatives of *yeeyeh*, the immoral father.

We shall now turn to oral aspects of the Apache myth of creation.

As noted earlier, the symbols to be found in dreams and myths can be representations of self-images of the dreamer. In the manifest story, *yeeyeh* and the Apache-speaking monsters devoured the first race of people and sought to eat Child-of-the-Water; they were, thus, cannibals.

Abraham (1916, pp. 253–258) suggested that the orally fixated individual sometimes has the wish to incorporate the object which had attracted his wish-fantasies by means of eating that object or its substitute, as noted before. Lewin (1950, pp. 102–165) has written of the desire to be reunited with a lost love object by being eaten.

The Apaches use a single word to mean envy, jealousy and greed and appear to equate the three states. Klein differentiates among them as follows:[1]

> Envy is the angry feeling that another person possesses and enjoys something desirable . . . . and goes back to the earliest exclusive relation with the mother. Jealousy is based on envy, but involves a relation to at least two people; it is mainly concerned with love that the subject feels is his due and . . . is in danger of being taken away from him by his rival . . . At the unconscious level, greed aims primarily at completely scooping out, sucking dry, and devouring the breast: that is to say, its aim is destructive introjection . . . greed is mainly bound up with introjection and envy with projection. [Klein, 1957, p. 607.]

One facet of the creation myth is that the mother-representatives of the girl are devoured. Although I do not have material from Apache patients or informants which proves that in this myth, the wish of the White Painted Lady to be reunited with her mother by being eaten by her parents (or parent: *yeeyeh* as father, surely, and perhaps the monsters as mother), I have ample data to indicate that all primary process mechanisms which are found to be operative in my analytic patients are likewise present in the Apaches. A clear example of the use of reversal to be found in the creation myth appears in a version of the slaying of Antelope monster (Opler, 1942, p. 11). After he killed Antelope, "Child-of-the-Water takes pieces of the meat of the antelope and blows on them, naming and thus creating the various animals as he does so".

[1] Although I agree with Zetzel's (1956) criticisms of Klein and her followers, she has contributed insights which I have found to be immensely helpful in the understanding of patients, particularly those who suffer from psychoses and severe character disorders (Kernberg, 1972).

Two other facets of the creation myth merit underlining in our attempt to understand its relationship to Apache orality.

With the aid of supernaturally endowed, friendly animals, animals which in most instances were likewise the foodstuffs of the monsters, Child-of-the-Water was able to persuade some of the flesh-eating animals to become standard meat for the Apaches. They who had been cannibals agreed to become the victims of the cannibals. Whom do the friendly animals symbolize in the family constellation of the child? After the Apache child's displacement from the relatively exclusive relationship with his mother by the arrival of a new nursling, he turned to food and his older siblings for solace.

In some versions of the myths which deal with the killing of Giant and the monsters, Child-of-the-Water hunts with Killer-of-Enemies, another child of White Painted Lady. The informants from whom Hoijer and Opler obtained their renditions of these myths were all adults. Elsewhere, I present evidence which I have interpreted to mean that adult Apaches are better able to use prose narrative to support their repressions than are teenagers (Boyer, L. B., 1975). In his rendition of the myth of the slaying of *yeeyeh* and the monsters, an adolescent boy said, referring to the episode in which Child-of-the-Water is assisted by Gopher in the killing of Bull or Antelope, "Child-of-the-Water told Gopher he wanted to kill that antelope and *his brother* told him what to do." It seems justifiable to ascribe to the friendly animals the meaning of siblings. They turn in unison upon their parents (or mother, if we assume the monsters represent mother), who have been endowed with the oral sadism of the displaced children, to destroy them and incorporate them through symbolic cannibalism. However, we have another complication. In at least one version of the myth of the slaying of the monsters, Gopher is a monster (Hoijer, 1938b, pp. 12–13). I believe we can resolve this apparent paradox when we recall that Apaches have great ambivalence toward their siblings, who, although they serve at times as helpers and tranquillizers, are likewise the targets of intense hostility. Today such hostility makes itself apparent, especially when Apaches are intoxicated (Boyer, L. B., 1964; Boyer and Boyer, 1972). In this context one of the over-determined meanings of the monsters is that of hated siblings.

In the origin myth one facet is reminiscent of the magic power of the voice which was found to be operative in the legend of the acquisition of *gahe* power. There, saying "*Sht*" kept the teeth, upon which had been projected the oral-sadism of the child, from eating the protagonist. In the origin myth *tubajíshchineh*'s voice could destroy *yeeyeh*'s logs–stones–arrows. Attention was called previously to the child's belief in the magic of his voice, which is presumed to have its origin in the mother's response to his calls.

So far as the symbology of stone is concerned, the version of the origin myth which was presented adds another meaning to those found in the *gahe* power acquisition legend. The arrows of both *yeeyeh* and *tubajíshchineh* were alternatively called stones; they were used for the purpose of destruction through penetration. We have no associative data from informants or obvious information in the myth itself to help us interpret the stone armour of *yeeyeh* beyond the obvious meaning of the stone as a symbol of bodily defence.

References

ABRAHAM, KARL (1916). The first pregenital stage of the libido. In *Selected Papers on Psycho-Analysis* (1948), pp. 249–279. Hogarth Press, London.

ABRAHAM, KARL (1924). The influence of oral erotism on character-formation. In *Selected Papers on Psycho-Analysis* (1948), pp. 393–406. Hogarth Press, London.

ADAIR, JOHN J. (1948). A study of culture resistance: the veterans of World War II at Zuni Pueblo. Ph.D. dissertation, University of New Mexico.

ARLOW, JACOB, A. (1961). Ego psychology and the study of mythology. *Journal of the American Psychoanalytic Association*, **9**, 371–393.

BASCOM, WILLIAM (1954). Four functions of folklore. *Journal of American Folklore*, **67**, 333–349.

BASEHART, HARRY W. (1959). Chiricahua Apache subsistence and socio-political organization. (Mimeographed.) University of New Mexico Mescalero-Chiricahua Land Claims Project, Alberquerque.

BASEHART, HARRY W. (1960). Mescalero Apache subsistence patterns and socio-political organization. (Mimeographed.) University of New Mexico Mescalero-Chiricahua Land Claims Project, Alberquerque.

BOYER, L. BRYCE (1964). Psychological problems of a group of Apaches: alcoholic hallucinosis and latent homosexuality among typical men. *The Psychoanalytic Study of Society*, **3**, 203–277.

BOYER, L. BRYCE (1975). The man who turned into a water monster: a psychoanalytic contribution to folklore. *The Psychoanalytic Study of Society*, **6**, 100–133.

BOYER, L. BRYCE (1977). Mythology, folklore and psychoanalysis. In *International Encyclopedia of Psychiatry, Psychology, Psychoanalysis and Neurology* (Ed. Benjamin B. Wolman), vol. 17, pp. 423–429. Aesculapius Publishers Inc. and Van Nostrand Reinhold Co., New York.

BOYER, L. BRYCE (in press). *Childhood and Folklore: A Psychoanalytic Study of Apache Personality*. Library of Psychological Anthropology, New York.

BOYER, L. BRYCE and BOYER, RUTH M. (1972). Effects of acculturation on the vicissitudes of the aggressive drive among the Apaches of the Mescalero Indian Reservation. *The Psychoanalytic Study of Society*, **5,** 40–82.

BOYER, L. BRYCE and BOYER, RUTH M. (1976). Prolonged adolescence and early identification: a cross-cultural study. *The Psychoanalytic Study of Society*, **7,** 95–106.

BOYER, L. BRYCE and BOYER, RUTH M. (1977). Understanding the individual through folklore. *Contemporary Psychoanalysis*, **13,** 30–51.

BOYER, L. BRYCE and BOYER, RUTH M. (in press). Additional data concerning the mountain spirits and the sacred clown of the Chiricahua and Mescalero Apache folklore and ritual. *Western Folklore*, **37.**

BOYER, RUTH M. (1962). Social structure and socialization among the Apache of the Mescalero Indian Reservation. Ph.D. dissertation, University of California, Berkeley, California.

BOYER, RUTH M. (1964). The matrifocal family among the Mescalero: additional data. *American Anthropologist*, **66,** 593–602.

DEVEREUX, GEORGE (1953). Why Oedipus killed Laius: a note on the complementary Oedipus complex in Greek drama. *International Journal of Psycho-Analysis*, **34,** 132–141.

DEVEREUX, GEORGE (1955). A counteroedipal episode in Homer's Iliad. *Bulletin of the Philadelphia Association for Psychoanalysis*, **4,** 90–97.

DUNDES, ALAN (ed.) (1965). *The Study of Folklore*. Prentice-Hall, Englewood Cliffs, New Jersey.

ERIKSON, ERIK H. (1939). Observations on Sioux education. *Journal of Psychology*, **7,** 101–156.

ERIKSON, ERIK H. (1950). *Childhood and Society*. Norton, New York.

FISHER, CHARLES (1954). Dreams and perception: the role of preconscious and primary modes of perception in dream formation. *Journal of the American Psychoanalytic Association*, **2,** 389–445.

FLEISS, ROBERT (1957). *Erogeneity and Libido: Addenda to the Theory of the Psychosexual Development of the Human*. International Universities Press, New York.

FRANKEL, FRED H. (1974). Trance capacity and the genesis of phobic behavior. *Archives of General Psychiatry*, **31,** 261–263

FREEMAN, DANIEL M. A. (1968). Adolescent crises of the Kiowa-Apache Indian male. In *Minority Group Adolescents in the United States* (Ed. Eugene B.

Brody), pp. 157–204. Williams and Wilkins, Baltimore, Maryland.

FREUD, SIGMUND (1900). *The Interpretation of Dreams*. Standard Edition, vols 4 and 5 (1953). Hogarth Press, London.

FREUD, SIGMUND (1915). *The Unconscious*. Standard Edition, vol. 14 (1957), pp. 159–215. Hogarth Press, London.

FREUD, SIGMUND (1923). *The Ego and the Id*. Standard Edition, vol. 19 (1961), pp. 1–66. Hogarth Press, London.

GILL, MERTON M. and BRENMAN, MARGARET (1959). *Hypnosis and Related States*. International Universities Press, New York.

HARTMANN, HEINZ (1939). *Ego Psychology and the Problem of Adaptation* (1958). International Universities Press, New York.

HARTMANN, HEINZ, KRIS, ERNST and LOEWENSTEIN, RUDOLPH M. (1949). Notes on the theory of aggression. *The Psychoanalytic Study of the Child*, **3–4**, 9–36.

HIPPLER, ARTHUR E., BOYER, L. BRYCE, BOYER, RUTH M., DAY, RICHARD and DEVOS, GEORGE (1978a). A Psychoethnography of the Upper Tanana Indians. Unpublished monograph.

HIPPLER, ARTHUR E., BOYER, L. BRYCE, BOYER, RUTH M., DAY, RICHARD and DEVOS, GEORGE (1978b). A psychoethnography of the Western Tanaina Indians. Unpublished monograph.

HOIJER, HARRY (1938a). The southern Athabaskan languages. *American Anthropologist*, **40**, 75–87.

HOIJER, HARRY (1938b). *Chicicahua and Mescalero Apache Texts*. University of Chicago Press, Chicago, Illinois.

HOLLISTER, C. S. (1903). *The Navajo and his Blanket* (1972). Rio Grande Press, Glorieta, New Mexico.

JACOBSON, EDITH (1964). *The Self and the Object World*. International Universities Press, New York.

KERNBERG, OTTO (1972). Critique of the Kleinian School. In *Tactics and Techniques in Psychoanalytic Therapy* (Ed. Peter L. Giovacchini), pp. 62–93. Science House Press, New York.

KESTENBERG, JUDITH S. (1956). On the development of maternal feelings in early childhood: observations and reflections. *The Psychoanalytic Study of the Child*, **11**, 257–291.

KLEIN, MELANIE (1957). *Envy and Gratitude*. Basic Books, New York.

LAFFAL, JULIUS (1964). Freud's theory of language. *The Psychoanalytic Quarterly*, **33**, 157–175.

LEWIN, BERTRAM D. (1950). *The Psychoanalysis of Elation*. Norton, New York.

LUBART, JOSEPH M. (1970). *Psychodynamic Problems of Adaptation: Mackenzie Delta Eskimos*. The Queen's Printer for Canada, Ottawa.

MAHLER, MARGARET S. and FURER, MANUEL (1968). *On Human Symbiosis and the Vicissitudes of Individuation*, vol. 1: *Infantile Psychosis*. International

Universities Press, New York.

MAHLER, MARGARET S., PINE, FRED and BERGMAN, ANNI (1975). *The Psychological Birth of the Human Infant: Symbiosis Individuation.* Basic Books, New York.

MURPHY, ROBERT F. (1957). Intergroup hostility and social cohesion. *American Anthropologist*, **59,** 1018–1035.

OPLER, MORRIS E. (1933). An analysis of Mescalero and Chiricahua Apache social organization in the light of their systems of relationship. Ph.D. dissertation, University of Chicago.

OPLER, MORRIS E. (1938). Myths and tales of the Jicarilla Apaches. *Memoirs of the American Folk-Lore Society*, vol. 36.

OPLER, MORRIS E. (1940). Myths and legends of the Lipan Apache Indians. *Memoirs of the American Folk-Lore Society*, vol. 36.

OPLER, MORRIS E. (1941). *An Apache Life-way.* University of Chicago Press, Chicago, Illinois.

OPLER, MORRIS E. (1942). Myths and tales of the Chiricahua Apache Indians. *Memoirs of the American Folk-Lore Society*, vol. 37.

OPLER, MORRIS E. (1945). The Lipan Apache death complex and its extensions. *Southwestern Journal of Anthropology*, **1,** 122–141.

OPLER, MORRIS E. (1946). Reaction to death among the Mescalero Apache. *Southwestern Journal of Anthropology*, **2,** 454–467.

RANGELL, LEO (1955). The role of the parent in the Oedipus complex. *Bulletin of the Menninger Clinic*, **19,** 9–15.

RASCOVSKY, ARNALDO and RASCOVSKY, MATILDE W. DE (1970). La matanza de los hijos. In *La Matanza de los Hijos y Otros Ensayos* (Ed. Arnaldo Rascovsky), pp. 9–38. Ediciones Kargieman, Buenos Aires.

REICHARD, GLADYS A. (1934). *Spider Woman. A Story of Navaho Weavers and Chanters* (1968). Rio Grande Press, Glorieta, New Mexico.

SJOBERG, ANDRÉE F. (1953). Lipan Apache culture in historical perspective. *Southwestern Journal of Anthropology*, **9,** 76–98.

SPERLING, MELITTA (1961). A note on some symbols and the significance of their change during psychoanalysis. *Journal of the Hillside Hospital*, **10,** 261–266.

SPERLING, MELITTA (1964). A case of Ophidiophilia. A clinical contribution to snake symbolism, and a supplement to "Psychoanalytic study of ulcerative colitis in children". *The International Journal of Psycho-Analysis*, **45,** 227–233.

SPIRO, MELFORD E. (1952). Ghosts, Ifaluk and teleological functionalism. *American Anthropologist*, **54,** 497–503.

SPIRO, MELFORD E. (1953). Ghosts: an anthropological inquiry into learning and perception. *Journal of Abnormal and Social Psychology*, **48,** 376–382.

STEKEL, WILHELM (1943). *The Interpretation of Dreams* (translation E. and C.

Paul), 2 vols. Liveright, New York.

WALDHORN, HERBERT F. and FINE, BERNARD D. (Eds) (1974). *Trauma and Symbolism*. International Universities Press, New York.

WEIGERT-VOWINCKEL, EDITH (1938). The cult and mythology of the magna mater from the standpoint of psychoanalysis. *Psychiatry*, **1,** 347–378.

WILSON, C. PHILIP (1967). Stone as a symbol of teeth. *The Psychoanalytic Quarterly*, **36,** 418–425.

ZETZEL, ELIZABETH R. (1956). An approach to the relation between concept and content in psychoanalytic theory (with special references to the work of Melanie Klein and her followers). *The Psychoanalytic Study of the Child*, **11,** 99–121.

Severed Heads that Germinate

Derek Freeman

HEAD-HUNTING, one of the most widespread and bizarre of the cults to have flourished in human societies, is defined in the *Shorter Oxford English Dictionary* as "the practice . . . of making incursions for the purpose of procuring human heads as trophies". My purpose in this brief essay is to look on head-hunting – and, in particular, on head-hunting as it once existed among the Iban of Borneo – as a mode of symbolic behaviour that must be interpreted to be understood.[1]

Most of the interpretations of head-hunting which have been offered by anthropologists have been explicitly sociological. For example, Downs (1955, p. 70) in his study of the Indonesian region, associates head-hunting with dual organization, and cites with approval J. P. B. de Josselin de Jong's view that "head-hunting belongs to the socio-religious complex of 'potlach'". More recently McKinley (1976, pp. 113 ff.) has advanced the egregious view that head-hunting has the symbolic function of "winning souls for humanity" (p. 125) by "the ritual incorporation of the enemy as friend" (p. 113) – the enemy's head being chosen as a ritual symbol "because it contains the face, which . . . is the most concrete symbol of social personhood" (p. 124).

Interpretations such as these give comfort, I suppose, to some; for me they have the defect of totally failing to detect any breath of the

[1] In this present paper I focus attention on the symbolism central to the Iban cult of head-hunting. In so doing, I would note that the beliefs and rites associated with head-hunting are most complex. I plan to discuss other aspects of the Iban cult of head-hunting in subsequent papers. For further information about the Iban, see Freeman (1970) and Jensen (1974).

symbolism integral to the cult of head-hunting which I myself have long pondered – that of the pagan Iban of the Baleh River and its fast-flowing tributaries.

In 1949, when I began my study of the Iban of Sarawak, the cult of head-hunting was still of passionate concern to them. Towards the end of the war against Japan numerous heads were taken, and I was able on several occasions to witness the enactment of the spectacular *gawai* in which a successful head-hunter celebrates his fell deeds and, by the ritual performance of a set of symbolic actions, seeks to ensure their repetition.

The climax of the remarkable allegory central to the Iban cult of head-hunting which, as it is chanted by bards is acted out by aspirant head-hunters, is a rite known as *ngelampang*, which literally means "to cut into pieces". In this part of the allegory a graphic description is given of the ritual splitting of a trophy head, or *antu pala*, by Lang Singalang Burong, the Iban god of war. Lang achieves this feat (which symbolizes the actual beheading of an enemy) with one swift blow of his sword, and from the head which he has split open there pours forth seed which when sown grows into a human crop – as did the dragon's teeth strewn by Cadmus on the plain of Boeotia.

A crucial question then, for anyone wishing to understand the Iban cult of head-hunting, is, "Why should a trophy head (of all things) contain seed?" In my field notes of the early 1950s, this question is posed in precisely these words. At that time it was an enigma to me. I could find no answer to it in the literature of anthropology, nor were my Iban informants of any great help. The best they could do was to tell me something I already knew: that the head-hunting allegory followed closely the theme of another most important ritual which has as its object the enhancing of the fertility of the hill rice, or *padi*, which the Iban cultivate in clearings in the rain forest. Of much greater help (as my attempts to fathom the symbolism of Iban head-hunting continued) was the literature of psychoanalysis, parts of which, I discovered, were directly relevant to the apparent enigma of severed heads that germinate. At this outcome, George Devereux (from whose writings I have long gained stimulus and insight) would not be in the least surprised.

We are concerned, it is evident, with three main elements: with trophies, with heads and with fertility. Fertility, as with all cultivators of the soil, is most highly valued by the Iban. Indeed, for pagan Iban the growing of *padi* is essentially a matter of ritual, their whole system of agriculture being based on an elaborate fertility cult. It is the fervent conviction of the Iban that their *padi*, like all other living things, possesses a soul of its own. "They imagine", as Sir James Frazer put it (1922, p. 414), "that in the fibres of the plant, as in the body of a man, there is a certain vital element which is so far independent of the plant that it may for a time be completely separated from it without fatal effects, though if its absence be prolonged beyond certain limits the plant will wither and die." This "vital element", or soul, is termed *semengat* by the Iban. The fertility of *padi* is believed to depend on the state of its *semengat*, and it is this state which the Iban strive to safeguard and enhance in their *padi* rituals.

In the same way the life of a human being is believed to depend on the presence in his body of his *semengat*. This *semengat*, the Iban believe, frequently leaves the body. An individual's dreams, they suppose, are the adventures of his soul as it wanders abroad. In these wanderings, should a *semengat* become lost or be waylaid by malevolent spirits, its owner will become ill, and it is with the recovery of souls and the returning of them to their rightful owners that Iban shamans (*manang*) are principally concerned. When a shaman is successful he emerges from his "trance" clutching the soul he has caught in his clenched fist which he then places on top of his patient's head, where the fontanelle once was, so enabling the *semengat* to reoccupy its proper abode. As this rite indicates, it is the belief of the Iban that the *semengat*, when it is in the body, resides in an individual's head. Thus, ear wax is called by the Iban *tai semengat*, or excrement of the soul.

While it is believed by the Iban that the possession of a soul is essential if life is to be sustained, there is no generalized belief in soul substance of the kind that has been reported from some other parts of Indonesia and South-East Asia. Rather, a *semengat* is conceived of as being *baka gambal kitai empu*; that is, it exactly replicates the appearance of the individual to whom it belongs. When in the head it is diminutive (no bigger than a match head, as one shaman put it), but when wandering abroad of ordinary human size.

In a paper entitled "The Significance of Head-Hunting in Assam" (1928, p. 403) J. H. Hutton argued that "the underlying purpose" in head-hunting is to secure the "fertilizing soul-matter" which resides in a human head, and is able to fructify crops. This theory may well hold for the Naga Hills, but it cannot be applied to the Iban, for the trophy head split open by Lang specifically contains not *semengat*, but *benih*, or seed, and it is this symbolism which must be interpreted if the significance of Iban head-hunting is to be comprehended.

Let us then turn to direct consideration of the human head as a symbol. As De Vries indicates in his *Dictionary of Symbols and Imagery* (1974, p. 243), the human head has been given a multiplicity of meanings, ranging from wisdom and authority to virility and fertility. In the present case it is obviously with the head as a symbol of virility and fertility that we are mainly concerned. This theme has been brilliantly explored by Professor R. B. Onians (1951, pp. 93 ff.). The psyche, as Onians documents (ibid, p. 119), was believed by the ancient Greeks to be present in seed or semen, and the seed was thought to be enclosed in the skull and the spine in the shape of "generative marrow". The head and the male genitals were regarded as the principal repositories of this generative power, and so were identified, the one with the other. Almost identical beliefs were held by the ancient Romans. Thus, the genius (or life-soul) was thought to reside in the head which was also "the source of seed" (ibid, p. 129).

From this evidence we may recognize the head as being, in some cultures, a phallic symbol, as standing, that is, for the phallus as a primary source of "the generative power of nature". This conferring on the head of a phallic significance is, the evidence suggests, both ancient and widespread. It may be seen, to cite but a few examples, in the horned head of the Devil (Jones, 1949, p. 172), the mitre of Osiris, the Phrygian cap of Mithras, and in the head of the phallic Shiva crowned by tresses of hair that, to use the words of Zimmer (1946, p. 166), broadcast "as it were, on their magic waves the exuberance and sanctity of vegetative life, the charm, the appeal, the solemn command, of the generative forces of procreating Māyā".

Not unexpectedly the symbolic identification of head and phallus came to the attention of Freud in his researches on human dreams and fantasies. In 1900 he recorded a dream in which a hat was accorded phallic significance (Freud, 1900, p. 360); and in 1916 he noted that "in phantasies and in numerous symptoms the head too appears as a symbol of the male genitals, or, if one prefers to put it so, as something standing for them" (Freud, 1916, p. 339). The symbolic equation Head = Phallus has since been confirmed in the writings of very many other psychoanalysts, and may be accepted as one of the basic symbolic identifications of many human cultures.

In what follows I shall consider the interpretation that the trophy heads by which the Iban set such store have a phallic significance as symbols of the generative power of nature. This means, of course, that a trophy head, in terms of unconscious symbolism, is another kind of "golden bough" (cf. Freeman, 1968, p. 371). I would not be surprised, furthermore, if this were the symbolic indentification basic to many of the other head-hunting cults in Indonesia, South-East Asia and elsewhere. In an account written in the 1850s Spenser St John (1863, vol. I, p. 204) has described how among the Land Dayaks of Borneo, a trophy head, newly taken, is believed "to make their rice grow well, to cause the forest to abound with wild animals, to enable their dogs and snares to be successful in securing game, to have the streams swarm with fish, to give health and activity to the people themselves, and to ensure of fertility to their women". Among the Rungus Dusun of North Borneo (G. N. Appell, personal communication) an infertile woman is treated by having a trophy head placed between her thighs.

The primary evidence in the Iban case for a trophy head having phallic significance is the culturally accepted fantasy that such a head contains seed. Further evidence of the symbolic significance of trophy heads is contained in the metaphors used to describe them in the *timang* which is chanted during a head-hunting *gawai*. These metaphors, for the most part, refer to fertility and abundance as when trophy heads are equated with a cluster of betel nuts (*sit pinang kunchit*) or a mass of durian fruit (*tambong rian melujong*); or are implicitly phallic as when a trophy head is referred to as a pointed red pepper, a quick river fish, or a scalded, pendant cucumber (*langgu rampo betu*) (cf. Jones, 1949, p. 38). One is put in mind of that timeless Welsh allegory, *Under Milk Wood*, with its talk of brilliantined trout and of Sinbad, whose "goat beard was a tuft of wiry fire" and who, to Gossamer Beynon, was "all cucumber and hooves" (Thomas, 1954).

Before turning to a descriptive analysis of the content of the allegory that accompanies Iban head-hunting rituals, let me comment briefly on the head as a trophy. The term trophy is derived from the Greek *tropos* which refers to the turning away of an adversary, and thus to triumphing over a foe. A trophy is some material object from the field of battle carried off as a memento of victory and a badge of valour. The weapons of a vanquished foe are very commonly taken as trophies but, in the case of males, there are two trophies, in particular, which provide unequivocal proof that an adversary has been utterly vanquished: his genitals and his head.

The taking of an enemy's genitals (in whole or in part) is an ancient human practice (Menninger, 1938, p. 238). David was commanded by King Saul to bring to him 100 foreskins of the hated Philistines: and the castration of vanquished enemies to provide trophies has persisted into modern times, as among the Danakil (or Afar) of Ethiopia (Lewis, 1955). Trophies of this kind are obviously not durable; whereas the head, with its bony skull, may be preserved for very long periods. It is this durability, I would suggest, that has made the head the most prevalent of all bodily trophies.

Among the Iban certainly the head of an enemy was, beyond all compare, the most highly valued of trophies, being regarded as a *tanda brani*, or sign of fighting prowess. It was by taking a head, above all else, that a man acquired prestige among his fellows. As the Iban phrase it: *"Sapa enda brani, enda bulih antu pala, enda brita."* "Those who are not daring, who do not take heads, lack renown."

When he had taken a head, and only then, was an Iban male entitled to have the back of his hands tattooed. With this achieved his prowess was on constant display. On formal social occasions he could bask in the adulation of the women who, sitting before him on the public gallery of the long-house, would ply him with rice wine (*tuak*), chant his praise for all to hear, and incite him to further deeds of derring-do. A successful young head-hunter, it is said, could have his pick of the most desirable young women, and was much sought after as a husband. In contrast, a man who had never taken a head, or who was known to be reluctant in battle, would be told by the women he courted:

Dulu niki tiang;
Dulu belabong isang.
(First scale the posts of an enemy long-house;
first bedeck your hair as does he who has taken a head.)

With these and comparable values being paramount, it is understandable that the collecting of trophy heads became the principal obsession of Iban males and prompted the emergence of a complex series of rituals in which the feats of the head-hunter are extolled and trophy heads accorded a symbolic significance of exceptional importance.

Let me now return to a description of a head-hunting ritual, or *gawai*, and of the allegory that accompanies it. *Gawai* are always performed by a *bilek* family for one or more of its male members. The preparations are protracted and costly, with as many as a score of guests being invited for the seven or so days for which the *gawai* lasts. In a large long-house the total number of guests at a *gawai* often runs into hundreds. The most important rite after the arrival of the guests (made up as far as possible of men renowned for their prowess as head-hunters) is the setting up of shrines, or *ranyai*, on the *ruai*, or public gallery of the long-house – one for each of the participating families. A shrine consists of a bamboo framework over which *ikat* fabrics (which commonly depict the feats of head-hunters) are draped. On the outer surface of the shrine are hung swords, and various ritual objects with phallic connotations.[1] Under Iban custom it should be set up by a man who has himself taken a head.

Once erected, a shrine becomes the centre-piece for the rites that follow and, in particular, it becomes the abode, during the course of the *gawai*, of Lang Singalang Burong. Lang is a sky-god – an amalgam of Jupiter and Mars, with a dash of Bacchus. In his human form he is an imposing man of heroic proportions, who, despite his mature age, is in full command of his great physical powers. His animal form is the Brahminy Kite: a predatory bird of great strength and beauty. Above all else Lang is the god of head-hunting: the custodian of severed heads from the beginning of time.

Lang's attendance at a head-hunting *gawai* is secured by especially commissioned *lemambang*, or bards. Here, as in the case of the shaman, the theory of the separable dream-soul holds. As the bard chants his invocation his soul, so it is believed, leaves his body and ascends to the skies (in the company of two culture heroes) to conduct Lang and his supernatural associates to the long-house where his mortal hosts have prepared shrines, offerings and sacrifices. As this journey is supposedly taking place, the bard and his assistants describe its course in graphic and moving mytho-poetic words as they parade up and down the gallery of the long-house.

The journey begins with the traversing one by one of the haunts of the tutelary spirits of a long succession of weapons and devices of war

[1] At a head-hunting ritual (*gawai nanga langit*) which I attended in Sungai Amang, Kapit District, in June 1949, a small basket containing sacred rice seed (*raga benih padi pun*) was suspended from the shrine. This seed was said (by the officiating *lemambang*, or bard) to symbolize the trophy heads which those performing the ritual hoped to take at some time in the future.

(such as the sword, the spear and the caltrop), and of animals such as the cobra, the crocodile and the serpent, which have a significance both phallic and aggressive.

Mythical serpents are particularly associated with the Iban cult of head-hunting. Almost every renowned head-hunter of former days was aided by a dream-derived spirit helper. The most wished for of all these spirit helpers was the *nabau*, a mythical serpent, or water dragon, which was believed to accompany the head-hunter, aiding him in his gruesomely heroic task. The canoe used by head-hunters was said to be like a snake and no menstruating woman was allowed to touch it. In the *gawai siligi* performed before a raid a spear was magically metamorphosed into a snake, which accompanied the head-hunters on their mission. This preoccupation with snakes and serpents is also conspicuous in the *gawai kenyalang*, or hornbill ritual (cf. Freeman, 1960), which is commonly performed by head-hunters. In this ritual the carved effigy of a rhinoceros hornbill is erected on a lofty pole. This pole, it is believed, turns into a serpent which joins the hornbill it supports in damaging attacks on enemy long-houses.

The bard's soul, having reached Lang's long-house in the skies, invites him to attend the rites on earth below. Lang eagerly accepts the invitation and summons his daughters and their husbands – the augural birds of the Iban – to accompany him. When they have assembled, the daughters point out, somewhat petulantly, that they have no gift to take with them and ask their father and their husbands to procure a freshly taken head. The husbands and father, with alacrity, agree and set out at once for the haunts of Bengkong, the tutelary spirit of trophy heads.

When the party reach Bengkong's domain they begin (on Lang's instructions) to flatter him. On hearing this flattery one of the heads in his possession becomes anxious, begins to whimper, and is nursed by Bengkong's wife, the head being depicted as an infant.

Then, this agitated infant (whose head is about to be taken) relates to Bengkong's wife a dream he has just had, saying:

> I dreamt of being bitten by a huge and threatening snake, from which my head hurts even more than if it had been struck against a great upstanding stump.

This dream, Bengkong's wife interprets thus:

> I fear, child, that you are about to be speared, and your head carried off in a cane container.

This is exactly what happens.

Lang and his followers, having a trophy to take with them, set off for the world below. Their journey is marked by numerous adventures. Finally, they descend the rainbow and make their way through the rain forest to the long-house where the head-hunting ritual is being held.

The chanting of this part of the invocation takes one whole night. Lang and his party enter the long-house at dawn. At this juncture, pigs are sacrificed and their livers divined, it being believed that in this way Lang makes known to aspirant head-hunters their chances of success. The hepatomancy over, Lang and his party enter the gallery of the long-house, where they are welcomed by the Orang Panggau – the culture heroes of the Iban. On his back Lang has a basket. There is intense curiosity as to what it contains, but this Lang refuses to divulge. Later, as, half-drunk, he is performing the dance of the head-hunter, which imitates the soaring flight of the Brahminy Kite, the basket falls from Lang's shoulders, and out on to the floor rolls a severed head. At this the women present recoil, and, in revulsion, exclaim that it is not the fine and shining object talked of by their husbands – but, as ugly as a barbecued bat. On hearing this the head, just as though it were an infant, begins to cry. But the women persist in their denigration, likening the head to a "pointed red pepper". This is even more hurting, and the head, insulted, cries inconsolably.

In an attempt to still its crying the head is nursed by a long succession of female spirits. And while this is described in the invocation, living women ritually act out its words, taking down actual trophy heads which they nurse like infants as they parade up and down the gallery of the long-house.

Despite being nursed by all manner of female spirits, the head remains inconsolable and will not stop crying. Finally it is handed to a group of transvestite male shamans (*manang bali*). They too nurse it. At once the head ceases its crying, and laughs aloud. This laughter, as the words of the invocation indicate, is caused by the droll appearance of the transvestite shamans, with their female attire all awry, their unformed breasts, and their broken and dangling penises. Here, I would suppose, we have a projection of male ridicule of the transvestite homosexual, but also, it would seem, the head stops crying because it feels more secure and happy in the care of a transvestite shaman, whose hands are without envy and only wish to possess and fondle.

The head having been comforted, the transvestite shamans announce that it has really been crying because it wants to be planted – to be thrust into the earth like the sucker of a banana plant, or a taro shoot.

Lang agrees to do this. But the head, he says, must first be split open. This he then does, using his war sword. This splitting open of the head is explicitly symbolic of the act of beheading an enemy. At the same time as Lang's actions are being described in the invocation, they are ritually acted out by the men for whom the *gawai* is being held (Figs 1 and 2). However, instead of splitting open an actual trophy head, each aspirant attempts to split open with one blow a husked coconut, around the centre of which a red thread has

FIG. 1. The rite of *ngelampang* about to be performed. In the centre, on an upturned war shield, lies an old trophy head (*antu pala*), together with three husked coconuts. The three aspirants, in ceremonial attire, are seated to the right. In the background, each with a staff in his hand, are the *timang* party who describe the actions of the war god, Lang Singalang Burong. The scene is on the *tanju*, or open platform, of the longhouse of Pengulu Kuleh, Sungai Imang, Baleh region, Sarawak, Borneo. (2 July, 1949.)

been tied. Here again, the splitting of the coconut is symbolic of the beheading of an enemy, and the success of an aspirant in performing this rite is taken as a measure of his future prowess as a head-hunter.

The head split open by Lang contains all manner of seed, and, most prominently, the seed of the sacred rice *(padi pun)* of the Iban. This precious seed, says Lang, is to be planted.

At this culminating point of a head-hunting ritual then, trophy heads and the rice seed *(benih padi)*, on the fertility of which the welfare of the Iban principally rests, are directly equated. Indeed, the trophy head, phallic and procreative, becomes a veritable fount of fertility – a most potent object which not only confers an undying prestige on the warrior who has procured it, but becomes, for his community, a source from which their sacred *padi* may draw an ever-continuing fecundity. So, as Jensen reports (1974, p. 188), in times of drought when there is felt to be a danger of the rice seed not germi-

FIG. 2. A trophy head *(antu pala)* used during the rite of *ngelampang*. The head is on a war shield which is resting on an ikat fabric *(pua kumbo)*. The piece of rice in front of the trophy head is a placatory offering. Rumah Kuleh, Sungai Imang, Baleh region, Sarawak, Borneo. (2 July, 1949.)

nating, "a trophy head *(antu pala)* from the long-house is sprinkled with water while the Iban implore the spirits for rain to drench the rice".

The rite of *ngelampang* completed, and the seed, from the trophy head split open by Lang, prolifically at hand, the *timang*, or invocation, takes the form of a protracted allegory based on the cultivation of hill rice. This, I shall describe in very condensed form.

The allegory begins with the preparation of a swidden. The felling of trees is symbolic of the killing of enemies, and the firing of the swidden of the burning down of an enemy long-house. Next comes the action of dibbling, which is seen as symbolic of sexual intercourse; and, this done, the seed from the trophy head is planted just as though it were *padi*.

From this seed there springs an abundant crop of what appears to be rice. But, on closer inspection, as Lang is the first to point out, it is seen to be a human crop; a crop of the enemies of the Iban, who are, of course, their competitors in getting a living from growing rice in the Borneo rain forest.

At the sight of this human crop, Lang and his Iban devotees are elated, for it represents a further supply of trophy heads, waiting to be gathered in. While it grows, as does *padi* in a swidden, this wished-for crop is most carefully tended. Then comes, in the words of the *timang*, the reaping of Lang's *padi*, which represents beheading. Not a head remains unharvested. Next comes the sunning of the crop, which is likened to the smoking of trophy heads, and, finally, the storing away of the harvest, which stands for the hanging of trophy heads in the gallery of a long-house.

It was the faith of the pagan Iban that by this prefiguration in symbolic form they would be certain to succeed in capturing further heads in minutely planned raids into alien territory, so ensuring the fertility of the *padi* they aspired eventually to plant there. And inspired by this ruthless faith they swept all before them.

The head-hunting rituals which I have delineated in this paper provided the Iban with a system of social prestige in a society lacking hereditary rank. Only those men who had taken a trophy head were qualified to complete the ritual cycle of the great *gawai*. The whole complex was a male cult with the trophy head having, as I have indicated, a phallic and procreative significance.

With the recognition of this symbolism it becomes apparent why the taking of trophy heads was regarded as so enormously enhancing of masculine prowess, and as contributing to the well-being and fertility of the long-house community as a whole.

Light is also cast on the remarkable expansion of the Iban during the nineteenth century, when head-hunting was still rife. At that time the Iban were cultivators of hill rice whose advancement was achieved by repeated incursions into enemy territory on head-hunting raids, which so terrorized its inhabitants as to compel their flight or capitulation.

Among the Iban, then, head-hunting was a highly aggressive masculine cult through participation in which ambitious individuals achieved an audacious lustre (Fig. 3), while capturing from alien tribes fresh tracts of rain forest for the cultivation of the abundant crops on which their prosperity depended. It is not, I would suggest, surprising that such a venturesome people should have taken to their

FIG. 3. Nyala anak Sikau, an Iban leader and long-house headman (*tuai rumah*) in the ceremonial dress of an accomplished warrior and head-hunter. The tufts of hair attached to the sides of his beaded helmet have been taken from trophy heads. Rumah Nyala, Sungai Sut, Kapit District. (9 April, 1949.)

hearts the piquant fantasy – *fecund with both death and life* – of severed heads that germinate.

References

DE VRIES, A. (1974). *Dictionary of Symbols and Imagery*. North-Holland Publishing Co., Amsterdam.

DOWNS, R. E. (1955). Head-hunting in Indonesia. *Bijdragen Tot de Taal- Land- en Volkenkunde*, **111,** 40–70.

FRAZER, SIR JAMES (1922). *The Golden Bough* (abridged edition). Macmillan, London.

FREEMAN, DEREK (1960). A note on the *Gawai Kenyalang*. In *The Birds of Borneo* (Ed. B. E. Smythies), pp. 99–102. Oliver and Boyd, Edinburgh.

FREEMAN, DEREK (1968). Thunder, blood and the nicknaming of God's creatures. *The Psychoanalytic Quarterly*, **37,** 353–399.

FREEMAN, DEREK (1970). *Report on the Iban* (2nd edition). Athlone Press, London.

FREUD, SIGMUND (1900). *The Interpretation of Dreams* (second part). Standard Edition, vol. 5 (1953), pp. 339–627. Hogarth Press, London.

FREUD, SIGMUND (1916). A Connection between a Symbol and a Symptom. Standard Edition, vol. 14 (1957), pp. 339–340. Hogarth Press, London.

HUTTON, J. H. (1928). The significance of head-hunting in Assam. *Journal of the Royal Anthropological Institute*, **58,** 399–408.

JENSEN, E. (1974). *The Iban and Their Religion*. Clarendon Press, Oxford.

JONES, ERNEST (1949). *On the Nightmare*. Hogarth Press, London.

LEWIS, I. M. (1955). *Peoples of the Horn of Africa: Somali, Afar and Saho*. International African Institute, London.

MCKINLEY, R. (1976). Human and proud of it! A structural treatment of headhunting rites and the social definition of enemies. In *Studies in Borneo Societies: Social Process and Anthropological Explanation* (Ed. G. N. Appell), Special Report no. 12, pp. 92–126. Center for Southeast Asian Studies. Northern Illinois University.

MENNINGER, KARL (1938). *Man against Himself*. Harcourt, Brace and Co., New York.

ONIANS, R. B. (1951). *The Origins of European Thought*. Cambridge University Press, Cambridge.

THOMAS, DYLAN (1954). *Under Milk Wood*. Dent, London.

ST. JOHN, S. (1863). *Life in the Forests of the Far East; or Travels in Northern Borneo*. vol. 1. Smith, Elder and Co., London.

ZIMMER, H. (1946). *Myths and Symbols in Indian Art and Civilization*. Pantheon Books, New York.

Queen of Night, Mother-Right, and Secret Male Cults

L. R. Hiatt

MY ANTHROPOLOGICAL interest in *The Magic Flute* was aroused when I read in some record notes a while ago that the conflict between the Queen of Night and Sarastro represents an evolutionary struggle in ancient society between two principles of royal succession, one matrilineal and the other patrilineal (Mann, 1964). Although unconvinced, I was nevertheless alerted to some problematic aspects of their relationship; and after seeing a performance in the Sydney Opera House early in 1974, I started to think a piece of work I was doing then on myth and ritual among the Australian Aborigines might contribute to an understanding of the libretto. In pursuing the possibility in the present essay, I am not proposing a direct historical link between Aboriginal Australia and ancient Egypt, or anything of that sort. Rather, I am suggesting that certain general features and functions of male secret cults, clearly discernible in the Australian case, play a role in shaping Mozart's Masonic representation of the cult of Isis and Osiris.

I begin by recounting the role of Prince Tamino, though I omit his association with Papageno. Then, to provide a background to matters of interpretation, I briefly discuss the authorship and sources of the plot, and the principles and practices of Freemasonry. I next consider a number of interpretations of the relationship between Sarastro and the Queen of Night. Finally, after introducing the Aboriginal material, I present my own argument.[1]

The plot

At the beginning of Act 1, Prince Tamino is pursued by a serpent. Three Ladies, attendants to the Queen of Night, rescue him and later show him a portrait of the Queen's daughter, Pamina, with whom he immediately falls in love. The Queen enters and tells Tamino that Pamina has been abducted by a villain named Sarastro. She commands him to be her daughter's saviour and gives him a magic flute for protection.

Tamino leaves the Queen's domain and reaches Sarastro's temple. He finds Pamina and they fall into each other's arms. Sarastro orders that they be taken away and ritually purified.

At the beginning of Act 2, Sarastro announces that Tamino wishes to enter the order of Isis and Osiris and proposes to the assembled priests that he be put to the test. If successful, he will be given Pamina in marriage.

Tamino is instructed in the untrustworthiness of women. When the Three Ladies arrive secretly in the temple to see how he is progressing in the quest to retrieve Pamina, he gives them a cool reception. The Queen herself arrives and orders Pamina to kill Sarastro. By now, however, Pamina's first loyalty is to Tamino, whose immediate concern is to gain acceptance into the cult of Isis and Osiris. After further trials and separation from Pamina, Tamino is reunited with his beloved and together they undergo the final trial of fire and water. Sarastro accepts them both into the order. The Queen of Night makes a last assault on the temple but is destroyed and sinks into the ground.

Authorship and sources of the libretto

Numerous Mozart scholars have written at length on the authorship and sources of the libretto. The issues have been recently reviewed in

[1]This paper was presented at the symposium on psychoanalysis and the interpretation of symbolic behaviour, ANZAAS, January 1975. I read a preliminary version to the Sydney University Anthropological Society in May 1974, and in March 1975 I addressed the Musicological Society of Australia, whose permission to publish the present article is gratefully acknowledged; an earlier, though essentially similar, version of this paper appears in *Musicology* V (in press). I appreciate the many helpful comments made in discussion on all three occasions.

scholarly detail by Jacques Chailley in his book *The Magic Flute, Masonic Opera* (1971), to which I refer the interested reader for details omitted in the following summary.

The accredited author of the libretto is Emanuel Schikaneder, who adapted it from a fairy-tale called *Lulu, or The Magic Flute*. It has been suggested, however, that several others had a hand in it, either directly or indirectly, and that, as one commentator has put it, the author of the libretto was less Schikaneder than "the Shikaneder firm" (Saint-Foix quoted in Chailley, 1971, p. 15; for a similar opinion see Brophy, 1971, p. 10). In 1818, twenty-seven years after the first production in 1791, one of the "silent partners" spoke up – Johann Metzler, also known as Giesecke, previously a minor actor and assistant librettist in Schikaneder's troupe, by this time a Professor of Mineralogy at Trinity College, Dublin. During a visit to present a scientific collection to the Imperial Museum in Vienna, Giesecke allegedly told a group of old friends in a restaurant that Schikaneder (who played Papageno) had written only the Papageno episodes, while he (Giesecke) had written the rest.

The question of Giesecke's participation in the libretto is still a matter of lively debate.[1] Another, and more generally acknowledged, influence is that of Baron Ignaz von Born, Masonic theoretician, classical scholar, and Grand Secretary of the Vienna Lodge of the True Unity. Haydn was a member of this lodge and Mozart a regular visitor. Mozart, who belonged to another Viennese lodge, was admitted into Freemasonry in 1784 and, as is well known, continued to be an ardent Mason until his death in 1791. There is reason to believe that von Born and Mozart knew each other well and that von Born was sympathetic to the idea of an opera that would express the lofty sentiments of Freemasonry.

Schikaneder seems to have taken Freemasonry less seriously, and was expelled from his lodge on the grounds of moral turpitude. Giesecke was also a Mason, though there is some obscurity about the details of his affiliation.

The sequence of events surrounding the composition of the plot of *The Magic Flute* may have been something like this. Schikaneder approached Mozart to write the music for a libretto based on *Lulu, or The*

[1] Brophy (1964, 1971) and Chailley (1971) conclude that Giesecke probably made a contribution under Schikaneder's general direction, while Branscombe (1966) and Batley (1969) strongly contest all claims made on Giesecke's behalf.

Magic Flute. Mozart, disinclined to take on such a lightweight story, may have suggested the incorporation of a Masonic theme. Schikaneder conceivably assigned the task to Giesecke,[1] while Mozart under von Born's tutelage maintained a close scrutiny.

The libretto's representation of the cult of Isis and Osiris was probably based on an article by von Born in the *Journal of Freemasonry*, entitled *On the Mysteries of Egypt*, and on a work called *Sethos* by the Abbé Jean Terrason (Professor of Greek and Latin at the Collège de France). Published in 1731, *Sethos* described the initiation of an imaginary Egyptian prince into the mysteries, and was well known to Freemasons in the eighteenth century.

Freemasonry[2]

In feudal England stonemasons moved from one building project to another. They were under the control of neither a feudal overlord nor a municipal corporation, and so they became known as "freemasons". They constructed living quarters for themselves on site – the original "masonic lodge". Like other craft guilds, the masons had trade secrets, passwords, and initiation ceremonies. There were three degrees of masonic achievement: Entered Apprentice (as entered on the lodge rolls after seven years' instruction); Fellow Craft (after another seven years); and Master (in charge of a building project).

Modern Freemasonry, known as "speculative" masonry to distinguish it from its "operative" counterpart, began in the seventeenth century. The circumstances of its origin are obscure, though the desire of cultivated men of the Enlightenment to undersand the principles of architecture was no doubt an important factor. Later the subject was used as an idiom for "a science of morality, veiled in allegory, and illustrated by symbols" (Mackey, 1869, p. 10). Thus God is the Great Architect, the plumb stands for rectitude, the level for equality, the trowel for harmony, the square for duty, and so on.

A good deal of Masonic symbolism is available in published form, not being considered a matter of secrecy. Masons, however, are bound to secrecy on Masonic ritual ("May my throat be cut across, my

[1] Cf. Einstein (1971, p. 479): "But if he [Giesecke] wrote any of it at all, it was at most Tamino's discourse with the Speaker . . ."

[2] My main sources are Jones (1967) and Mackey (1869), though numerous other works were consulted.

tongue torn out by the root, and buried in the sand of the sea at low water mark . . .") but several detailed disclosures have appeared (Hannah, 1952; Jones, 1967).

Following the operative model, Freemasons are inducted into the degrees of Entered Apprentice, Fellow Craft, and Master. The ritual of induction into the Master's degree (through which Mozart passed) is based on the legend of Hiram Abiff, Master Mason in the construction of King Solomon's temple. Abiff was murdered by underlings seeking his secret knowledge (he stayed silent to the end). The candidate undergoes a symbolic death by similar violence, is laid in a grave and lifted back to life.

From the Enlightenment onwards, Masons speculated about the origins of Freemasonry in classical antiquity. In a handbook for Masons, Mackey (1869) devotes a chapter to the ancient mysteries, with special reference to Isis and Osiris. Hiram Abiff is supposed to have been the leader of a Dionysian cult and his importance for Masons depends in part on the assumption that he brought together Classical and Hebraic traditions.

Problems and interpretations

A long-standing issue, going back to 1840,[1] concerns an apparent inconsistency in the presentation of the Queen of Night and Sarastro, as between Act 1 and Act 2. In Act 1, the Queen of Night is a wronged woman pitted against the villainous Sarastro; in Act 2, Sarastro appears as a wise and benevolent philosopher-king, while the Queen of Night is transformed into the fanatical leader of an underground terrorist organization.

One school of thought holds that the change in characterization is so radical that it can be explained only by assuming that the original conception of the plot was revised after the first act had been completed (see, for example, Dent, 1913, pp. 328–331; Istel, 1927, p. 519; Brophy, 1964, pp. 131–202). A common explanation for the supposed revision is that, while work on *The Magic Flute* was still in progress, a rival company presented a new opera called *The Magic Zither, or Kaspar the Bassoon-player*, also adapted from *Lulu, or The Magic Flute,*

[1] See Deutsch (1965, pp. 555–556).

and that Schikaneder changed direction to avoid a charge of plagiarism.[1] Brigid Brophy (ibid.) argues, however, that the change was occasioned by a growing realization that the original conception, allegedly a visit to the Underworld, would entail revealing too much of the secrets of Freemasonry (see also Brophy, 1971). Again, an unsigned article in *Opera News* claims that Mozart and Schikaneder "decided midway in the first act to alter the course of the story to honor the recent death of a masonic leader, Ignaz von Born. This accounts for the discrepancy between the first appearance of the Queen of the Night as a sympathetic mother and her subsequent role as villainess." (1973, p. 26.)

The opposing school of thought denies any substantial alteration in the plot (see, for example, Batley, 1969; Chailley, 1971, chapter 4; Einstein, 1971, p. 480). The altered perspectives on the Queen of Night and Sarastro can, it is argued, be explained in terms of an internal dramatic development: in Act 1 Tamino accepts the Queen's version, in Act 2 he is disabused (see Broder, 1964, p. 329). Chailley, after reviewing the evidence for the "fear of plagiarism" hypothesis, concludes (1971, pp. 27–28): "What is certain is that in no case can we consider the libretto . . . to have been formed by soldering together two independent sections . . . At once miscellaneous and homogeneous, the opera is the one and the other at the beginning as much as at the end. And of Mozart's music . . . we can affirm that not a single eighth-note was composed to the possible first version of the libretto."

Chailley's judgment seems to me compelling, and I shall try later to add something to this side of the argument. But let me turn now to a more important issue: the basis for the antagonism between Sarastro and the Queen of Night.

The conspicuous cause of the Queen's animosity is Sarastro's abduction of her daughter. "A villain ran off with her", she tells Tamino. Sarastro justifies his action to Pamina by saying that her happiness depended on being removed from her mother. Later, he tells the assembled priests that Pamina is destined by godly decree to marry Tamino, which is why she had to be taken from the Queen. The latter hopes, through deceit and superstition, to beguile the populace and destroy the temple.

[1] This supposition derives from Ignaz von Seyfried, who joined Schikaneder's company eight years after the first production of *The Magic Flute* in 1791 (Deutsch, 1965).

A rarely reproduced speech by the Queen[1] indicates that her hostility to Sarastro predates the abduction of Pamina. It occurs in Act 2, just before her second aria ("The vengeance of Hell boils in my heart . . .").

PAMINA: . . . O let us flee, dear mother! Under your protection I will brave every danger.

QUEEN: Protection? Dear child, your mother can protect you no more. With your father's death my power went to the grave.

PAMINA: My father . . .

QUEEN: Voluntarily handed over the sevenfold Sun-Circle to the initiates. Sarastro wears this potent Sun-Circle on his breast. When I discussed the matter with your father, he spoke with wrinkled brow: "Wife, my last hour has come – all the treasures that were my exclusive property are yours and your daughter's." "The all-consuming Sun-Circle", I quickly interposed . . ."It is assigned to the initiates", he replied. "Sarastro will be its male custodian, as I have been till now. Ask me not one word more. Do not enquire into matters which are incomprehensible to the female spirit. Your duty is to give yourself over, and your daughter also, to the leadership of wise men."

A little later in the dialogue:

QUEEN: . . . Do you see this dagger here? It is whetted for Sarastro. You will kill him and deliver the potent Sun-Circle to me.

William Mann infers from the Queen's statement that the struggle between her and Sarastro personifies the historical transition from Mother-right to Father-right. He says:

The Queen was the wife of the Priest of the Sun; as such she expected that the sovereignty would descend by matrilinear succession, that is, according to the tradition of husband-sacrifice, characteristic of myths in which all men are subservient to the mother-goddess. The Old Law prescribed that, upon the death of Pamina's father, Astrafiammante [Queen of Night] would take another husband who in turn would have to die after a term of office, and so on until Pamina became Queen. But in all these myths the second stage of civilization arrives when one husband rebels and establishes male succession, abolishing the rite of husband-sacrifice. Pamina's father has evidently prepared for this, just before his death, by giving the emblem of his sovereignty, the seven-fold circle of the sun, into Sarastro's keeping. The Queen very naturally wished to counter this revolution, but Sarastro took Pamina, the heir to the throne of Night, under his own wing so that she might in time serve as consort to his own successor, thus re-establishing the old link between night and day on a new and proper patriarchal footing. [Mann, 1964, p. 4.]

[1] Translated here from the edition of W. Zentner, Reclam-Verlag, Stuttgart, 1953, kindly made available to me by Ms. I. Sültemeyer, German Department, University of Sydney. I am grateful to Margaret Clunies Ross for advice on the translation.

The nineteenth-century theory that patriarchy displaced matriarchy in the broad course of social evolution (see, for example, Bachofen, 1861, 1967; Engels, 1902) would find little support among anthropologists today (see, for example, Lowie, 1937, pp. 40–43; Radcliffe-Brown, 1952, pp. 13–31; Harris, 1968, pp. 188–189, 196). Nevertheless it is noteworthy that George Devereux, in an intriguing essay on the sociopolitical functions of the Oedipus myth, affirms the notion that in ancient Greece patrilineal succession to kingship displaced indirect matrilineal succession and husband-sacrifice, and he argues, moreover, that the Oedipus myth reflects and ratifies the transition (Devereux, 1963). However this may be, no justification can be found in the libretto of *The Magic Flute* for Mann's inference that this is what the struggle between Sarastro and the Queen of Night signifies. There is no mention of husband-sacrifice or matrilineal succession nor is there any suggestion that Sarastro is a monarch or that Tamino is to succeed him either in that capacity or as High Priest of Isis and Osiris (cf. Sarastro's words of encouragement to Tamino, ". . . if in time you wish to rule as a wise prince . . ."). Nevertheless, the notion that the opera is about a transition from Mother-right to Father-right is very interesting, and I shall return to the matter later.

Chailley's central thesis is that *The Magic Flute* is "a symbolic illustration of the conflict between two worlds, the Masculine and the Feminine, the conflict to be resolved, after the necessary purification, by the new, perfect union in the Mystery of the Couple" (1971, pp. 92–93). The libretto certainly contains anti-female propaganda. When Tamino inveighs against Sarastro on behalf of the Queen, the Priest chides him for believing the babbling of a woman, who "does little, talks much". Sarastro tells Pamina that she must allow a man to guide her feelings, otherwise she will step beyond her proper sphere. Two Priests instruct Tamino to "beware of women's tricks, that is the first duty of the Order". And when the Three Ladies appear in the temple seeking Tamino, the priestly chorus sings: "The holy threshold is desecrated, away to hell with the women."

That these and other remarks add up to an ideology of male domination cultivated within a priestly religious order could hardly be denied. Chailley's assertion that they symbolize a conflict between the Masculine and the Feminine introduces an abstract dimension for which the evidence would be somewhat less substantial. Even if it could be shown that this is what the librettist had in mind, we would still be inclined to ask what the substance of this alleged conflict is supposed to be. A similar point might be made about the notion of a "perfect union in the Mystery of the Couple", which is held to resolve the conflict.

Chailley regards the Queen's speech to Pamina, quoted earlier, as "the capital passage for understanding the libretto" (ibid., p. 93). The Solar Circle, he says, symbolizes Masculinity and Wisdom. Deprived of wisdom, the Queen is relegated to the Kingdom of Night (that is, ignorance). She attempts through her daughter to destroy Sarastro, symbol of male supremacy, but she fails. The Queen of Night's great error, according to Chailley, is her refusal to submit to male domination. When her daughter is taken from her to form the perfect couple with Tamino, her fury is unbounded. "Irreverently", says Chailley, "one might say that the basis of the story is the rebellion of the mother-in-law." (ibid., p. 95.)

The last proposition would be difficult to reconcile with the fact that the Queen's hatred of Sarastro begins with the loss of the sevenfold Sun-Circle. She opposes him not because he is giving her daughter away in marriage but because he heads a cult that has robbed her of her power. Far from being a reluctant mother-in-law, she commits herself twice to such a prospect in return for support against her enemy – first, when she promises Tamino: "You shall be my daughter's saviour, and when I see you victorious, then shall she be yours forever"; and again at the end she tells Monostatos: "I keep my word; it is my will, my child shall be your wife."

Chailley's general insight, to which the above throw-away line makes no particular contribution, is that we are dealing with some kind of universal struggle between men and women. But whereas he is, by and large, content to represent the conflict at an abstract and ideological level (as between Masculine and Feminine, Good and Evil, Wisdom and Ignorance, Day and Night), I am keen to explore its concrete dimensions in the context of male secret cults. To do this, I turn now to the Australian Aborigines.

Secret male cults among the Australian Aborigines

In most Aboriginal tribes of Australia, the men belonged to one or more religious lodges or cults from which women and children were rigorously excluded. Youths were initiated into the cults soon after reaching sexual maturity, and typically the induction procedures began when the novices were led off to a secret place ostensibly to be destroyed there by a supernatural being. Eventually, through the good offices of the men, the lads were returned safely to their mothers, though from now on they lived separately in bachelors' camps. A man did not normally acquire his first wife until the age of about twenty-five or thirty, whereas women married at puberty. In most communities a system of polygyny prevailed in which virtually all the sexually mature females were monopolized by men over thirty. Adultery was considered an offence, and no formal provision was made for the sexual needs of bachelors. Young men were expected to be preoccupied with religious education and warfare (a redirection of their energies upwards and outwards, so to speak).

In several recent papers I have presented examples of the induction of youths into secret male cults in various parts of Australia, together with associated myths (Hiatt, 1971, 1975). Here I offer a small selection.

The climax of the Engwura ceremony among the Aranda (Spencer and Gillen, 1927, pp. 289–291) centred around a representation of the amnion (or caul). The rite, which took place at night, was divided into three phases. First, at a signal from the old men, the novices left the sacred ground carrying bundles of burning sticks. They then rushed towards the women and children, assembled close at hand, and hurled the sticks over their heads, causing "a scene of indescribable confusion" (ibid., p. 289). When their ammunition was exhausted, the youths ran rapidly back to the ceremonial ground. Second, the leader of the ceremony grasped the representation of the amnion and, with a supporter on each side, moved it up and down all night. It was believed that if their strength failed, the novices (who lay silent and immobile throughout) would die. Third, at dawn the same three men, followed by the novices, left the ceremonial ground carrying the amnion. They proceeded in silence towards the assembled women, then suddenly threw themselves headlong on the ground, hiding the sacred object from view. Immediately afterwards the novices fell on top of them. After remaining thus for several minutes, the novices rose and formed a square, through which they hustled the three leaders away from the women, back to the secret ground.

It seems that, by attacking the women with firesticks, the novices obeyed an adult male command to give up childish attachments. Then representatives of the all-male group sat up throughout the night "giving birth". Finally, the "male mothers" in the company of their "new-born" sons flaunted the instrument of birth in full view (almost) of real mothers.

The Mara of south-eastern Arnhem Land recounted the following myth to R. M. Berndt.

> A long time ago an old woman called Mumuna lived alone with her two daughters. By making a smoky fire, she attracted men to her camp, then welcomed them with food and invited them to spend the night with the daughters. Later, while they slept deeply from sexual exhaustion, she dropped boulders on them. The next morning she cooked and ate them, then regurgitated them onto an ant-bed. Their bones can be seen today in the form of stones.
>
> The attitude of the daughters was equivocal. On the one hand they relished the sexual role that their mother encouraged them to play. On the other, they deplored the old woman's cannibalism and feared its consequences. In particular, they were disturbed by her habit of hanging up the genital organs of the dead men on a tree and proposing to the girls that they eat them – an invitation they steadfastly refused.
>
> Mumuna's grisly practices were finally put to an end by a man named Eaglehawk, a light sleeper who woke up in time to kill her before she killed him. The daughters ran away. As the old woman died, she called out *brr*, and her blood splashed onto every tree. Afterwards, in her memory, Eaglehawk cut down a tree and made a bull-roarer, which contained the old woman's dying cry.
>
> [After Berndt, 1951, pp. 148–152.]

This myth was the charter of a secret male cult (Berndt, 1951, pp. 144–184). The initiation rite began with the swinging of the bull-roarer near the general camp and the seizure of the novices who were hurried away into the bush. Officially, the women believed that Mumuna had swallowed them. At the end of the ritual, several months later, the men at the secret ground offered food symbolically to Mumuna and ate it on her behalf. In return she was said to regurgitate the novices. The latter were then smeared from head to foot with red paste and displayed to the women and children back at the general camp. The men said: "Look at the colouring they have on their bodies: they are smeared with the inside liquids of Mumuna's womb."

Among the Murinbata of Port Keats (Northern Territory), the induction of young men into the cult of the Old Woman was the highest rite in the ritual repertoire. Called *Punj*, it was sanctioned by a myth recorded by W. E. H. Stanner.

The people said [to Mutjingga, the Old Woman]: "We shall leave the children with you while we find honey; you look after them." She agreed, and the people went off to hunt. After the children had bathed, they settled down to sleep near her. Bringing one close on the pretext of looking for lice, she swallowed it. Then she swallowed the others, ten altogether, and left.

A man and his wife returned to the camp for water and realised what must have happened. They gave the alarm, and the others came back. Ten men set off in pursuit and eventually overtook Mutjingga crawling along a river bed. A left-handed man speared her through the legs and a right-handed man broke her neck with a club. They then cut her belly open and found the children, still alive, in her womb. They had not gone where the excrement is. The men cleaned and adorned the children and took them back to the camp. Their mothers cried with joy on seeing them and hit themselves until the blood flowed. [After Stanner, 1963, pp. 40–42.]

The rite of *Punj* (Stanner, 1963, pp. 6–9) began when the postulants were taken to the secret ground and told they would be swallowed alive by Mutjingga and then vomited up. On the third day men began swinging bullroarers near the ceremonial ground and slowly converged on the assembled novices, who were told that the Old Woman was coming. Suddenly the men leapt into view, and the secret of the bullroarers was revealed. Each novice was given a bull-roarer which was thrust between his thighs in the position of an erect penis.

The ceremony ended away from the secret ground when the novices crawled towards their mothers through a tunnel of legs formed by the initiated men. As each youth emerged he sat momentarily in front of his mother, with his back to her, while all the women wailed and lacerated their heads. The youths then returned through the tunnel, and all the men rushed with loud shouts back to the secret ground. After another week the young men resumed ordinary life in the community, though they were not allowed to go near their mother's camp.

As a final example, I give a myth recorded by M. J. Meggitt among the Walbiri of Central Australia. It was associated with a secret male cult called Gadjari.

A long time ago there were two Mulga-tree brothers, each with a wife and several sons. Because the area they inhabited was suffering from drought, the two men decided to take leave of their families and explore other regions for food. Before departing, they secretly circumcised their sons and inducted them into the clan totemic cult. Their wives heard about the ceremonies and became angry at their exclusion; and when the men refused to allow them to accompany them on their travels, saying they must stay behind and look after the boys, their anger increased.

The husbands responded to their demands by soundly thrashing them with boomerangs. They then jumped into the air and began their journey.

After various adventures, they returned home. As they alighted from the sky, they called out happily to their wives, but there was no answer. Puzzled and apprehensive, they searched the vicinity of the camp site and to their alarm discovered evidence of a violent struggle. Leading away from the spot were two sets of footprints, which they identified as their wives'. Then they guessed what must have happened: the two women, furious at being excluded and left behind, had killed and eaten their sons.

The two men followed the tracks to a cave, around the mouth of which flies were swarming. Quickly fashioning torches they entered a large chamber where, among the boulders on the floor, they saw the putrescent remains of their sons. The flies, however, were streaming past the corpses and going further into the cave. The men raised their torches and cautiously advanced. At the end of the cave, they saw the two women, crouching like hideous demons, with flies swarming into their gaping, blood-stained mouths. The men realised that they had vomited up the lads and were ready to swallow them again. So terrifying was the scene of carnage that the men ran in terror from the stinking cavern. Outside, their courage returned. They rushed back in with armfulls of dry grass, threw it over the women and set fire to it. The women were completely destroyed.

Badly shaken by these events, the two brothers returned to their original camp where they mourned the passing of their sons. Then they pondered the question of how to replace the lads now that they were without wives and without prospects of acquiring more. That night the older brother dreamt of a magical formula that enabled the two men not only to resurrect their sons but to produce an unlimited supply of children without the aid of women. [After Meggitt, 1967, pp. 55–60.]

On the basis of the data exemplified above, we can say that in Australia the metaphorical rebirth of boys as initiated men was frequently, though not invariably, carried out on a model of natural parturition. Given the formal separation of sons from mothers that regularly preceded the ceremonies, the basic message from the men was something like: "This boy is your offspring; we must take him now and destroy his attachment to you; then we will reproduce him as one of us." Ogress myths reinforced this message by imputing malevolence to women and by emphasizing the protective propensities of men. Typically in the myths, initial trust is reposed in women; the trust is betrayed when the women wantonly attack those living under their auspices; and the victims are avenged or saved by men.

Thus the rituals and their supporting myths removed the sexually maturing male from his mother and sisters and, through the symbolism of parturition, placed him in a situation of dependence upon older men. Through the authority of the cult, these men guided and governed the sublimation of his energies during a lengthy period of enforced bachelorhood.

Conclusion

The three main structural components of the initiation theme in *The Magic Flute* are the initiates (Sarastro and his priests), the candidate (Tamino) and the excluded females (Queen of Night and her Three Ladies). With the foregoing Australian material in mind, it is interesting to note an initial identification between Tamino and the females, followed by a limbo in which he is instructed in the untrustworthiness of women, and finally his incorporation into the male cult. The switch in his sympathies, which gave rise to the "revised plot" controversy, follows the natural movement of masculine affinities from childhood to adulthood. In the opening scene, Tamino, fleeing from a phallic monster, is saved by the three matrons, who dwell on his beauty as a mother dotes on her baby. Through them, he meets the Queen who addresses him as "my dear son". By the closing scenes, his attachments to these original female protectors have been completely destroyed; and his identification with Sarastro and the male cult is consummated as a victory of light over darkness.

Pamina's simultaneous acceptance into this stronghold of anti-feminism is anomalous. It is also incompatible with the precept and practice of Freemasonry: the 1723 Constitution limited admission to "men of good reputation" and excluded "slaves, women, and immoral or disgraced men" (Chailley, 1971, p. 75). Here we should remember that the original model for *The Magic Flute* was *Lulu, or The Magic Flute*, and that Lulu is a prince to whom a Fairy Queen promises her daughter if he assists in rescuing her from an evil magician. In consequence, we can say that unless Schikaneder's foreshadowed libretto is to be completely emasculated in deference to Mozart's desire for a Masonic content, then the Queen's daughter must stay in. To that extent, her admission to the cult is a literary compromise, not to say a theatrical necessity.

This does not mean that Pamina's marriage to Tamino is anomalous; like the wife of an Aboriginal cultist, she is the reward for his trials. Moreover, their union completes the natural transition in male sexual development from love of mother to love of wife, as mediated by adult male authority. To overcome the constraints imposed by the Lulu story, we should ignore the one given blood relationship and regard the Queen, Sarastro, Tamino, and Pamina as archetypes for Mother, Father, Son, and Son's Wife respectively. Equipped with a magic phallus,[1] the Son sets out to assail the Father. When his animosity changes to admiration, he rejects the Mother and marries a woman of the Father's choice.

I referred above to the nineteenth-century theory that matriarchy preceded patriarchy. The evidence comes mainly from a widely distributed class of myths ascribing power to women, and the assumption is made that the myths are a kind of historical record. My own view is that they are more like dreams; and that in the present instance they express the memory, not of a prehistoric revolution, but of a crucial change in the early life of every individual male. The alleged historical transition from Mother-right to Father-right is in reality the ontogenetic transition from the maternal succour of childhood to the paternal authority of youth. By transposing it to a social plane and projecting it back to the time of the gods, the myth both ratifies the process and increases the gap between wistful fancies and their realization.

It is from this position that I would approach the symbolism of the "sevenfold Sun-Circle" *(der siebenfachen Sonnenkreis)*. As we have seen, Chailley says the Solar Circle stands for Masculinity and Wisdom. Although he does not give us his authority for this interpretation, I would gather from his acknowledgements that he is depending here on Masonic sources, including personal communications. There is no doubt that Masonic exegesis is the appropriate one, since in all likelihood we are dealing at this point of the libretto with the influence of von Born. But I venture to say that the symbolism as stated by Chailley is incomplete. Let me summarize the section headed "The Point within the Circle" in Mackey's *Symbolism of Freemasonry*.

According to Mackey, the "point within a circle" is a symbol of great importance. The usual meaning offered among Freemasons is that the point stands for the individual, the circle the boundary line of his duty to God and man. But behind this trite exegesis lies a deeper and more ancient meaning: worship of the generative principle in nature. In eastern religion this is signified by *linga* and *yoni*. In classical antiquity, Mackey maintains, all the deities can be reduced to the two different forms of the generative principle – active male,

[1] Even though the phallic properties of flutes are well known (see De Vries, 1974, p. 195), I would not make such an apparently facile and gratuitous association here but for the fact that, according to Pamina, her father cut the magic flute from an oak tree in the midst of thunder and lightning. The phallic significance of this complex in classical mythology has been convincingly demonstrated by Freeman (1968).

passive female, as represented by Jupiter and Juno, Bacchus and Venus, Osiris and Isis. Their union was frequently symbolized by the point within the circle, the point indicating the sun and the circle the universe, invigorated and fertilized by his generative rays (Mackey, 1869, pp. 111–116).

The Circle of the Sun, as distinct from the Sun itself, is therefore to be seen as a symbol of female reproductivity. That is what has been handed over to the male cult, and we recall that the Queen of Night says that then she was robbed of her power. The ascription to women of an original mystical power which was appropriated by men and preserved within a secret male cult is a widespread myth motif of the kind alluded to earlier in the discussion of Mother-right and Father-right. As well as clarifying the cause and nature of the Queen's anger, its occurrence in a key passage confirms my belief that *The Magic Flute* can be illuminated by an understanding of the ritualization of human male ontogeny. Inasmuch as this is a matter of fundamental significance in the evolution of human nature and culture, the libretto, far from being a hodgepodge of nonsense, would seem to offer the composer a theme worthy of his genius.

Postscript

In his recent film version of *The Magic Flute*, Ingmar Bergmann departs from the libretto in order to present Sarastro and the Queen of Night as husband and wife, Pamina as their daughter. Sarastro shows manifest fondness for Pamina, with hints of something more. Through Pamina, he gives Tamino his flute; at the end it is returned to him and, after giving Pamina an affectionate farewell, he looks significantly at it. The Queen of Night gives Sarastro a knowing smile as she disappears into oblivion.[1]

Bergmann's interpretation of the struggle between Sarastro and the Queen of Night is thus the mirror image of my own: a resolution of father-daughter attachment rather than son-mother attachment. Sarastro's incestuous inclination towards his daughter excites his wife's hatred; but, in the event, he organizes Pamina's marriage and,

[1] For two relevant reviews of the film, see Evidon (1976) and Osborne (1976).

through the symbolism of a phallic gift,[1] renounces his sexual interest in favour of Tamino.

Although this is a serious and interesting attempt to make sense of the relationship between Sarastro and the Queen of Night, it leaves the central difficulty unresolved: why is the relative moral status of Sarastro and the Queen of Night, as presented in Act 1, reversed in Act 2? Indeed, Bergmann aggravates the problem: in Act 1, Tamino sets out to rescue Pamina from her abductor who, we now learn, is her incestuous father; yet, in Act 2, he accepts the latter as the epitome of goodness. To say he does so merely in order to obtain Pamina as his wife would be to attribute a cynicism to the Prince for which there is no warrant either in the libretto or its high-minded Masonic conception.

A further objection is that Bergmann's interpretation takes no account of the sevenfold Sun-Circle which, according to the libretto, is the basic cause of the conflict between Sarastro and the Queen of Night. My own theory seeks to explain this matter, as well as the change in Tamino's attitude to Sarastro and the Queen of Night, in terms of a cult ideology designed to deflect the attachment of maturing males from their mothers to their fathers.

While putting the finishing touches to this paper, I was surprised and pleased to discover that the kernel of its argument was advanced a few years ago by a Roman Catholic priest, Father Lee, Professor of Classics at the Franciscan House of Studies in Chicago. In the course of a brief note in *Opera News*, Father Lee writes:

> The Queen of Night . . . is a personification . . . of motherhood, which cannot – much as the child might wish it – be indulgent and protective forever . . . Sarastro . . . is that bright consciousness which is the beginning of reason, which builds cities and civilizations, and is associated archetypally with the father figure . . . So Tamino moves from the mother's natural paradise, where serpents are slain and beautiful ladies baby him, to the father's civilized kingdom, where the emphasis is on trial, virtue and achievement. Like Homer's Achilles and Virgil's Aeneas, he is at first mother-bound but comes eventually to see the values of the father–son relationship.
>
> [Lee, 1973, pp. 28–29.]

References

BACHOFEN, J. J. (1861). *Das Mutterrecht*. Schwabe, Basel.

BACHOFEN, J. J. (1967). *Myth, Religion and Mother Right* (translation R. Manheim). Routledge and Kegan Paul, London.

[1] As Sarastro is Pamina's father in Bergmann's version, it would follow that it was he who cut the magic flute from the oak tree (see footnote 1, p. 261).

BATLEY, E. (1969). *A Preface to the Magic Flute*. Dobson, London.

BERNDT, R. M. (1951). *Kunapipi*. Cheshire, Melbourne.

BRANSCOMBE, P. (1966). *Die Zauberflöte:* some textual and interpretive problems. *Proceedings of the Royal Musical Association*, **92,** 45–63.

BRODER, NATHAN (1964). *The Great Operas of Mozart*. Norton, New York.

BROPHY, BRIGID (1964). *Mozart the Dramatist*. Faber, London.

BROPHY, BRIGID (1971). Introduction to *Die Zauberflöte*. In W. A. Mozart, *Die Zauberflöte; Die Entfuhrung aus dem Serail*. Cassell, London.

CHAILLEY, JACQUES (1971). *The Magic Flute, Masonic Opera*. Knopf, New York.

DENT, E. J. (1913). *Mozart's Operas: A Critical Study*. Chatto and Windus, London.

DE VRIES, A. (1974). *Dictionary of Symbols and Imagery*. North-Holland Publishing Co., Amsterdam.

DEUTSCH, O. E. (1965). *Mozart: A Documentary Biography*. Black, London.

DEVEREUX, GEORGE (1963). Sociopolitical functions of the Oedipus myth in early Greece. *The Psychoanalytic Quarterly*, **32,** 205–214.

EINSTEIN, ALFRED (1971). *Mozart: His Character – His Work*. Panther Books, London.

ENGELS, FREIDRICH (1902). *The Origin of the Family, Private Property and the State* (translation Ernest Untermann). C. H. Kerr and Co., Chicago, Illinois.

EVIDON, R. (1976). Bergmann and "The Magic Flute". *The Musical Times*, **117,** no. 1596, 130–131.

FREEMAN, DEREK (1968). Thunder, blood and the nicknaming of God's creatures. *The Psychoanalytic Quarterly*, **37,** 353–399.

HANNAH, W. (1952). *Darkness Visible*. Augustine Press, London.

HARRIS, MARVIN (1968). *The Rise of Anthropological Theory*. Routledge and Kegan Paul, London.

HIATT, L. R. (1971). Secret pseudo-procreation rites among the Australian Aborigines. In *Anthropology in Oceania* (Eds L. R. Hiatt and C. Jayawardena), pp. 77–88. Angus and Robertson, Sydney.

HIATT, L. R. (1975). Swallowing and regurgitation in Australian myth and rite. In *Australian Aboriginal Mythology* (Ed. L. R. Hiatt), pp. 143–162. Australian Institute of Aboriginal Studies, Canberra.

ISTEL, E. (1927). Mozart's "Magic Flute" and Freemasonry. *The Musical Quarterly*, **13,** 510–527.

JONES, M. (1967). Freemasonry. In *Secret Societies* (Ed. N. Mackenzie), pp. 152–177. Aldus, London.

LEE M. O. (1973). A delicate balance. *Opera News*, **38,** no. 7, 28–29.

LOWIE, R. H. (1937). *The History of Ethnological Theory*. Farrar and Rinehart, New York.

MACKEY, A. (1869). *The Symbolism of Freemasonry*. Clark and Maynard, New York.

MANN, W. (1964). Introduction and Synopsis. Booklet accompanying a recording of *The Magic Flute* by the Philharmonic Orchestra and Chorus. His Master's Voice.

MEGGITT, M. J. (1967). *Gadjari among the Walbiri Aborigines of Central Australia*. *Oceania* monograph no. 14. University of Sydney, Sydney.

Opera News (1973). vol. 38, no. 7, 26.

OSBORNE, C. (1976). The "Flute" on film: it works. *High Fidelity*, **26**, no. 2: *Musical America*, 16–18.

RADCLIFFE-BROWN, A. R. (1952). *Structure and Function in Primitive Society*. Cohen and West, London.

SPENCER, W. B. and GILLEN, F. J. (1927). *The Arunta*. Macmillan, London.

STANNER, W. E. H. (1963). *On Aboriginal Religion*. *Oceania* monograph no. 11. University of Sydney, Sydney.

Phantasy and Symbol: A Psychoanalytic Point of View

R. H. Hook

THIS PAPER has two aims: to look at certain aspects of the psychoanalytic concepts of symbol and symbol formation, especially in relation to phantasy, and to consider by means of examples drawn from the literature how these concepts may contribute to the understanding of ethnographic material. It is not intended to enter into debate about what is "psychoanalytic" or "symbolic", nor to summarize or evaluate different points of view, but only to note, with regard to the former, that "psychoanalytic" has, in its broadest use, come to include almost anything related to, or deriving from, the work of Sigmund Freud, whilst, in a narrower sense, it may, with ample justification, be limited to certain restricted, and definable, techniques and theories. In surveying the scope and meaning of "symbol", Raymond Firth (1973, p. 54, footnote) recorded Melford E. Spiro's protest that in a symposium entitled "Forms of Symbolic Action" it was not clear why some of the contributors imagined that they were studying symbolism at all. It is hoped that my own use of these terms will become clear as the discussion proceeds.

Primary process thinking

Freud's great contribution to psychology was to offer a new and revolutionary model of the mind, with tremendous potential for the elucidation of otherwise obscure phenomena – still largely unexplored. For thousands of years man has been so preoccupied with the task of acquiring and consistently using logical and rational thought, so necessary for mastering the external world of physical and social reality, that he has had little inclination to investigate another system of thinking, which is, at least superficially, incompatible. Investigation of this other system of thinking is disturbing to man's sense of security for it would show him how he deludes himself into believing that he is other than he is; but it is only because this delusion so often breaks down in frank neurotic or psychotic illness that the source of man's somewhat tenuous adjustment to reality came to be investigated in the first place and this second system of thinking discovered. The effects of this other system of thinking – at least in so far as they arose to conscious awareness – were usually treated as irrational, and hence, inexplicable; or, for want of a more adequate aetiology, were attributed to demons or other superhuman powers.

Psychoanalysis would turn thinking on its head: ordinarily one starts from the assumption that man is rational and logical and when, as in dreams and neurosis, it appears that he is not, it is the irrational that has to be explained. So this is what every patient who consults a psychiatrist asks; this is what we say when we recall a dream; this was Freud's point of departure when he set out to study neurotic symptoms: why do we think, dream, this irrational nonsense? Freud showed that it is, in fact, the other way around: by nature man has an undiscriminating preference for whatever offers immediate gratification and it is only harsh reality that forces him to be rational. He attempts mentally to construct the world as he desires it and it is only when that world does not work that he is obliged to start again, only this time taking frustrating reality into account. In investigating thinking, psychoanalysis does not start with the rational world of the scientist and the logician – the "adult" of the sophisticated Western world – but would look rather at the world of the infant and the primitive.

Psychoanalysts are not alone in recognizing the ubiquity of the primitive and the irrational. In the Preface to *The Greeks and the Irrational*, E. R. Dodds quotes Lévy-Bruhl's opinion that "dans tout esprit humain, quel qu'en soît le développement intellectuel, subsiste un fond indéracinable de mentalité primitive", and that of Nilsson that "primitive mentality is a fairly good description of the mental behaviour of most people today except in their technical or consciously intellectual activities", whilst Dodds himself asks, "Why should we attribute to the ancient Greeks an immunity from 'primitive' modes of thought which we do not find in any society open to our direct observation?" (Dodds, 1951, p. viii). Indeed, why should we?

If we turn to the neurotic, we find Freud, in *Project for a Scientific Psychology* (begun at least as early as 1895), describing "hysterical *excessively intense ideas*" and "*hysterical compulsion*" as "(1) *unintelligible*, (2) *incapable of being resolved by the activity of thought*, (3) *incongruous* . . ." (Freud, 1950 [1895], p. 348). Such ideas are unintelligible and irrational because they operate according to a "logic" different from that of rational thinking. Freud called this different type of thinking "primary process thinking" to distinguish it from rational, logical, reality-oriented thinking, which he called "secondary process". The "logic" of the primary process is not only that of neurosis and psychosis, it is also to be discovered in so-called "normal" activities of the mind, dreams and parapraxes *(actes manquées)* and, it might be added, in myth and ritual, infused though these undoubtedly are with elements drawn from external day-to-day reality.

Dreams, as recalled, may be reduced to two fractions: the manifest and the latent content, the former, the dream story, being drawn from the events of daily life, frequently from the recent past. The importance of the manifest content is that it is used to represent, and so to give expression to, another series of mental events – phantasies, ideas or wishes – the latent content. Even in the process of being recalled the dream undergoes a further development called secondary revision. This is a reworking by secondary process thinking, which has the effect of making the dream more intelligible and more acceptable.

Freud discovered that the latent content, the *real* meaning of the dream, can best be understood as a reflection of wishes or ideas which can only be tolerated when expressed in a suitably disguised form. The type of thinking by means of which the latent content is ordinarily represented is primary process, characterized by such features as omnipotence of thought, hallucinatory wish-fulfilment, absence of negation, representation of the whole by a part or by the opposite, or by distortions due to displacement and condensation. Moreover, in primary process thinking, time and space have an altered significance, and, if represented at all, are dealt with in a manner altogether different from that of secondary process. These are also the mechanisms by means of which symbols are formed and we may expect to find a close relationship between the study of symbolization and symbolic thinking and an understanding of primary process.

With a revised concept of thinking we are able to move on from the simple notion of primitive or non-rational elements embedded in rational thinking to a more adequate conceptualization of the relationship of the non-rational to the rational, which would require a model similar to that used by Freud to depict the relationship of the unconscious to the conscious, viz., that of an iceberg the major portion of which, the unconscious – here primitive, non-rational, primary process thinking – lies beneath the surface, but is able, with a shift in internal dynamics, to overturn the whole mental "iceberg", including the rational, secondary process tip.

The earliest psychoanalytic concept of the symbol, that of "stable translations" of unconscious repressed impulses (Freud, 1916, p. 151) was neatly summarized by Rodrigué (1956, p. 150).

> The notion of symbols as special entities encouraged us to conceive them only as separate units. The possibility of complex symbolic structures lies outside the realm of our classical assumptions. Consequently Freud, instead of regarding the whole "form assumed by dreams" as symbolic, concluded that dreams contain symbolic units in their non-symbolic fabric. The same conclusion was maintained with regard to myths, proverbs and other modes of thought.

Freud's earliest view of the symbol was that of an idea or image present to the conscious mind, awake or in dreams, which translated an unconscious impulse or wish that had undergone distortion for the purpose of eluding the (dream) "censor". The symbol arises out of the distortion and serves to give expression to what would otherwise be inexpressible, because unacceptable. Symbol formation is a necessary part of the dream work, and interpretation reverses the process, turning symbols back into the (formerly) unconscious wishes which they represent.

The language of the primary process, and of the latent dream thoughts, is that of the symbol.

> . . . it may be pointed out that the interpretations made by psycho-analysis are first and foremost translations from an alien method of expression into the one which is familiar to us. When we interpret a dream we are simply translating a particular thought-content (the latent dream-thoughts) from the "language of dreams" into our waking speech. In the course of doing so we learn the peculiarities of this dream

language and it is borne in upon us that it forms part of a highly archaic system of expression. [Freud, 1913, p. 176.]

The "alien", "highly archaic system of expression" is that of the primary process; the one which is familiar to us is that of our waking speech, secondary process, logical, spatio-temporally organized and propositional.

Freud regarded primary process as ontogenetically and phylogenetically prior to secondary process. Heuristically, this is a useful distinction but its significance may be easily distorted. As with the not unrelated notion of "ego"– that part of the mind that relates to, and interprets, reality – some rudimentary secondary process, as some rudimentary ego function, must have been present from the beginning, for from its beginning life has had to cope with external reality or cease to exist.

Phantasy

There are two separable notions covered by the term "phantasy" and the distinction between them is enshrined in the two ways of spelling the word in the English language. James Strachey drew attention to this in the Introduction to *The Standard Edition of the Complete Psychological Works of Sigmund Freud* (1966, p. xxiv), whilst the distinction was further emphasized and incorporated into a theoretical framework by Susan Isaacs (1948, p. 80). Strachey, following a lead given by the Oxford English Dictionary, used the *ph* form for "the technical psychological phenomenon" and the *f* form when the idea of "caprice, whim, fanciful invention" predominates. Susan Isaacs used the *ph* form to denote "*unconscious* mental content, which may or may not become conscious", but it should be noted that this distinction is not universally accepted and some psychoanalytic writers contest its validity on the grounds that it is not in harmony with the complex nature of Freud's thought (cf. Laplanche and Pontalis, 1971, p. 156).

There were three significant stages in the development of the psychoanalytic theory of fantasy: Freud's early discovery that, contrary to what he at first thought, fantasy is more significant than the memory of an actual historical event for the subsequent course of mental development;[1] Anna Freud's clarification of the role played by

[1] A discovery which introduces another, and largely unknown, variable into studies of the relationship between child rearing practices – or even the specific culture in which the child grows up and lives – and adult personality.

fantasy as an ego defence (1936, pp. 69 ff.); and finally the contribution of Melanie Klein, Susan Isaacs and Hanna Segal to the concept of phantasy as the content of primary process thinking.

Susan Isaacs (1948, p. 81) defined phantasy as "the primary content of unconscious mental processes", with the implication that everything that happens in the unconscious happens in terms of phantasy; for instance, defence mechanisms operate on and modify phantasies. It is a phantasy that undergoes projection, as a phantasy of something being expelled from inside the body and being put into something or someone outside; or conversely, of being taken inside the body in the case of introjection. In condensation, elements of two or more phantasies are taken out and combined to form a third, condensed phantasy; whilst in displacement, cathectic energy attaching to one phantasy is transferred to another so that the second stands in place of the first in the distribution of energy cathexes. When, through the operation of mechanisms such as condensation and displacement, there is a change in the distribution of cathectic energy, the replacing phantasy may be said to stand in the relation of symbol to the phantasy it replaces.

When a symbol is formed, interest is transferred from the phantasy symbolized to the phantasy which stands in its place. The features of the latter which enable it to receive such a transfer of interest (in technical language, cathexis) are specifiable: they are the features of similarity, contiguity, part for whole, and so on, which we saw to be characteristic of primary process thinking. The primary units of thinking are phantasies, simple or complex, and the basic operation of the primary process is their manipulation by symbolization, one coming to stand in the place of another in an endless series. This is the basis of Ernest Jones's statement that civilization is the result of an endless process of symbolic substitutions, whilst Melanie Klein saw in symbolization the process by means of which the infant apprehends reality and endows it with value. Failure of symbolic substitution leads to a state of autism in which the external world is lacking in interest, as it was for "Dick", described by Melanie Klein (1930, pp. 236 ff.).

It might be objected that (like W. R. Bion's alpha-function) such a concept of phantasy attempts to explain too much and so loses explanatory force but it must be remembered that it was the observation of the drastic consequences for personality development (as in schizophrenia and autism) of the failure of some basic and important function that led to the need to widen the concept of phantasy, and also led Bion to postulate his alpha-function.[1]

The mental representative of an instinct is a phantasy, and the operation of an instinct is represented by a phantasy of the satisfaction of that instinct by its appropriate object. The earliest object is the breast or nipple. Criticism of this concept of the breast as the earliest object usually runs along neurological lines: that the myelinated tracts upon which such a representation might depend are not at that time available in the infant brain. It would seem, however, that there must already be in existence tracts adequate for the searching behaviour which the human infant has in common with the young of other species and which must be the outcome of innate patterning. What the psychic representation of this "instinctual" behaviour is we can only surmise but it seems not unreasonable to suppose that some trace must be left which would have consequences for later development. It is doubtful if we have any knowledge which would enable us to be more precise.

However, the starting point for a psychoanalytic theory of thinking cannot be merely the satisfaction derived from contact with the breast or nipple, for were satisfaction immediate and constant there would be no need for thought. The initial stimulus must be an absence, a void, or a frustration, because the object is not present at all or because it is incompletely satisfying or – and it amounts to the same thing – it has to be given up. Response may be by motor discharge or by "thinking". For Bion, the latter depends upon the possibility of alpha-function which, in the first instance, the infant derives from

[1] W. R. Bion, in his penetrating essays into the psychoanalytic theory of thinking, postulated two basic mental functions which, in order to avoid importing such overtones as would inevitably be inferred had he used terms drawn from everyday use, he called "alpha-function" and "beta-function". He then set out to discover what was to be included in these functions, which produce respectively what he called "alpha-" and "beta- elements". Beta-function is the more primitive and is concerned with elements which cannot be assimilated or "digested", which cannot become unconscious or transformed into memories, and accordingly can have no subjective significance and have to be got rid of by being projected. On the other hand, the postulated alpha-function, which is essential for normal development, enables objects to be distinguished from their mental representations and makes possible memory, emotional experience, the distinction between unconscious and conscious, and the possibility of dreaming, so that maturation also becomes possible. The process of symbolization is an attribute of alpha-function.

contact with the alpha-function of his mother and her capacity for what Bion calls "reverie" (1962b, pp. 36–37).[1]

The earliest phantasies are about bodies and represent instinctual aims towards objects, serving from the beginning as a defence against tension and anxiety. As phantasies of introjection and projection appear very early in mental life, we have an important reason why body language, and "gut" responses in particular, figure so prominently in language expressing emotion in all peoples.

Symbol

The Greek *symbolon*, from *symbalein*, to put together, means each of two halves or corresponding pieces of an object, such as a potsherd, broken into two fragments which could be rejoined for the purpose of recognition or identification in the manner of an "indenture" (a document in duplicate torn, or "indented", for the same reason). The derivation of "symbol" indicates its essential feature: that it comprises two parts which, though separate, belong together in some significant respect and may be recognized as belonging together.

Freud's early analysis of symbol is to be found in *Project for a Scientific Psychology* (1950 [1895], pp. 348–349).

> Before the analysis, *A* is an excessively intense idea, which forces its way into consciousness too often, and each time gives rise to weeping. The subject does not know why he weeps at *A*; he regards it as absurd but cannot prevent it. After the analysis, it has been discovered that there is an idea *B*, which justifiably gives rise to weeping . . . The effect of *B* is not absurd; it is intelligible to the subject and can even be combated by him. *B* stands in a particular relation to *A*. For there has been an occurrence of *B*+*A*. *A* was an incidental circumstance; *B* was appropriate for producing the lasting effect . . . it is as though *A* had stepped into *B*'s place. *A* has become a substitute, a *symbol* for *B*.

The formative relationship here adduced by Freud is one of simple association or contiguity: "there has been an occurrence of *B*+*A*".

[1] It is difficult to be sure that one has fully understood Bion, but it seems that if the infant is extremely aggressive, greedy or unable to accept frustration, or – and it amounts dynamically to the same thing – if the mother is unable to receive the "projections" of the infant and reduce them to a tolerable form, there is likely to be a failure of alpha-function and only beta-function is possible. Beta-elements cannot be converted to alpha-elements and can be dealt with only by expulsion or projection, that is, by resort to flight *vis-à-vis* frustration rather than by a modification of the frustration of the kind which would result from the operation of alpha-function. Flight here means a massive use of the mechanisms of splitting, repression and denial; whilst modification means replacing the lost object in thought without at the same time denying its absence. (A useful discussion, in French, of Bion's ideas is to be found in Luzes, 1969, p. 798 ff.).

The relationship of the symbol, *A*, to the thing symbolized, *B*, may be formed otherwise than by association or contiguity: it may resemble it, it may be part of it, or it may stand in relation to it as opposite, and so on. Freud emphasized the *tertium comparationis*, the feature common to both *A* and *B*, which links *A* to *B* and causes *A* to arise in place of *B*.

In this account of the formation of an hysterical symptom or idea, the symbol is personal and fortuitous, that is, idiosyncratic. In his study of dream symbolism Freud recognized also symbols which were sufficiently constant, and common, to be regarded as "stable translations" permitting interpretation of the dream, or at least of parts of it, *without questioning the dreamer* (Freud, 1916, p. 151). That is, symbols may also be general rather than personal and not fortuitous but, having constant features, may be presumed to arise from a predisposition of the mind or from the fact that minds and bodies are what they are and function as they do.

Drawing attention to the fact that in some cases the element common to the symbol and to what it represents, the *tertium comparationis*, is obvious whilst in others it is concealed, Freud suggested a genetic relationship:

> Things that are symbolically connected to-day were probably united in prehistoric times by conceptual and linguistic identity. The symbolic relation seems to be a relic and a mark of former identity. [Freud, 1900, p. 352.]

The nature of this former identity is suggested in the sections of this paper dealing with phantasy and symbolic behaviour but, for the moment, it is sufficient to note that symbols may be idiosyncratic and specific, or general and more widely available but that, in both cases, we are dealing with symbols in the more restricted sense of the term, that used by Sándor Ferenczi, one of the earliest psychoanalytic writers on symbolism.

> Only such things (or ideas) are symbols in the sense of psycho-analysis as are invested in consciousness with a logically inexplicable and unfounded affect, and of which it may be analytically established that they owe this affective over-emphasis to *unconscious* identification with another thing (or idea), to which the surplus of affect really belongs. Not all similes, therefore, are symbols, but only those in which the one member of the equation is repressed into the unconscious . . .
>
> This being so, it is more prudent not to assume that the conditions under which symbols arise are identical with those for analogy-formation in general, but to presuppose for this specific kind of analogy-formation specific conditions of origin, and to search for these. [Ferenczi, 1913, pp. 277–278.]

Although Ferenczi here restricts the psychoanalytic concept of symbol to those things which, when conscious, have "a logically inexplicable and unfounded affect" and of which "one member of the equation is repressed into the unconscious"– thereby following closely Freud's early analysis of symbol formation in relation to hysterical symptoms – it would seem that this need not be taken to imply that one member of the equation must necessarily be conscious. On the contrary, Freud recognized that symbols used in dreams are not always formed by the dream work but rather that:

> . . . dreams make use of any symbolizations which are *already present* in unconscious thinking, because they fit in better with the requirements of dream-construction on account of their representability and also because as a rule they escape censorship.
> [Freud, 1900, p. 349 (my italics).]

Two essential ingredients of early psychoanalytic views on symbolism are the displacement of affect (cathexis or attachment of libidinal energy) from what is symbolized, the "idea *B*", to the symbol which stands in its place, "*A*", and the unconscious nature of this displacement, one element (at least) being repressed, that is, unconscious. Whilst retaining the notion of displacement of cathexis, later psychoanalytic thinking has tended to emphasize symbolization as a basic and more general function or capacity of the mind, manifesting itself both in the formation of idiosyncratic and specific symbols and in the "complex symbolic structures" of which Rodrigué speaks, so that symbolization may be seen as the process by means of which the external world is invested with libidinal energy (cathected) and so apprehended or appropriated.

Displacement of cathexis is not an indifferent or two-way process but is always from the idea of an object or activity of primary instinctual interest on to the idea of an object of less instinctual interest, the latter becoming the symbol of the former. "*A*" is always of less instinctual interest than "*B*". Symbolization is a "centrifugal, one-way process" (Rycroft, 1968, pp. 53–54). Ernest Jones said the same thing in different words. "I do not in any sense mean that [trends on the surface] are to be neglected, or in their turn, underestimated, but simply that one should not put the cart before the horse and talk of something secondary and less important being *symbolised* by something primary and more important." (Jones, 1916, p. 125.)

Rycroft points out that the phallic *symbols*, dagger, watering-can, gun, aeroplane and snake, refer to different affective conceptions of the penis, and to different aspects of its functions, in which cases cathexis is displaced from the object of primary instinctual interest, penis, on to the ideas, or symbols, of less instinctual interest, dagger, watering-can, etc., though the fact that an object or activity is itself of primary instinctual interest is no bar to its being used as a symbol. Displacement of cathexis can also occur in the opposite, or centripetal, direction, when it "is usually called 'regression', though it could as appropriately, and perhaps less confusingly, be called 'desymbolization'. . . the reverse of symbolization, not a special form of it" (Rycroft, 1968, p. 54). Displacement of significance from one activity or object to another is capable of infinite repetition and, once established, tends to persist.

Ernest Jones called civilization the result of an endless process of symbolic substitutions,[1] a view which may be compared with that of Melanie Klein and also with that of Ernst Cassirer[2] in his treatment of symbolic function as the process by means of which the mind constructs its universes of perception and discourse, and which mediates between reality and the mind's apprehension of reality.

Rycroft excludes the processes of symbolization and displacement from the concept of primary process on the grounds that to include them would imply, firstly, "that the modes of unconscious and conscious mental activity are qualitatively absolutely different" and, secondly, "that symbolization is a feature of unconscious mental

[1] The importance of symbolization for cultural development is widely attested. Cf. Lévi-Strauss: "Toute culture peut être considérée comme un ensemble de systèmes symboliques au premier rang desquels se placent le langage, les règles matrimoniales, les rapports économiques, l'art, la science, la religion" (1950, p. xix).

[2] Paul Ricoeur (1965, p. 19) thinks that Cassirer's view of symbolism is too wide and would restrict the concept of symbolism to the interpretation of language: "Selon nous le symbole est une expression linguistique à double sens qui requiert une interprétation, l'interprétation un travail de compréhension qui vise à déchiffrer les symboles" (1965, p. 18), and, ". . . le problème du symbole s'est égalé à celui même du langage. Il n'y a pas de symbolique avant l'homme qui parle . . ." (1965, p. 25). It would seem likely, however, that man acquired both symbolism and the capacity to speak, to use language, in the process of becoming human: both are fundamental human characteristics and humanity is not conceivable without them. If anything, it would appear that language depends upon a capacity for symbolizing. Ricoeur limits the concept "symbol" to the act of interpreting: ". . . je propose de délimiter le champ d'application du concept de symbole par référence à l'acte d'interprétation. Je dirai qu'il y a symbole là où l'expression linguistique se prête par son double sens ou ses sens multiples à un travail d'interprétation." (1965, p. 26.) Important though the act of interpretation is, and it is, of course, central to the psychoanalytic process, interpretation is a logical construction and symbolization cannot be defined only in reference to it. To follow Ricoeur would be to remain on the secondary process level and to fail to penetrate to the roots of symbol formation.

activity and does not occur in conscious thinking" (1968, p. 47). Rycroft's objection to the idea that symbolism is confined to unconscious mental activity may be accepted without thereby denying that symbolization is typical of primary process thinking. Primary process should not be equated with unconscious mental activity, nor is secondary process to be treated as co-extensive with conscious mental activity. There is considerable overlap, but they are in any case differing categories. Unconscious mental activity differs qualitatively from conscious mental activity in regard to accessibility to consciousness; primary process differs from secondary process in regard to certain features, such as mobility of cathexes, distortion (or absence) of time and space, absence of negation, omnipotence of thought and wish-fulfilling fantasies, which are distortions of reality and are not compatible with reality-oriented, secondary process thinking.

It is not, of course, contended that symbolization does not occur in conscious thinking: what is suggested is that both symbolization and the mechanisms of which it is the consequence, displacement, condensation, representation of whole by part, etc., are characteristic of primary process thinking. However, once formed, symbols may be rapidly converted to secondary process use and may, indeed, fit their new use so well as to appear expressly formed for just such purpose. Symbols may also be invented and used by the secondary process, as are the symbols of mathematics and logic. When these are arbitrarily allotted representations they may be called "signs" to distinguish them from symbols (cf. Langer, 1942). The latter, in the psycho-analytic sense, require to have an affective significance, or cathexis. Things which were, in origin, symbols may be converted into signs by having their affective, that is, symbolic, significance withdrawn in the course of being taken over by the secondary process. They become de-cathected, or in Hartmann's term, "neutralized", and the reverse may occur: things which in themselves were neutral may have special, or symbolic, significance attached to them, a process which may be observed to occur when words appear in dreams, or in schizophrenia when words are used in a private and idiosyncratic way.

The dream and its apprehension and recall is an example of what happens at the interface between primary and secondary process. Dreams are largely, if not entirely, primary process in formation and are experienced directly in pictorial form, though sensory modalities other than visual may be represented; in schizophrenia primary process type thinking may be apprehended consciously and directly, a fact which in part accounts for both the anxiety to be seen in the early stages of the condition and the characteristic disturbance of reality testing. When dreams are translated into words for the purpose of recall, review and revision, secondary process comes into play. Another example of the relationship between the two kinds of thinking may be seen in a story told of the discovery of the benzene ring by the chemist, Kekulé. Seated on the top deck of a London bus and tired from his day's work, Kekulé's reveries corresponded to the well-known fantasy of snakes chasing, or swallowing, their tails (the *uroborus*) with primary process qualities, but in this instance it was grasped by Kekulé and applied to the problem occupying his mind at the time, with dramatic results.[1] In a similar way, through the mechanism of sublimation, primary process "play" becomes secondary process "work".

In so far as secondary process thinking is in terms of words and other symbols, it is limited, and distorted, by the symbols available to, and used by, the thinker. It may be similarly limited and distorted by primary process formations which act in a facilitating or inhibiting manner, the result of pleasure or anxiety operating at a deeper and unconscious level. Secondary process thinking may be seen as operating between the twin poles of what is allowed, or required, by the (unconscious) primary process, and what is allowed, or required, by reality.

Language occupies an important and central place in the study of symbolism.[2] Grammar and semantics are concerned with the ways in which language serves the purposes of logical, secondary process thinking, whilst the language of mathematics and logic is entirely designed for this purpose, but another aspect of language closer to the symbolic function typical of primary process thinking is its use in expressing feeling and emotion, as in poetry and other literature. In evocative language, the mechanisms by means of which symbols are formed, resemblance, part for whole, and temporal and spatial association, etc., characteristic of primary process, are repeated in the

[1] Apparently Kekulé was in London prior to 1856, whereas his brilliant discovery was made in 1865. But even if the story is apocryphal, the point remains.

[2] A contrasting view is that of Jacques Lacan, who treats the unconscious as being itself structured, its structure being that of language (cf. Laplanche and Pontalis, 1971, p. 474, "Symbolique"; Steiner, 1976, p. 255).

corresponding figures of speech, simile and metaphor, synecdoche and metonymy.

Of the many uses of the concept, symbol, to be discovered in the psychoanalytic literature, the two aspects highlighted here are, firstly, the earlier and more restricted use which limits symbols to particular elements embedded in fantasies and dreams – or in myth and ritual; and the later, more extended view, which would see not only "the whole form assumed by dreams", or myths, as symbolic but would treat all complex patterns of behaviour, and even the apprehension of reality itself, as involving symbolization. Both views are explicit in Ernest Jones's classical paper, "The Theory of Symbolism" (1916), in which he emphasizes that in psychoanalytic usage the symbol itself is conscious but represents, and so allows for limited discharge of, what is unconscious and must remain repressed, but he also saw that symbolism makes possible the apprehension and extension of the individual's "outer world".

Symbolic behaviour

The productions of a civilization – literature, music, graphic and constructional art, as well as the myths and rituals of both civilized and primitive people – may seem a long way removed from the child's first frustrations and experience of loss.[1] Susan Isaacs pointed out the connection between frustration and achievement:

> Disappointment may be the first stimulus to adaptative acceptance of reality, but the postponement of satisfaction and the suspense involved in the complicated learning and thinking about external reality which the child presently accomplishes – and for increasingly remote ends – can only be endured and sustained when it itself satisfies instinctual urges, represented in phantasies, as well. [1948, p. 94.]

Anna Freud shows how play can express instinctual urges:

> The dismantling of toys because of the wish to know what is *inside* betrays sexual curiosity. It is even significant in which manner a small boy plays with his railway:

[1] In the Kleinian view, symbol formation is the outcome of loss, not only in the "depressive position" when symbol formation is ". . . a creative work, involving the pain and the whole work of mourning", but more generally, "every aspect of the object, every situation that has to be given up in the process of growing, gives rise to symbol formation" (Segal, 1973, p. 76). The symbol preserves the lost object.

whether his main pleasure is derived from staging crashes (as symbols of parental intercourse); whether he is predominantly concerned with building tunnels and underground lines (expressing interest in the inside of the body); whether his cars and buses have to be loaded heavily (as symbols of the pregnant mother); or whether speed and smooth performance are his main concern (as symbols of phallic efficiency). [1965, pp. 19–20.]

In a similar way, Anna Freud goes on to show how a little girl's horse craze reveals her emotional needs.

Bénassy and Diatkine see in play a bridge between phantasy and reality and point to a reciprocal relationship between the two:

. . . because [play] is manifest behaviour connected with latent fantasy, and we can proceed from one to the other. Fantasy could be described as interiorized play and fantasy can itself be exteriorized in overt activity, play. [1964, p. 175.]

The same may be said of artistic production and aesthetic experience, play with shapes, forms, colours and sounds, commonly in a traditional or stylized manner, but nonetheless stimulating and gratifying internal phantasy. Artistic production links phantasy and reality and offers a suitable medium for the operation of the psychological mechanisms of projection, projective identification, re-introjection and re-projection, as well as others such as condensation, often in multiple determination. A single feature may be this as well as that: not this or that only, but both at the same time. Anthony Forge brings out well this multiple function in Sepik art:

It seems to me that Abelam flat painting is a system in which a limited number of motifs, some themselves simple graphic elements, most with several alternative meanings, are combined and arranged in harmonious designs, ancestrally sanctioned, and believed to be intrinsically powerful. The total design may or may not have a name or "represent something" in our terms, what is important is the expression of relationship between the parts and the meanings of those parts . . . to identify a "representation" is not to find out what the painting means, it is merely one element in a complex web of meaning which is to be found in the relationships of the parts that compose them. [1973, p. 187.]

From the psychoanalytic point of view many meanings are always present and they need not, indeed often cannot, be put into words for they are a response to, and satisfy, unconscious phantasies. The total design of an artistic production, a myth, ritual sequence, or dream, may be perceived as a gratifying whole, expressing complex phantasies, and is, itself, able to undergo condensation and pass into further combinations without diminishing the importance of the parts and the relationship between them.

Elementary phantasies are not lost but persist and undergo transformation by the mechanisms we have been considering into complex phantasies which may be taken over by the secondary process and built into such complicated constructions as models or pictures of world order – a recurrent interest of primitive mythologies – and other culturally important derivatives. Cassirer gives examples to show how differentiation of parts of the body serves as a basis or model for the mental representation of other spatial configurations. Differentiated and re-integrated as a "... self-enclosed and intrinsically articulated organism, [the body] becomes, as it were, a model according to which [man] constructs the world as a whole" (1953, vol. I, p. 206). He constructs language in the same way, as a number of recent studies have also argued.[1] Cassirer, quoting H. K. Brugsch, cites the ancient Egyptian word *kod*, which meant originally "to turn around, to turn in a circle", but came to represent, via the notion of the turning of the potter's wheel, the potter's formative activity, and then acquired the significance of form, create, build, work, travel, sleep, and substantively, likeness, image, similarity, circle, and ring, as well as to be a potter and to make pots (Cassirer, 1953, vol. I, p. 288, footnote). Cassirer further instances the great diversity and precision "... in general designations of locality, and in special designations for the situation of a thing and the direction of a movement ..." (1953, vol. I, p. 210) to be found in the case structure of the Ural-Altaic family of languages, and quotes Friedrich Müller:

> "These languages do not simply stop outside the object, but penetrate, one might say, into the object and create a formal opposition between its inside and outside, its top and its bottom. The three conditions of rest, motion towards the object and motion away from the object, combine with the categories of 'inside', 'outside' and in some languages 'above', to create an abundance of case forms for which our languages have no feeling at all, and which we can therefore not adequately render. [Cassirer, 1953, vol. I, p. 210.]"

Central features of the above illustrations are the notions, in slightly expanded form, of circle and movement (or position and movement in relation to the circle, or "point within a circle"),[2] top and bottom,

[1] Cf., for example, Thass-Thienemann (1973).

[2] See the paper in this volume by Dr Hiatt, who points out that "point within a circle" is a symbol with an ancient meaning, viz. the worship of the generative principle in nature, signified in Eastern religion by the *linga* in the *yoni*; the point also indicates the sun and the circle the universe, invigorated and fertilized by his generative rays (pp. 261–262, quoting Mackey).

above and below, inside and outside (or coming out–going in). These are secondary process representatives of primary process phantasies and are widely spread, as evidenced, in addition to the above-mentioned examples, by material from a culture widely removed in time and distance from ancient Egypt and from the speakers of the Ural-Altaic group of languages – that of the Walbiri of Central Australia. It might be objected that these are necessary logical categories and that it would not be possible to order the material in any other way. However, Nancy Munn points out that the Walbiri make the sexual connotation quite explicit, an observation that supports psychoanalytically based inferences about the origin of these notions. In the case of the Walbiri, "'coming out – going in' and its visual correlates provide a way of thinking and communicating about the nature of the cosmos" (Munn, 1973, p. 217). "Coming out–going in" has sexual reference both in terms of birth and death and in terms of intercourse:

> . . . the circle in its two senses of camp site or country and female body or "mother" is a container; a visible form within which life is carried. Walbiri interpretations suggest the concentricity of the circle conveys the internal structure of the country or body. The essential contrast between centre and periphery is that the former is a hole or waterhole where the life sources are localized, while the latter is a solid enclosing form, i.e. the country or body, the container itself. . . . the relation between the hole or waterhole and the camp site is itself ambiguous, for the former mediates between the bottom or "underneath part" of the country and the surface. On the one hand, the centre is the bottom of the hole, and therefore under the country; on the other, the centre is a visible topographical form on the surface of the country, ringed by the camp. We have to remember that the waterhole, like all topographical features, was created by the Dreamings, and functions as visible proof of their existence. But it also marks the point where the Dreaming exists hidden underground, or where he existed before emergence, before the waterhole was made.
>
> The same sort of double reading can be phrased in terms of the body. From one point of view the centre is inside the woman's body, while the peripheries are the body surface. In another sense, the centre is the vaginal hole through which entry is effected into the body in sexual intercourse and from which the child is born.
>
> [Munn, 1973, p. 213.]

It will be appreciated that this sort of thinking suggests the possibility of freer and richer phantasy representation than is common in "civilized" society and must greatly facilitate cathexis of the physical environment thereby giving it greater emotional significance. The primary phantasy origin of the material just quoted is still clear but in other instances it has entirely disappeared and it is at times possible to illustrate the process of disappearance. In the British Museum there is a series of earthenware vessels from the Lusatian Culture (1400–700 B.C.) of Eastern Germany and Western Poland. The earliest vessels, which could have been used for drinking or for the presentation of food, were ornamented with a vigorous bossed and fluted decoration inspired by the human breast, but this later degenerates into fluted areas surrounding a central nipple, whilst the fluting becomes more geometric, with filled triangles a common motif. In the development of Sumerian cuneiform writing during the period from about 3000 B.C. to 600 B.C., the signs for "man" and for "woman", which in the earliest phase were clearly representations of genitalia, became in the course of time so transformed that all indication of their genital origin was lost and the meaning became formally rather than explicitly attached (cf. Niederland, 1964, p. 108).

We are now in a better position to understand Freud's view that "things that are symbolically connected to-day were probably united in prehistoric times by conceptual and linguistic identity . . . in a number of cases the use of a common symbol extends further than the use of a common language . . ." and, in a footnote added in 1925, Freud notes Dr Hans Sperber's opinion "that all primal words referred to sexual things but afterwards lost their sexual meaning through being applied to other things and activities which were compared with the sexual ones" (1900, p. 352). The processes which may be seen to be operating are extension by symbolization and repression of the sexual component, leaving the non-sexual element to stand as a *symbol* of the forgotten sexual one. The connection between the two elements may still be seen in those languages where, for instance, words for offensive weapons like knife and spear are also used for penis (cf. Alfred Gell's discussion of *tadv* relations at pp. 138 ff. of this volume).

Myth and primary process

Like the dream, myth has an underlying fabric of phantasy which constitutes the thought of the myth. The work of the myth, like the dream work, is to turn these phantasies into a form acceptable to the ego; like the dream, the manifest content of the myth is made up of elements drawn from the daily life and experience of the people, as well as from material generally regarded as suitable for myth-making. Myth differs from dream in that, belonging to a social group, it has a continuing external form which is able to be modified with the passage of time and so to undergo variations. Devereux called these phantasies, at least in one of their aspects, "ego dystonic insights, which are at once too powerful to be repressed and too painful to be applied to oneself", and continued:

> The "mythopoeic position" appears to be the following: "This is the truth, but it happened not to me, but to someone else; it applies not to me, but to someone else." Such inventions are accepted by the listeners, and are transmitted to future generations because the listener's unconscious echoes the latent content of the myth while the manifest content of the myth – the fact that it *is* a myth – enables the listener *not* to apply the insight to himself. [1957, p. 400.]

Both myth and dream are extensively overdetermined, each part answering to many associations and satisfying several wishes or needs, and emerging only as clear and definite in the process of being worked over. Material from a study of the mythology of Śiva by Wendy O'Flaherty illustrates well the primary process quality of myth.[1]

> . . . Indian mythology impresses us with its apparent formlessness; there is no one "myth" but rather a vague, ectoplasmic substance whose outlines constantly change, containing somewhere within it the essence of the myth. [O'Flaherty, 1973, p. 314.]

Śiva may be seen as admirably cast for the projection of wishes like those of infantile omnipotent narcissism. The caste system and the related doctrine of *svadharma* ("one's own particular duty in life") led to restriction or loss of freedom of choice but, to quote Dr O'Flaherty again,

> . . . these frustrations are relieved in the myths, where Śiva embodies *all* of life, in *all* of its detail, at every minute. He alone need make no choice; through him all of the conflicting challenges are accepted at once. [1973, p. 315.]

And, in more general terms:

> By refusing to modify its component elements in order to force them into a synthesis, Indian mythology celebrates the idea that the universe is boundlessly various, that everything occurs simultaneously, that all possibilities may exist without excluding each other. [1973. p. 318.]

[1] It may be thought that the illustrations of symbolic constructions taken from the work of Cassirer, Forge and O'Flaherty and quoted in this paper have been taken out of context, but it is suggested that the statements which these authors make about their respective materials are consonant with the view of the primary process origin of symbolism put forward here and are, moreover, what would be expected if this view is correct.

Through the process of externalization by projection on to a social screen (in dream, projected on to a private screen), internal conflicts are given form in a verbal tradition which becomes capable of further modification according to the needs of the narrator or hearers, or, in the case of ritual, actors. Devereux indicated the defensive function of myths:

> . . . culture, in providing myths or beliefs for the "cold storage" of certain fantasies and insights, keeps them out of "private circulation". This view is quite in accordance with the thesis proposed elsewhere [Devereux, 1956] that culture provides a set of standard defences against, and solutions for, "type conflicts" characteristic of a given cultural milieu. [Devereux, 1957, p. 400.]

It is for this reason that many hitherto unformulated psychoanalytic facts which seldom, if ever, make an appearance in the psychoanalytic chamber, may ultimately be derived from the study of myths, beliefs and the like (cf. Devereux, 1957, p. 400).

Myth is not basically a rational product, though it is capable of revision and rationalization (by offering an explanation or reinterpreting as a metaphysical system) and, reflecting primary process, will tend to be timeless and will contain no negations or, if it does, they will be interpreted in a positive or affirmative sense, whilst apparent contradiction and incompatibility will serve to draw attention to important elements of the myth closely related to significant conflicts.

Too narrow a view of what is psychoanalytic or "Freudian", will obscure the real psychoanalytic meaning. "Freudian" is often taken to connote the unusual or bizarre, especially when expressed in anal, genital, or more narrowly oedipal themes. What is significantly attributable to Freud is not only recognition of the universality and extent of what may meaningfully be called "sexual", but, and equally important, of the role of unconscious and repressed impulses and their derivatives, expressed in phantasies, in influencing conscious thought and behaviour. Aggressive and destructive impulses co-exist, fused in varying degrees, with the sexual as may be seen in sadism and masochism. They are interwoven in the mythology of Śiva and, as Dr O'Flaherty points out, ". . . the basic concept underlying the corpus of seduction myths [is] that the sexual act is dangerous, causing the loss of power and sometimes of life itself" (1973, p. 180).

Psychoanalytic interpretation

Psychoanalytic interpretation is concerned with the unconscious and seeks to make explicit underlying impulses, wishes and phantasies. For this reason it does not, *cannot*, clash with interpretations made on a different level, or using a different mode of analysis, but is complementary to them (Devereux, 1972). The interpretation of individual behaviour is the legitimate field and the home base of psychoanalysis where it is able to work with its own special technique, the understanding and interpretation of transference. Transference phenomena are not properly interpretable outside of the analytic situation, for transference interpretation is validated by the material that emerges subsequent to it. The data of the ethnographer are usually obtained using a different technique. How then can the psychoanalyst offer interpretations of value or interest to the anthropologist?

What the psychoanalyst finds when he studies the reports of ethnographers is that the material "rings true" in terms of observations made in the psychoanalysis of individuals. That is to say, on the level of primary process the psychoanalyst's observations made within the framework of Western society correspond with observations made on material from other cultures widely dispersed in time and space.[1] If this were not so, it is not only unlikely that the psychoanalyst would have anything relevant to say to the ethnologist, but the ethnologist himself would be unable to develop empathy for, or achieve much significant understanding of, the behaviour of other cultures. Interpretations offered by psychoanalysis may throw fresh light on the data and suggest further avenues for exploration by the ethnographer, using his own methods.

The elucidation of the psychoanalytic meaning of cultural products, such as myths, depends upon the existence of primitive phantasies and a "psychic apparatus" common to all men – both of which it has been the achievement of psychoanalysis to investigate and clarify. Myths and legends, of which the classical example is *Oedipus Rex*, have furnished psychoanalysis with some of its most fecund material and have, in the past, contributed more to psychoanalysis than has psychoanalysis to the study of myth.

[1] This and other references to similarities between cultures widely dispersed in time and space is not to be taken as implying support for "diffusionist" theories, but rather as evidence for the universality of certain basic human responses.

What is important is the model of the mind provided by psychoanalysis. Primary phantasies undergo transformation by mechanisms which are now fairly well known: by symbolic substitution they come to embrace more and more diverse aspects of reality, which thereby acquire interest and emotional value. All human behaviour has a symbolic component, but is not all equally interpretable in terms of underlying phantasies. The first step in interpreting those elements which are clearly symbolic will be to trace the phantasies they express and, where possible, the mechanisms involved and the underlying needs they serve. It may then be possible to show how a particular piece of behaviour, myth or artistic production satisfies core phantasies and reduces anxiety and tension. For instance, aggressive and destructive phantasies may be more safely dealt with when projected in the form of devils and evil spirits –"Externalization makes possible the containment of terror" (Bruner, 1960, p. 277).

The function of symbol formation is the binding and discharge of psychic energy. In experiments in which the subject has been prevented from dreaming by being awakened at the onset of dreaming, the result has been restless anxiety. It would seem that one function of myth and ritual is to bind energy which would otherwise issue in unbearable anxiety, or in less desirable social consequences.

> When the symbolization is poor, when the condensation, the displacement and dramatization are rudimentary, the energy, imperfectly bound up, is liable to be unleashed from one moment to the next . . . [De M'Uzan, 1974, p. 464.]

Binding makes sublimation possible: discharge is controlled in socially useful ways.

References

BÉNASSY, M. and DIATKINE, R. (1964). On the ontogenesis of fantasy. *The International Journal of Psycho-Analysis*, **45**, 171–179.

BION, W. R. (1962a). The psycho-analytic study of thinking. *The International Journal of Psycho-Analysis*, **43**, 306–310.

BION, W. R. (1962b). *Learning from Experience*. Heinemann, London.

BION, W. R. (1963). *Elements of Psycho-Analysis*. Heinemann, London.

BRUNER, J. S. (1960). Myth and identity. In *Myth and Mythmaking* (Ed. H. A. Murray), pp. 276–287. Braziller, New York.

CASSIRER, ERNST (1953). *The Philosophy of Symbolic Forms* (translation R.

Manheim). 3 vols. Yale University Press, New Haven, Connecticut.

DE M'UZAN, M. (1974). Analytical process and the notion of the past. *International Review of Psycho-Analysis*, **1**, 461–466.

DEVEREUX, GEORGE (1956). Normal and abnormal: the key problem of psychiatric anthropology. In *Some Uses of Anthropology: Theoretical and Applied*, pp. 23–48. Washington Anthropological Society, Washington, D.C.

DEVEREUX, GEORGE (1957). The awarding of a penis as compensation for rape. A demonstration of the clinical relevance of the psycho-analytic study of cultural data. *The International Journal of Psycho-Analysis*, **38**, 398–401.

DEVEREUX, GEORGE (1972). *Ethnopsychanalyse Complémentariste*. Flammarion, Paris. (English translation: *Ethnopsychoanalysis: Psychoanalysis and Anthropology as Complementary Frames of Reference* (1978). University of California Press, Berkeley, California.)

DODDS, E. R. (1951). *The Greeks and the Irrational*. University of California Press, Berkeley.

FERENCZI, SÁNDOR (1913). The ontogenesis of symbols. In *First Contributions to Psycho-Analysis* (1952), pp. 276–281. Hogarth Press, London.

FIRTH, RAYMOND (1973). *Symbols, Public and Private*. Allen and Unwin, London.

FORGE, ANTHONY (1973). Style and meaning in Sepik art. In *Primitive Art and Society* (Ed. A. Forge), pp. 169–192. Oxford University Press, London and New York (for Wenner-Gren Foundation for Anthropological Research Inc.).

FREUD, ANNA (1936). *The Ego and the Mechanisms of Defense*. In *The Writings of Anna Freud*, vol. II (1966). International Universities Press, New York.

FREUD, ANNA (1965). *Normality and Pathology in Childhood*. International Universities Press, New York.

FREUD, SIGMUND (1900). *The Interpretation of Dreams*. Standard Edition, vols 4 and 5 (1953). Hogarth Press, London.

FREUD, SIGMUND (1911). *Formulations on the Two Principles of Mental Functioning*. Standard Edition, vol. 12 (1958), pp. 213–226. Hogarth Press, London.

FREUD, SIGMUND (1913). *The Claims of Psycho-Analysis to Scientific Interest*. Part II (A), The Philological Interest of Psycho-Analysis. Standard Edition, vol. 13 (1955), pp. 176–178. Hogarth Press, London.

FREUD, SIGMUND (1916). *Introductory Lectures on Psycho-Analysis*. Part II, Dreams. Standard Edition, vol. 15 (1963), pp. 83–239. Hogarth Press, London.

FREUD, SIGMUND (1923). *The Ego and the Id*. Standard Edition, vol. 19 (1961), pp. 3–66. Hogarth Press, London.

FREUD, SIGMUND (1925). Negation. Standard Edition, vol. 19 (1961), pp. 233–239. Hogarth Press, London.

FREUD, SIGMUND (1950) [1895]. *Project for a Scientific Psychology.* Standard Edition, vol. 1 (1966), pp. 281–397. Hogarth Press, London.

HARTMANN, HEINZ (1964). *Essays on Ego Psychology: Selected Problems in Psychoanalytic Theory.* Hogarth Press, London.

ISAACS, SUSAN (1948). The Nature and Function of Phantasy. *The International Journal of Psycho-Analysis,* **29,** 73–97. Also in *Developments in Psycho-Analysis* (Ed. Joan Riviere) (1973). Hogarth Press, London.

JONES, ERNEST (1916). The theory of symbolism. In *Papers on Psycho-Analysis* (5th edition, 1950), pp. 87–144. Ballière, Tindall and Cox, London.

KLEIN, MELANIE (1930). The importance of symbol-formation in the development of the ego. In *Contributions to Psycho-Analysis 1921–1945* (1948), pp. 236–250. Hogarth Press, London.

LANGER, SUSANNE K. (1942). *Philosophy in a New Key: A Study in the Symbolism of Reason, Rite and Art.* Harvard University Press, Cambridge, Massachusetts.

LAPLANCHE, J. and PONTALIS, J-B. (1971). *Vocabulaire de la Psychanalyse.* Presses Universitaires de France, Paris.

LÉVI-STRAUSS, CLAUDE (1950). Introduction à l'oeuvre de Marcel Mauss. In Marcel Mauss, *Sociologie et Anthropologie,* pp. ix–lii. Presses Universitaires de France, Paris.

LUZES, PEDRO (1969). Les troubles de la pensée en clinique psychanalytique. *Revue Française de Psychanalyse,* **33,** 727–844.

MUNN, NANCY D. (1973). The spatial presentation of cosmic order in Walbiri iconography. In *Primitive Art and Society* (Ed. A. Forge), pp. 193–220. Oxford University Press, London and New York (for Wenner-Gren Foundation for Anthropological Research Inc.).

NIEDERLAND, WILLIAM G. (1964). Some ontogenetic determinants in symbol formation. *The Psychoanalytic Study of Society,* **3,** 98–110.

O'FLAHERTY, WENDY DONIGER (1973). *Asceticism and Eroticism in the Mythology of Śiva.* Oxford University Press, London.

RICOEUR, PAUL (1965). *De l'Interprêtation: Essai sur Freud.* Editions du Seuil, Paris. (English translation: *Freud and Philosophy: An Essay on Interpretation* (1970). Yale University Press, New Haven, Connecticut.

RODRIGUÉ, EMILIO (1956). Notes on symbolism. *The International Journal of Psycho-Analysis,* **37,** 147–158.

RYCROFT, CHARLES (1968). Symbolism and its relationship to the primary and secondary processes. In *Imagination and Reality: Psycho-Analytical Essays 1951–1961,* pp. 42–60. Hogarth Press, London. (Also in *The International Journal of Psycho-Analysis,* 1956, **37,** 137–146.)

SEGAL, HANNA (1957). Notes on symbol formation. *The International Journal of Psycho-Analysis,* **38,** 391–397.

SEGAL, HANNA (1964). Fantasy and other mental processes. *The International*

Journal of Psycho-Analysis, **45**, 191–194.

SEGAL, HANNA (1973). *Introduction to the Work of Melanie Klein.* Hogarth Press, London.

STEINER, GEORGE (1976). A note on language and psychoanalysis. *International Review of Psycho-Analysis*, **3**, 253–258.

STRACHEY, JAMES (1966). Notes on some technical terms whose translation calls for comment. In *The Complete Psychological Works of Sigmund Freud.* Standard Edition, vol. 1, pp. xxiii–xxvi. Hogarth Press, London.

THASS-THIENEMANN, THEODORE (1973). *The Interpretation of Language.* vol. 1, *Understanding the Symbolic Meaning of Language;* vol. 2, *Understanding the Unconscious Meaning of Language.* Aronson, New York.

Subject Index

E

F

N

O

U

V

W

Y

Z